MW00380670

PRAISE

"*Encouraging Words at the Well: A 365 Daily Devotional* has blessed my soul by uplifting, inspiring, and motivating me every day. It reminds me and challenges me to be strong in the Lord and never give up or lose hope but stay focused on Jesus! Thank you Namie Sims, a remarkable woman of God for your dedication and humbleness to God by encouraging all of us daily with the Word of God!"

— **Lenzena (Lynn) Byrd,** AT&T (Retired)

"Mrs. Namie, you are phenomenal!! You have been faithful to us women with *Encouraging Words at the Well.* You guide us as godly women through your teachings and your shared daily posts. Thank you for creating a place for us women to share, learn, and be accepted!"

— **Christina Roberts-Burroughs,** Director,
Ecorah Comfort Homecare Services

"It has been a life-enriching experience to participate in daily devotionals with *Encouraging Words at the Well*...a fresh, encouraging word every morning to remind me of who I am in Christ, that He carries me every day, and that I have sisters in Christ who help me pray and keep me strong in the Word. Blessings and peace. Never surrender your joy!"

— **Debbie S. Ray,** Harnett County Schools/
Exceptional Children Program (Retired)

"*Encouraging Words at the Well* has been part of my daily devotions for over a year. I always learn something new, get encouragement, and am challenged to grow in my walk with the Lord."

— **Ravonda Moss,** ASL Interpreter and Deaf Outreach

"Get a REFRESHING drink of God's Word for every day of the year with Minister Namie's *Encouraging Words at The Well: A 365 Daily Devotional*! You will be captivated & challenged to reflect on life and His Word and be inspired to grow BETTER!! Prepare to be filled powerfully, refreshed, and ENCOURAGED!"

—**Elder Shelia Michelle Jackson,** Bible Way Church
of Atlas Road

"*Encouraging Words at the Well* has been a life jacket, lifeline, and buoy to me during the lowest point of my life. The daily scriptures kept reinforcing God's words and promises to me at a time when I was so troubled, I could not concentrate. The daily prayers and well wishes of the other women sustained me during my ten-day stay in ICU. Thank God for your vision."

—**Deloris Moss,** Social Worker, Child Abuse/Neglect/
Foster Care (Retired)

"I look forward to reading *Encouraging Words at the Well*. It has truly blessed my soul. The daily devotions are a great way to start my day. I wake up on a positive note each morning knowing that a new blessing is waiting for me to read. I believe reading will encourage you."

—**Sharan P. Scott,** Communications Specialist,
Prisma Health Richland

"The *Encouraging Words at the Well* daily devotional is an essential part of my life. The scriptures provide guidance on strength, encouragement, and faith. I enjoy sharing the message I obtain from them with my husband and family. I hope to gain continued knowledge from the inspiring words within the daily devotionals."

—**Lenora Watts,** Supervisor, South Carolina Department of
Disability and Special Needs (Retired)

"When I read *Encouraging Words at the Well*, I feel gratitude, joy, mercy, prayerful, and encouraged. I'm Buddhist, and I think that all religions encourages all readers to be grateful, considerate, cheerful, and humble in everyday life. I believe your book will bring peace and joy to readers of any faith."

—**Namie Okamoto**, Friend (Japan)

"*Encouraging Words at the Well: A 365 Daily Devotional* helps me start my day with powerful promises from God! Each devotional is supported by scriptures, which allows me to dig deeper into God's Word. These devotionals reaffirm my faith! Finally, I can meditate and spend quiet with God. If you're looking to start your day with blessings from God, pick up a copy to read and join Women @ the Well. You will thirst no more because the Word will quench your spiritual thirst!"

—**Sharon D. Pollock**, Human Resources Executive

"*Encouraging Words at the Well: A 365 Daily Devotional* is an outpouring from Norma Sims, founder of Women @ the Well. She has been faithful to encourage women from all ages and walks of life to feel God's presence daily. I encourage anyone who feels dry or thirsty for more to pick up a copy and be refreshed."

—**Renee Fisher,** Author & Life Coach

All rights reserved. No part of this book may be reproduced, stored in a retrieval system, or transmitted in any form or by any means—electronic, mechanical, digital, photocopy, recording, or any other—except for brief quotations in printed reviews, without the prior permission of the author.

Copyright © 2021 by Norma Sims
NamieJeanMinistries.com
Published by Namie Jean Ministries
P.O. Box 460
Blythewood, SC 29016

Unless otherwise identified, all scripture quotations in this publication are taken from GOD'S WORD Translation (GW) Copyright © 1995, 2003, 2013, 2014, 2019, 2020 by God's Word to the Nations Mission Society. All rights reserved.

Scripture taken from the:

New Century Version® (NCV), Copyright © 2005 by Thomas Nelson, Inc. Used by permission. All rights reserved. † The Message Translation (MSG), Copyright © 1993, 2002, 2018 by Eugene H. Peterson. Used by permission. All rights reserved. † Holman Christian Standard Bible (HCSB), Copyright © 1999, 2000, 2002, 2003, 2009 by Holman Bible Publishers, Nashville Tennessee. All rights reserved. † New Revised Standard Version Bible, (NRSV), copyright © 1989 the Division of Christian Education of the National Council of the Churches of Christ in the United States of America. Used by permission. All rights reserved. † The Living Bible (TLB), copyright © 1971 by Tyndale House Foundation. Used by permission of Tyndale House Publishers Inc., Carol Stream, Illinois 60188. All rights reserved. † New Living Translation (NLT), copyright © 1996, 2004, 2015 by Tyndale House Foundation. Used by permission of Tyndale House Publishers, Inc., Carol Stream, Illinois 60188. All rights reserved. † Amplified Bible (AMP), Copyright © 2015 by The Lockman Foundation, La Habra, CA 90631. All rights reserved. † Amplified Bible (AMPC), Copyright © 1954, 1958, 1962, 1964, 1965, 1987 by The Lockman Foundation † The New King James Version® (NKJV), Copyright © 1982 by Thomas Nelson. Used by permission. All rights reserved. † The Holy Bible, English Standard Version. ESV® Text Edition: 2016. Copyright © 2001 by Crossway Bibles, a publishing ministry of Good News Publishers. † Holy Bible, New International Version®, NIV® Copyright ©1973, 1978, 1984, 2011 by Biblica, Inc.® Used by permission. All rights reserved worldwide. † NIV Reverse Interlinear Bible: English to Hebrew and English to Greek. Copyright © 2019 by Zondervan. † The Passion Translation®. (TPT), Copyright © 2017, 2018, 2020 by Passion & Fire Ministries, Inc. Used by permission. All rights reserved. thePassionTranslation.com † King James Version, (KJV), is public domain. † Common English Bible (CEB), Copyright © 2011 by Common English Bible † New American Standard (NASB)

Cover & Interior Layout Design: © Nelly Murariu at PixBeeDesign.com

ISBN Paperback: 978-0-578-93792-2
ISBN eBook: 979-8-9852812-0-0

Encouraging Words at the Well

A 365-DAILY DEVOTIONAL

NORMA SIMS

Dedication

It is with a grateful heart that I would like to first dedicate this book to God the Father, Son, and Holy Spirit. Thank You for loving me, saving me, and leading me in Your ways, and teaching me not to be afraid but obedient to be the person You created me to be.

I'm forever appreciative to my husband of forty-three years—my high school sweetheart—and to our four children, Tunesia, Janir, LaVetra, and Rock, Jr. Thanks to all of you for believing in me and for encouraging me to go after my dream.

To my late Grandmother Century, who once told me it was her desire to be a missionary going all over the world to spread God's Word. I dedicate this book to you for leaving me with a legacy of faith.

To all the members of our Facebook group, Women @ the Well, and the subscribers to my blog on Namie-JeanMinistries.com—each of you with your unfailing commitment of showing up, your prayers, comments, and help with growing the group by inviting your friends gave me my voice and the encouragement and determination to keep writing.

INTRODUCTION

It has been a lifelong dream of mine to write and publish a book.

This book came into existence partially because of all the women who joined my Facebook group, Women @ the Well.

I want to thank this group of women who helped me find my voice through the daily publication of these heartfelt and straightforward devotions during a time when the COVID-19 pandemic put a hold on the world.

After standing on the serenity prayer for a couple of years, I eventually began to surrender everything to God and decided to be intentional about showing up in the world for Him and what He has for me. After realizing that God had placed me in a place of peace, I committed to meeting with Him at 3:30 a.m. every morning to show my gratitude, not knowing it would turn into a devotional.

Forsake Not the Assembling

On this Sunday, let us thank God for the opportunity to gather in a place where we can share our faith. Despite it being God's plan for us as His people to assemble in the body of Christ, we may not always be able to physically meet together every time, but we can still find ways to connect. May He continue to bless everyone according to His will.

"Not giving up meeting together, as some are in the habit of doing, but encouraging one another—and all the more as you see the Day approaching." (Hebrews 10:25, NIV)

"'Sir,'" the woman said, 'I can see that you are a prophet. Our fathers worshiped on this mountain, but you Jews claim that the place where we must worship is in Jerusalem.' Jesus declared, 'Believe me, woman, a time is coming when you will worship the Father neither on this mountain nor in Jerusalem. You Samaritans worship what you do not know; we worship what we do know, for salvation is from the Jews. Yet a time is coming and has now come when the true worshipers will worship the Father in spirit and truth, for they are the kind of worshipers the Father seeks. God is spirit, and his worshipers must worship in spirit and in truth.'" (John 4:19-24, NIV)

LESSON † Let us continue to praise and worship God. There is power in coming together, praising and worshiping God, but we must be true worshipers who worship in spirit and truth no matter where we worship.

In what ways have you initiated coming together to worship with loved ones and others?

Happy on Monday

Today, let's lift each other up in our prayers. I have and continue to pray for God's will to be done in each of our lives!

Although Mondays are mostly associated with dread and mundane tasks, we can and should be happy on Mondays. Monday is the day that allows us to set the tone for the rest of our week, so it is wise for us to begin the day with prayer, plans, and purpose to set our path for the entire week.

> "This is the day which the LORD hath made; we will rejoice and be glad in it." (Psalms 118:24, KJV)

LESSON † Each new day we live, we should acknowledge that it's a day that the Lord has made, and we should look forward to what God has for us.

Most people don't like Mondays. What do you like or dislike about Mondays?

What Type of Hat?

Thank God for diversity! We come from all walks of life, have many different titles, and have experienced many different seasons of life, but we are all one in Christ.

Living during a season when we are faced with many roles in life can prove to be challenging. We can and will navigate through each role, but in different ways.

> "Who can find a virtuous woman? for her price is far above rubies." (Proverbs 31:10, KJV)

> "She equips herself with strength [spiritual, mental, and physical fitness for her God-given task] And makes her arms strong." (Proverbs 31:17, AMP)

LESSON † **Some—if not all—of us will see our inner strength and recognize our true worth. We wear many different hats, and each hat requires something different from each of us.**

What type(s) of hat(s) do you find yourself wearing during this current season of life?

Foolproof

Thank God that, through His Holy Spirit, He gives us the wisdom and the ability to make good choices and not foolish ones. Because the Holy Spirit leads, guides, and teaches us, we don't have to be anybody's fool today or ever!

I love a good joke, but sometimes what's funny to me may not be funny to others. God doesn't want us to hurt each other. We must be considerate and sensitive about the things that we joke about. Not all jokes are good jokes. We must take into consideration the circumstances of others and what's going on in their lives. Let's learn, instead of playing jokes on each other, to pray for and share God's knowledge with each other. Let's live foolproof lives!

> "The fear of the LORD is the beginning of knowledge, but fools despise wisdom and instruction." (Proverbs 1:7, NIV)

LESSON † To live foolproof days, let us choose to start and finish each day with God. There is no one like the Lord. He knows and can see everything coming at us and gives us the wisdom to manage and live through it.

Is there a time when you or someone played a joke and it didn't go well? What do you think God wants you to learn from it?

Carrying Your Own Water

I pray today for lighter burdens and that God will continue to provide for and protect each of us individually and collectively.

I was carrying water to water my plants the other day, and God brought back a personal childhood experience to my mind. Long story short, I grew up with the old water pump, and when it would freeze in the winter, my cousin would allow us to carry water from her house. Carrying water today reminded me of how good God is! I was carrying water for my plants because I wanted to, but I had to carry water back then because it was a necessity.

The woman at the well, who met Jesus there, did not need her water vessel after her encounter with Him. She ran off and left it. Her burdens were lifted!

> "Then the woman left her water jar and went back into the city. She told the people, 'Come with me, and meet a man who told me everything I've ever done. Could he be the Messiah?' The people left the city and went to meet Jesus."
>
> (John 4:28-30)

Yes, we each carry our own experiences. They are our own, and we must learn from them. Jesus tells us to give them to Him! Visit https://healthpositiveinfo.com/the-story-of-the-glass-of-water.html to read an illustraion The Glass of Water, and think about the weight of what you are carrying, I encourage you to give it to God![1]

> **LESSON** † It's important to remember to let go of your stresses. As early in the evening as you can, put all your burdens down. Don't carry them through the evening and into the night.

What weight would you say you are carrying but need to give to God?

Ministry vs. a Job

I pray that each of you has had a safe and productive work week! Let us continue to pray for all those who are committed to their ministries and jobs.

Although we may find ourselves living during days that are difficult and unrecognizable for most, we must continue to trust God and each other! There will be days of uncertainty. They too shall pass!

> "So, my dear brothers and sisters, stand strong. Do not let anything move you. Always give yourselves fully to the work of the Lord, because you know that your work in the Lord is never wasted." (1 Corinthians 15:58, NCV)

LESSON ✝ God has equipped each of us with gifts that will qualify us with the opportunity to practice those giftings for the call that He has on our lives. He doesn't call for us to be perfect whether we consider ourselves working a job or in a ministry. In fact, working a job and being in ministry should be one in the same. We must work as unto the Lord.

How would you say that you use your gifts from God in your job or in your ministry?

God Answers Knee-Mail

Each day, let us make a habit of praying for our well-being and for the well-being of those we love. During times in life when things come up and are challenging and difficult, we can always pray to God, and He will lift us so that we can make it through them.

> "Never stop praying. Whatever happens, give thanks because it is God's will in Christ Jesus that you do this."
>
> (1Thessalonians 5:17-18)

LESSON † Thank God that He answers knee-mail! No matter the circumstances, we can always depend on Him and know that He promises to be with us and never leave us.

What prayer do you consistently pray to God?

Set Free

Let us honor and praise the Lord for His goodness! Let us remember all that He has done for us! There is something about Jesus that changes us. He makes all things right!

> "Shout and cheer, Daughter Zion! Raise your voice, Daughter Jerusalem! Your king is coming! a good king who makes all things right, a humble king riding a donkey, a mere colt of a donkey." (Zechariah 9:9, MSG)

> "When they neared Jerusalem, having arrived at Bethphage on Mount Olives, Jesus sent two disciples with these instructions: 'Go over to the village across from you. You'll find a donkey tethered there, her colt with her. Untie her and bring them to me. If anyone asks what you're doing, say, "The Master needs them!" He will send them with you.'"
>
> (Matthew 21:1-3, MSG)

LESSON † On His way to Jerusalem, Jesus had a donkey that was tied up set free, and He rode humbly into the city on that donkey. Similarly, He wants to set us free so that we can be used by Him. Let us allow Him to free us from whatever is holding us, and let Him use us for His glory.

What things are keeping you from being set free to serve God?

Holy Week Monday

With all that is going on in our world today, I pray this morning that each of us will walk into this new week prepared and hungry for new beginnings!

There may be turmoil or trouble in our lives, but we must not let it stop us from praising God! Let us walk like Jesus did toward resurrection morning with prayer, pure hearts, and clean hands.

> "When he entered Jerusalem, the whole city was in turmoil, asking, 'Who is this?' The crowds were saying, 'This is the prophet Jesus from Nazareth in Galilee.' Then Jesus entered the temple and drove out all who were selling and buying in the temple, and he overturned the tables of the money changers and the seats of those who sold doves. He said to them, 'It is written, "My house shall be called a house of prayer"; but you are making it a den of robbers.'"
>
> (Matthew 21:10, NRSV)

LESSON ✝ We must believe that Jesus has come as King of Peace to save us! And to reign with Him, there must be some preparation.

On a daily basis, how do you prepare yourself to interact with God?

Cleansing the Temple

Blessings to each of you this morning! I pray for everything that concerns each of us! Let us give it to our Father who is in Heaven, because He knows all about them.

As we continue to follow the example of the steps of Jesus in scripture, we see Jesus and the disciples back in the Temple, where Jesus had thrown out the merchants and money changers the day before.

> "Then he was back in the Temple, teaching. The high priests and leaders of the people came up and demanded, 'Show us your credentials. Who authorized you to teach here?' Jesus responded, 'First let me ask you a question. You answer my question and I'll answer yours.'" (Matthew 21:23, MSG)

Jesus confronts the hypocrisy of the Jewish leaders.

According to Lexico, the definition of hypocrisy is the practice of claiming to have moral standards or beliefs to which one's own behavior does not conform; pretense.

Jesus, being all-knowing and seeing through their scheme, answered them with a seemingly unrelated question that exposed their real motives. They didn't want an answer to their question. They only wanted to trap Him.

LESSON † Acting like Pharisees, we only want the truth when it affirms our views and causes. Jesus revealed to them then and to us now that He is the King Eternal, King of Kings, and Lord of Lords with divine authority! Jesus has been given all authority in heaven and on earth! And He will show us who He is by revealing to us who we are!

Do you believe in Him? What areas of your life might need to be confronted and cleaned up by the Holy Spirit?

A Bribe to Betray Jesus

Trusting that all is well with each of you! Let us continue to pray because our world remains in unchartered waters, our emotions are everywhere, and most of all, many hearts are hurting. The world is literally plagued by disease and greed! Lord, help us to find peace and comfort in Your love and in each other.

Coming together can be a powerful thing. Matthew 18:20 (KJV) lets us know, "'For where two or three are gathered together in My name, there am I in the midst of them.'"

In scripture during Holy Week/Passion Week, on the day known as Spy Wednesday, there was a bribe to betray Jesus. Jesus's path to His crucifixion was met with the betrayal of Him by a close disciple and friend named Judas Iscariot.

> "Then one of the twelve apostles, Judas Iscariot, went to talk to the leading priests. He said, 'What will you pay me for giving Jesus to you?' And they gave him thirty silver coins. After that, Judas watched for the best time to turn Jesus in."
> (Matthew 26:14-16, NCV)

LESSON † **God's mission is our focus!!!**

Has there ever been a time when you were betrayed? How did it make you feel?

Last Supper

I pray every day that we *don*'t get weary in well-doing! Instead of getting weary, let us search within ourselves and be reminded of the life lessons we have learned since we have met Jesus and what He has done for us.

He's our most excellent teacher and our Lord! We must ask God to help us learn from His examples. We must ask for the strength to walk faithfully with Him, even when the road becomes difficult and we feel lost. We must remember that He is faithful!

The Last Supper with Jesus and His disciples before He was crucified is called Maundy Thursday. They had gathered for Passover meal, the meal which remembers when God freed His people, the Israelites, from captivity.

Jesus tells us to take Communion to remember his death and "proclaim the Lord's death until he comes." Communion not only reminds us what Jesus did, but that He will return!

> "'I give you a new command: Love each other. You must love each other as I have loved you. All people will know that you are my followers if you love each other."
>
> (John 13:34-35, NCV)

LESSON † We are facing many of the same difficulties that Jesus did. That day was also marked by the betrayal and denial. However, Jesus didn't quit. He knew this was the calm before the storm and spent this time teaching and establishing a new commandment with His disciples and with us today!

What significance does communion have to you? How often do you partake?

Crucify Him

This is the day that the Lord has made, and I pray that each of you can truly rejoice and be glad in it.

We all have had expectations of someone or something that has let us down, only to find out that the someone or that something either didn't or couldn't give us what we expected. Despite the cries to crucify Him, Jesus moved ever so humbly toward Black/Good Friday, the day He would die on the cross. For those who expected Jesus to save them, they thought all hope was gone that day. The chief priests shouted for the crowd to chant "crucify him."

> "Pilate knew that the people turned Jesus in to him because they were jealous. While Pilate was sitting there on the judge's seat, his wife sent this message to him: 'Don't do anything to that man, because he is innocent. Today I had a dream about him, and it troubled me very much.' But the leading priests and elders convinced the crowd to ask for Barabbas to be freed and for Jesus to be killed."
>
> (Matthew 27:18-20, NCV)

LESSON † It's not always what it looks like! The trauma of that first Good Friday/Black Friday undoubtedly broke the hearts of Jesus's disciples and all those who put their hope in Him.

The crowd turned on Jesus. Do you find it hard to love and forgive those who betray or deny you?

Jesus's Body in the Tomb

I praise God for each of you, and I trust that all is well. The steps of Jesus during that Holy Week led Him to the tomb, where He spent the day called Silent Saturday on the Jewish sabbath. Let us thank Him for enduring the cross for our sins.

> "Now there was a good and righteous man named Joseph. He was a member of the Jewish high council, but he had not agreed with the decision and actions of the other religious leaders. He was from the town of Arimathea in Judea, and he was waiting for the Kingdom of God to come. He went to Pilate and asked for Jesus' body. Then he took the body down from the cross and wrapped it in a long sheet of linen cloth and laid it in a new tomb that had been carved out of rock." (Luke 23:50-53, NLT)

Although Jesus died and was placed in the tomb, in the meantime, between His death and His Resurrection, His spirit descended into hell to set the captives free! While the earth was waiting, God in heaven was still working on behalf of the believers. There is no depth that God won't go to in order to save us!

LESSON † On that Saturday, the earth was silent, and the people were resting and waiting. We can all rest assured, knowing that Jesus paid the ransom for our lives and that death and hell have no hold on us! It couldn't hold Jesus and will not be able to hold us!"

Have you ever had the feeling that everything is lost—or at least it seemed like it was?

Resurrection

Let us give God all the honor and glory today! He has shown His wondrous and amazing love to the world by giving His only Son so that each of us can also be called His children. I pray that He will open our eyes so that we may see His extraordinary grace and that we will be glad and rejoice in our salvation through Him. Lord, we say thank You!

> "After the sabbath, as the first day of the week was dawning, Mary Magdalene and the other Mary went to see the tomb. And suddenly there was a great earthquake; for an angel of the Lord, descending from heaven, came and rolled back the stone and sat on it. His appearance was like lightning, and his clothing white as snow. For fear of him the guards shook and became like dead men. But the angel said to the women, 'Do not be afraid; I know that you are looking for Jesus who was crucified. He is not here; for he has been raised, as he said.'"
> (Matthew 28:1-6, NRSV)

There is no better news! The key to our Christian faith is the resur-rec-tion of Jesus Christ. Just as Jesus promised, He rose from the dead on the third day, and we can be assured that He will accomplish all He has promised.

LESSON † The resurrection is the basis for the church's witness to the world. Jesus is more than just a human leader; He is the Son of God and the ruler of God's eternal kingdom. Because we believe this, we do not have to be afraid. Tell someone and invite them into the kingdom of God today!

Has there been a time when you felt that you made a sacrifice for someone else?

Now What

As I take a deep breath, I say good morning, good afternoon, or good evening. I hope that each of us can say that today. No matter how you celebrated Easter, I trust that God's presence was felt!

Let us not move on so quickly with the next event in our lives. It's okay if we wait. Stop and reflect on the most significant event in history—the death, burial, and resurrection of Jesus Christ. Ponder what that means for us individually and collectively as a body of believers. We are called to be witnesses, commissioned to go!

> "And being assembled together with them, He commanded them not to depart from Jerusalem, *but to* wait for the Promise of the Father, 'which,' He said, 'you have heard from Me; for John truly baptized with water, but you shall be baptized with the Holy Spirit not many days from now.'" (Acts 1:4, NKJV)

LESSON † Jesus did what He did for us so that we will be able to live in unity and love. We have been given an opportunity to share God's love, mercy, and forgiveness every day by both what we say and what we do! We don't have to wait for Easter Sunday to honor Jesus's death, burial, and resurrection. Why? I read somewhere that, "Easter is a big Sunday! And every Sunday is a little Easter!"

Are you willing to be a witness? How can you boldly walk in the freedom and victory of what Jesus has done for us?

Picking Up the Pieces

I thank God for every one of you. I thank Him for allowing each of us to see another day! I pray that each of us will see and feel God's presence in our lives today, knowing that He is with us.

We all know that the world and our lives can feel broken at times. Life can throw some unexpected and painful situations our way! We must seek and trust God to bring us through them. As I was walking around picking up the dead fallen branches from the trees in my yard after a storm, I thought of Paul and the storm he faced on the ship to Rome and how God promised to protect them. I know each of you also have a story of how God has brought you through and the protection He has provided.

Those things and places were not to destroy us but to show us the power of God, the One who is in control.

> "After they had gone a long time without food, Paul stood up before them and said: 'Men, you should have taken my advice not to sail from Crete; then you would have spared yourselves this damage and loss. But now I urge you to keep up your courage, because not one of you will be lost; only the ship will be destroyed. Last night an angel of the God to whom I belong and whom I serve stood beside me and said, "Do not be afraid, Paul. You must stand trial before Caesar; and God has graciously given you the lives of all who sail with you." So keep up your courage, men, for I have faith in God that it will happen just as he told me. Nevertheless, we must run aground on some island.'" (Acts 27:21-26, NIV)

LESSON † God is trying to get us to, a place of wholenes and a place to be His witness! When we give God our broken pieces, He can make us whole!

How can you keep on trusting God during the trials of life?

When We Are Weak, He Is Strong

I pray that each of us has a great day today. We have all learned how hard it is to deal with the issues of life while going through physical/social separation. Let's continue to pray for God's protection and provisions.

Do something today to brighten someone's day. Send a text to someone working from home and to someone who is working the front lines of society despite the fearful and dangerous circumstances. If you're reading this and feel like you don't have anyone to encourage you, know that you are more than enough, and there is no need to feel a sense of unworthiness, a sense of discouragement, or that you are living a defeated life.

Say this out loud:

> "I can do all things through Christ which strengtheneth me."
> (Philippians 4:13, KJV)

LESSON † Be comforted knowing that no matter what season of life we find ourselves experiencing, everything is going to be all right!

In what ways have you seen God's protection in your life?

My Help!

When we're living in frightening times, our help comes from the Lord. It's evident that our world is constantly in trouble and will not get better without divine intervention. God is calling for us to stand in unity like never before.

> "Call for the wailing women to come; send for the most skillful of them. Let them come quickly and wail over us till our eyes overflow with tears and water streams from our eyelids. The sound of wailing is heard from Zion: "How ruined we are! How great is our shame! We must leave our land because our houses are in ruins."' Now, you women, hear the word of the LORD; open your ears to the words of his mouth. Teach your daughters how to wail; teach one another a lament."
>
> (Jeremiah 9:17, NIV)

How many of you remember S.O.S.? It's the international Morse code distress signal associated with the phrases, "Save our ship" or, "Save our souls." It is a cry for help. We all need help in life, and we all need God's help! He's our constant help in the time of trouble.

> "I lift up my eyes to the hills—from where will my help come? My help comes from the LORD, who made heaven and earth."
>
> (Psalm 121:1-2, NRSV)

Lesson: **God is fully capable of helping and protecting us, and He continues to call for us. He wants us to turn and to seek Him! Let us ask God for His divine intervention in healing not only our land, but for whatever healing we each may need in our personal lives.**

People of God, are you willing to stand in unity today? In what ways have you seen God's help in your life?

Be Steadfast

Good morning, good afternoon, or good evening! I trust that all is well as we come to the end of this work week for many. I pray that you have an excellent working weekend for those whose work continues and don't get weary in well-doing.

Many of us may have had struggles this week. If so, I pray that God gives each of us the courage and the strength to embrace the struggles and not quit but continue to be persistent in all that we do, knowing that only what we do for the Lord will last.

> "Therefore, my beloved brethren, be steadfast, immovable, always abounding in the work of the Lord, knowing that your labor is not in vain in the Lord."
>
> (1 Corinthians 15:58, NKJV)

LESSON † Quitting seems to be the easiest thing to do when we're facing oppositions or struggles in our ministries, our jobs, and our lives. For the Christian, quitting should never be an option when doing the Lord's will!

Has there ever been a time when you regret giving up on something or someone?

Encouraging Words at the Well

Bring Your Burdens to Jesus

May there be excitement and wonder as we continue to love and be committed to God and each other. In life, we show up every day not knowing what we will encounter. Thank God He is with us every step of the way.

We can become so worried about our problems, work, earthly desires, and needs that we lose our peace, joy, and contentment in our day-to-day lives. It is my prayer for each of you that you show up in life, that you feel inspired, and that you have had a God encounter.

> "Don't be upset because of evil people. Don't be jealous of those who do wrong, because like the grass, they will soon dry up. Like green plants, they will soon die away. Trust the LORD and do good. Live in the land and feed on truth. Enjoy serving the LORD, and he will give you what you want." (Psalm 37:1-4, NCV)

LESSON † No matter what we do or say, there will always be something missing in our lives if we delight more in the world and not in the Lord. I wish you a blessed Saturday! Please take what you need for today; tomorrow has its own worries.

Is there a time you experienced God's comfort during a difficult time? Do you offer God's comfort to others?

Believe

Good Sunday morning, afternoon, or evening. My prayer is that each of us will feel the joy of the Lord and that we will experience His peace in our lives.

As we have had to experience some difficult seasons in life, I wonder how many of you have asked the question W.I.G.I.A.T.—"Where is God in all this?" I know I sure have! You may have as well. As believers, we often don't want to appear that we don't know or understand for fear of being seen as weak, doubtful, or even unfaithful in our Christian walk.

Today we read about Thomas, one of Jesus's twelve disciples, labeled as a doubter because of his reaction when told of His resurrection. He said that he needed to see for himself. The idea of a risen Jesus was just too great to take someone else's word for it.

> "But Thomas, one of the twelve, called Didymus, was not with them when Jesus came. The other disciples therefore said unto him, We have seen the LORD. But he said unto them, Except I shall see in his hands the print of the nails, and put my finger into the print of the nails, and thrust my hand into his side, I will not believe." (John 20:24-25, KJV)

LESSON † **Thomas teaches us that faith does not remove doubt and questions. Neither does it take away moments when we wonder whether God is truly with us! We must choose whether we will believe the gospel Good News or others' opinions.**

Have there been times when you didn't ask for a better understanding? Or have you been the one who has said what everyone else was thinking?

Pray for Leaders

Let us pray specifically that God's will be done! Ask that our leaders, no matter who or what they may be leading, will lead with honesty and integrity. In Jesus's name!

I don't mean to be political, but every day we trust our leaders with our lives. We trust them to make the right and best decisions for us. I agree with those who say that we need to pray for our leaders of government, elected officials, clergy, supervisors, and managers— anyone who has to make decisions about the safety and protection of others.

> "First, I tell you to pray for all people, asking God for what they need and being thankful to him. Pray for rulers and for all who have authority so that we can have quiet and peaceful lives full of worship and respect for God. This is good, and it pleases God our Savior, who wants all people to be saved and to know the truth. There is one God and one mediator so that human beings can reach God. That way is through Christ Jesus, who is himself human. He gave himself as a payment to free all people. He is proof that came at the right time." (1 Timothy 2:1-6, NCV)

LESSON † We ought to pray always and without ceasing. Prayer and fasting are the birthing room for our breakthroughs.

Do you find it difficult to submit to those in authority over you who do not possess godly characters?

Help Us, Holy Spirit

May God's peace rest, rule, and abide within each of us today! In life we will continue to face many difficult situations and choices that we have never experienced. We may not always know what we should be praying for.

Because we have never experienced these things, making choices and decisions may cause us to feel helpless, confused, and even speechless in our prayer life. As Christians, we must embrace the fact that we don't live in the world that God said in the beginning was good. Because of sin, we live in a fallen world, and there will be pain and suffering. Fear not! We serve a God who knows the heart and promises never to leave us nor forsake us.

After Christ's ascent into heaven, He sent the Holy Spirit to help us, just as He had promised!!!

> "In the same way, the Spirit helps us in our weakness. We do not know what we ought to pray for, but the Spirit himself intercedes for us through wordless groans. And he who searches our hearts knows the mind of the Spirit, because the Spirit intercedes for God's people in accordance with the will of God." (Romans 8:26-27, NIV)

LESSON † God has a greater power, purpose, and plan for our lives that outweigh anything that we could dream or imagine! When we are weak, He is strong! Trust God's plan, the Holy Spirit!

In what ways have you seen God's protection in your life when you were weak?

Suitable for the Task

I pray this morning that each of you experiences the strength of the Lord and that you have a safe, productive, and joyful day.

We've heard so much about essential workers—who's essential and who's not. Let us be reminded of how crucial we all are, individually and collectively. Let's continue to support and lift each other. With the power of God's grace and mercy, our faith, and the help and support of the other women in our lives, there is nothing that we can't accomplish. Since the beginning of time, women have been found suitable for the task.

> "The LORD God said, 'It is not good for the man to be alone. I will make a helper suitable for him.'" (Genesis 2:18, NIV)

> "So the man gave names to all the livestock, the birds in the sky and all the wild animals. But for Adam no suitable helper was found. So the LORD God caused the man to fall into a deep sleep; and while he was sleeping, he took one of the man's ribs and then closed up the place with flesh. Then the LORD God made a woman from the rib he had taken out of the man, and he brought her to the man. The man said, 'This is now bone of my bones and flesh of my flesh; she shall be called "woman," for she was taken out of man.'" (Genesis 2:20-23, NIV)

LESSON † Both men and women were formed and equipped by God for various tasks, and they all lead to the same goal. They are honoring God!

Has there ever been a time when you didn't feel you were suitable for a task?

Grateful Thursday

Thank God for waking us up this Thursday! Let us thank God for life, health, and strength this day, for we know we have an enemy who is roaming the earth, seeking to devour us.

Let us continue to be grateful, alert, and do what is best for our lives because we have a personal responsibility to protect ourselves and to make healthy choices. The Word tells us that our bodies are temples, and we must take care of them!

> "You should know that your body is a temple for the Holy Spirit who is in you. You have received the Holy Spirit from God. So you do not belong to yourselves, because you were bought by God for a price. So honor God with your bodies."
>
> (1 Corinthians 6:19-20, NCV)

LESSON † If there are no ups and downs in your life, then you are not alive! Let us not focus on the troubles of today. Let us thank God for life, health, and strength.

Are there times when you don't feel grateful and accountable to God for how you treat your physical body?

Delight in the Simple Blessing of Today

Thank God for allowing us to see another day! He has safely brought us through another week. Let us continue to praise God and trust Him to see us through these troubled, uncertain, and overwhelming times.

Enjoy the simple blessings of today and rest knowing that the Lord is with us! When we give Him everything that concerns us, He will carry it for us!

> "'Take my yoke upon you, and learn from me; for I am gentle and humble in heart, and you will find rest for your souls. For my yoke is easy, and my burden is light.'"
>
> (Matthew 11:29-30, NRSV)

LESSON † There is knowledge and rest for the weary that comes through commitment and dedication to Christ.

Have there been times when you've experienced lighter burdens because of walking with Jesus?

Jumping for Joy

I pray that each of you will experience joy and happiness today! Too often, we spend much of our time waiting for the weekend— waiting for what could have been, or just simply waiting for things to get better.

The reality is that life will always have some disappointments and complications. There will always be something that will need to be done. Being raised having so many responsibilities as a young girl made me take life a little too seriously. Not only am I learning not to take life so seriously, but I'm also learning not to wait for things to get better before I can experience some of life's joy, happiness, and peace.

If we don't learn to be happy right now, we could run out of time. Choose to be happy and give God thanks right now! He created each of us for a purpose.

> "She is clothed with strength and dignity; she can laugh at the days to come." (Proverbs 31:25, NIV)

LESSON † Sometimes all we need is to break the routine and have some fun. Oh, the good ol' days of innocence, when we jumped for joy.

Are you aware that you can experience God's hope and joy within your everyday life? Are you willing to share Him as the reason for your hope and joy?

The Two on the Emmaus Road

Today I thank God for His Holy Word. I ask Him to open the eyes of our hearts. I pray that we continue to celebrate His constant presence in our lives and that His Word will give each of us hope and the strength to make it through each day.

Today's selection from the Word is only a glimpse of the two on the road to Emmaus. They left Jerusalem confused and feeling hopeless after the resurrection of Jesus, because they had expected a different ending.

They were walking away! They were met by who they thought was a stranger, who explained the scriptures about the Messiah to them. They were amazed, and it wasn't until He broke bread with them that they realized who He was, just before He disappeared from their sight.

> "They asked each other, 'Were not our hearts burning within us while he talked with us on the road and opened the Scriptures to us?'" (Luke 24:32, NIV)

LESSON † Jesus will meet us where we're at, especially during the times when we are most confused and feeling hopeless about our circumstances. We, too, can find help from the scriptures that will light a fire in us.

Have you ever expected something to happen or maybe to end a certain way, and when it didn't happen the way that you expected it to, you were sad, mad, disappointed, or perhaps brokenhearted?

Baggage Check

There is a lot of talk about a new normal. New requires change, and change can be scary. Truth be told, we can look at each day like it's new. I pray this morning that each of us will meet this new day with the faith and confidence that God is with us. He knows us, He hears us, and He sees us. I pray that we have the strength and courage to release and let go of any and every stronghold that presents itself in each of our lives.

Wouldn't it be nice if we could look back on the events of our lives and only see our mistakes as lessons and not regrets? Much too often, we do our best to hide our mistakes and challenges from others and ourselves, only to have them hold us back and weigh us down!

> "For the Lord is the Spirit, and wherever the Spirit of the Lord is, there is freedom." (2 Corinthians 3:17, NLT)

LESSON † We can't experience freedom if we continue to carry unhelpful thoughts that control and sabotage our minds. The sooner we let go and let God handle them, the freer we will be.

Are you ready to do an emotional baggage check so that you can release and let go of the extra, unhelpful weight?

Trouble Won't Last Always

I pray that each of you are feeling strong, encouraged, and that you are experiencing the peace of God, especially when life feels like a roller coaster ride.

Sometimes, our lives can be moving along just fine. And as if we don't already have enough to be concerned about, we find ourselves somewhere in the middle of a situation that just seems to come out of nowhere. We make our plans, and we are probably feeling good about ourselves and the accomplishments that we have already made, or maybe we have promised ourselves that we will do better. Either way, things just get turned upside down.

Despite all of our efforts to plan and be intentional about our lives, when troubles, large or small, arise, we tend to worry about them. May you rest and relax in the peace of God today. Let whatever you do today be good enough. Only what we do for Christ will last!

> "'Do you now believe?' Jesus replied. 'A time is coming and in fact has come when you will be scattered, each to your own home. You will leave me all alone. Yet I am not alone, for my Father is with me. I have told you these things, so that in me you may have peace. In this world you will have trouble. But take heart! I have overcome the world.'"
>
> (John 16:31-33, NIV)

LESSON ✝ Despite the troubles in this world, we are over-comers in Christ Jesus! We don't have to worry when we're trusting in Him.

Do you always see God as a part of your plans? Or do you include Him when they fail?

We Can Do All Things

Good morning! I thank God that He has brought us halfway through another week. Let us praise Him for what He has already done for each of us individually and collectively.

Let us thank God for giving us the strength to release and let go of the extra baggage and for the ability to rest and relax in His peace. I pray that His favor and blessings continue to be with us throughout this week. If you are already feeling weary and exhausted today, or just standing in need, ask the Lord to provide you with enough and strengthen you enough so that you can be and do what is required of you.

> "I know how to live when I am poor, and I know how to live when I have plenty. I have learned the secret of being happy at any time in everything that happens, when I have enough to eat and when I go hungry, when I have more than I need and when I do not have enough. I can do all things through Christ, because he gives me strength."
>
> (Philippians 4:12-13, NCV)

LESSON † It is the power of Christ within us that gives us spiritual strength and contentment so that we can do everything that pertains to the will of God. The power is also given to us to face the challenges that come from our commitment to doing His will.

What does it mean that you can do everything? Do you always believe it?

Grateful

Let us thank God for giving us life, health, and strength. Let us thank Him for our countless blessings and the people in our lives that help make life purposeful and fulfilling.

Despite our sometimes being unfaithful to God, we can always count on Him loving and being good to us. He's still working on our behalf. When we don't or can't see the blessings flowing, we need to know that He's still working things out for our good, but for His glory. He keeps on blessing us over and over again!

As children of God, let us make a daily habit of declaring the good things of God over our lives every day, every second of the day!

> "Give thanks to the LORD, for he is good; his love endures forever. Let the redeemed of the LORD tell their story—those he redeemed from the hand of the foe, those he gathered from the lands, from east and west, from north and south. Some wandered in desert wastelands, finding no way to a city where they could settle. They were hungry and thirsty, and their lives ebbed away. Then they cried out to the LORD in their trouble, and he delivered them from their distress." (Psalm 107:1-6, NIV)

LESSON † When the praises go up, the blessings come down!

How will you thank God more often every day?

Running on Empty

Thank God for each passing month, as He gives us another day to rejoice and be glad. I pray that you have been encouraged and strengthened by the Word of God so far this week.

For many of us, life can be consuming and overwhelming, so even the strongest of us can become weary. We give so much of ourselves away to relationships, children, families, jobs, and the list can go on and on. Maybe you're good physically, but you struggle emotionally and spiritually, and you don't know where to turn. You may feel that you don't have anything else to give. Your tank is running on empty, but you can't stop because others are depending on you.

> "'Come to me, all you who are weary and burdened, and I will give you rest. Take my yoke upon you and learn from me, for I am gentle and humble in heart, and you will find rest for your souls. For my yoke is easy and my burden is light.'"
>
> (Matthew 11:28-30, NIV)

LESSON † God's Word promises us that when we are weary, we can come to Him, and He will give us rest. He promises to fill us with the power of His Spirit and that His joy will be our strength. When we are running on empty, no one or nothing can re-energize or fill us like the Lord!

What are you doing to feed your spirit daily?

Weak without God!

As we make it to the weekend, some of us will probably get some well-deserved rest and relaxation. It is my prayer for those who still have to work that God strengthens you for the task.

As we face life situations, my prayer is that we will continue to trust, pray, and believe that God is with us. Let us seek ways to connect with God individually and as a community of believers each morning. To grow spiritually and learn God's perfect will for our lives, we must read, study, and know His Word.

We need Him daily!

> "'Live in me. Make your home in me just as I do in you. In the same way that a branch can't bear grapes by itself but only by being joined to the vine, you can't bear fruit unless you are joined with me. I am the Vine, you are the branches. When you're joined with me and I with you, the relation intimate and organic, the harvest is sure to be abundant. Separated, you can't produce a thing." (John 15:4-5, MSG)

LESSON † **Without Christ, we have no power over sin and Satan. With Him, we have everything!**

Has there ever been a time when you felt that you didn't need God, but then you realized that He was all you had?

Move On

Let us thank God for bringing us this far! Let us remember all that He has done for us.

When there's a shift in our lives, it may be difficult for some to keep the routines and the things that we have become accustomed to.

The enemy would have us feel like scattered sheep, alone and isolated. We can learn our greatest lesson about moving forward and not being stuck in the routine of rituals and habits from the story of Moses and the Israelites. They were having a hard time adjusting and moving on to their new way of life. They thought that going back to their old life was the answer to their survival.

> "Then the LORD said to Moses, 'Why are you crying out to me? Tell the Israelites to move on. Raise your staff and stretch out your hand over the sea to divide the water so that the Israelites can go through the sea on dry ground. I will harden the hearts of the Egyptians so that they will go in after them. And I will gain glory through Pharaoh and all his army, through his chariots and his horsemen. The Egyptians will know that I am the LORD when I gain glory through Pharaoh, his chariots and his horsemen." (Exodus 14:15-18, NIV)

LESSON † God always provides instructions and direction. Some things we will never understand until after we have moved on and time has passed.

While going through upsets, do you find it hard to move forward in your life and focus on Jesus and the spiritual rituals you have come to honor and respect?

Give Me a Drink

I pray today that the Lord will give each of us a fresh start as we begin this new week. If you are dealing with any trying or challenging circumstances, I pray that you will trust God to provide the help and resources needed to deal with them.

In our scripture today, we see the unnamed woman at the well, and she represents many of us and a lot of women in our lives—women whose souls are thirsty, women who are or at some point in life have been hurt, broken, and disappointed. We see that Jesus met this woman where she was at in her life. He did not change her circumstances. She still had a past, but now because she learned about and accepted the Living Water that Jesus offered, she had an even greater future, one that she ran to tell everybody about.

> "Jesus answered, 'Everyone who drinks this water will be thirsty again, but whoever drinks the water I give will never be thirsty. The water I give will become a spring of water gushing up inside that person, giving eternal life.' The woman said to him, 'Sir, give me this water so I will never be thirsty again and will not have to come back here to get more water.'"
> (John 4:13-15, NCV)

LESSON † There is a thirst of the soul that can only be satisfied by God. Through His mercies and compassion, He gives us a fresh start each new day! Jesus is as necessary for our spiritual life as water is for our physical life.

Jesus desires that everyone drinks from the Living Water! Will you ask Him today to give you a drink?

Pleasing God, Not People

It is my prayer today that each of us will step into the day knowing that the Lord orders our steps. I pray that we cheerfully do whatever we put our hands to do today. Let it be pleasing to the Lord.

I know that most of us have heard it said, "You can't please everyone," or, "You can't make everyone happy." We were divinely created to be helpers. We are also by nature nurturers. These are two great qualities and abilities that can often get used, abused, and often misdirected, causing what we do to become burdensome. We end up only getting hurt and being unfulfilled. We seldom get the response we want when we please anyone other than our Lord and Savior, Jesus Christ.

We must love God first and seek to please Him through our families, our relationships, and in all that we do. So let's ask Him to help us find that inner strength and peace in His love so that we can focus on pleasing Him.

> "In all the work you are doing, work the best you can. Work as if you were doing it for the Lord, not for people. Remember that you will receive your reward from the Lord, which he promised to his people. You are serving the Lord Christ. But remember that anyone who does wrong will be punished for that wrong, and the Lord treats everyone the same." (Colossians 3:23-25, NCV)

LESSON † Let pleasing God be bigger than pleasing people. Only our work that is done to the honor and the glory of Christ will bring us an everlasting reward.

Do you find yourself being tempted to conform to the world's ways instead of following Jesus's ways?

Blessed Because She Believed

We're several days into this week, I pray that each of you who are mothers have felt the joys and the honors of motherhood. And for those still waiting, that you continue to carry hope as you trust God's will for your life.

While motherhood has its joys and honors, it can also bring its heart-aches and pains. Mothers are expected to show up every day, no matter if they're exhausted or tired. In life, things don't always go as planned. On this journey of life, we all will need some help and encouragement. The good thing is that God will always see that we make it through the unexpected and challenging times by placing people in our lives who love us, understand us, and support us.

> "A few days later Mary hurried to the hill country of Judea, to the town where Zechariah lived. She entered the house and greeted Elizabeth. At the sound of Mary's greeting, Elizabeth's child leaped within her, and Elizabeth was filled with the Holy Spirit. Elizabeth gave a glad cry and exclaimed to Mary, 'God has blessed you above all women, and your child is blessed. Why am I so honored, that the mother of my Lord should visit me? When I heard your greeting, the baby in my womb jumped for joy. You are blessed because you believed that the Lord would do what he said.'" (Luke 1:39-45, NLT)

LESSON † **We must not quit or give up on God. He never asks us to do something and then sends us out alone to do it. He promises to never to leave us nor forsake us. Jesus says, "'Blessed rather are those who hear the word of God and obey it!'" (Luke 11:28, NIV)**

Having gone through some difficult and challenging times, do you still believe that God will do what He said? Why?

Thank You, Frontline Workers!

Let us make this "grateful Thursday" a day where we thank God for all the frontline workers.

During difficult times, our burdens can seem to be more than we can bear. We wonder how we can go on. We must remember that the Lord is our great burden-bearer who is able to keep us lifted up. Let's be reminded to let the peace of Christ rule in our hearts and let thankfulness overflow to those who we encounter during trying times.

THIS TOO SHALL PASS!

> "Your kingdom is an everlasting kingdom; Your rule is for all generations. The Lord is faithful in all His words and gracious in all His actions. The Lord helps all who fall; He raises up all who are oppressed. All eyes look to You, and You give them their food at the proper time. You open Your hand and satisfy the desire of every living thing. The Lord is righteous in all His ways and gracious in all His acts. The Lord is near all who call out to Him, all who call out to Him with integrity. He fulfills the desires of those who fear Him; He hears their cry for help and saves them. The Lord guards all those who love Him, but He destroys all the wicked. My mouth will declare Yahweh's praise; let every living thing praise His holy name forever and ever."
>
> (Psalm 145:13-21, HCSB)

LESSON † God is the source of all our daily needs and is ready to lift us up and bear our burdens if we turn to Him for help.

As a frontline worker or an essential worker, are your daily activities and decisions bringing life to others?

Happy with What You've Done

Thank God, we've made it to the end of this week! For many, the days seem to be running together, making it hard for us to know the days of the week.

It is my prayer that each of you is happy and satisfied with what you have done this week and that you're not focusing on what you may have missed. We will only be satisfied at the end of each day if we have done our best. We don't get to choose our days on the earth, but we do get to decide how we will spend them. We make every day count when we do our day-to-day work out of love for God. He gives each of us the same opportunities to use our time, gifts, and talents according to our abilities. He expects and desires us to invest them wisely until He returns.

> "'His master praised him for good work. "You have been faithful in handling this small amount," he told him, "So now I will give you many more responsibilities. Begin the joyous tasks I have assigned to you."'" (Matthew 25:21, TLB)

LESSON † Jesus is indeed coming back. The issue is not how much we have but how well we use it. We are responsible for using well what God has given us.

Are you satisfied with where you are in your relationship with God? If not, why?

Breathe

Praise God it's a new day with new mercies. I pray that each of us can let go of yesterday's worries and concerns so that we can have a fresh start at life today. Let us take nothing for granted this weekend and take every breath as a gift from God.

We often worry and carry our daily struggles by ourselves, which only shows that we have not fully trusted God with our lives. According to the Word, we must humble ourselves and admit that we need God's help. Have you ever thought that because you may have caused the struggles in your life by your sin and disobedience, that God's not concerned? The good news is that He is concerned! But we must turn to Him in repentance, recognizing that He cares, and He will bear the weight even of those struggles.

> "If you will humble yourselves under the mighty hand of God, in his good time he will lift you up. Let him have all your worries and cares, for he is always thinking about you and watching everything that concerns you." (1 Peter 5:6-7, TLB)

LESSON † Take a deep breath! Breathe and give all your worries and cares to God because He cares about what happens to us. We must not give in to our circumstances. We must give our circumstances to the Lord, who can control them.

Each breath is a gift! Have you ever noticed that your breath mimics what you think or how you are feeling? If you're feeling anxious, relax and just breathe.

All is Well

I'm trusting that all is well for all those belonging to the sisterhood of mothers, grandmothers, great-grandmothers, stepmothers, foster/adoptive mothers, godmothers, aunties, mother figures, those who have lost their mothers, those who have lost their child, all those waiting to be mothers, and all the fur babies' moms.

Being a mother is no easy task. The truth is, being a mother can be hard at times, but it also can be gratifying. If asked today, how you doing? How is your husband? Children? Are you able to make a declaration of faith and say that "all is well"?

In our scripture today (not to take away what the husband did) it was at the wife's request that they make room in her home for the man of God. Because of her devotion, God rewarded them above her greatest imagination.

Even at the death of her son, she kept her faith. She did not turn her back on God.

> "As she approached Mount Carmel, Elisha saw her in the distance and said to Gehazi, 'Look, that woman from Shunem is coming. Run and meet her and ask her what the trouble is. See if her husband is all right and if the child is well.' 'Yes,' she told Gehazi, 'everything is fine.'"
>
> (2 Kings 4:25-26, TLB)

LESSON † It's okay if all is not well today! Let us make room in our hearts and home for God, knowing that He loves us and that He has a plan and a work for us.

Has there been a time in your life when you've had to pause and ask God to help you understand what's happening in your life or your children's lives?

Life is Like a Camera

Thank God for the ability and the joy of seeing all the captured memories from our lives, especially those with our families and friends.

I'm sure that most, if not all, of us have heard the saying, "A picture is worth a thousand words, but memories are priceless."

Life is a blessing that we only get to live one day at a time. Let us not focus on the petty and negative things but the things worth cherishing that will make good memories.

> "From now on, brothers and sisters, if anything is excellent and if anything is admirable, focus your thoughts on these things: all that is true, all that is holy, all that is just, all that is pure, all that is lovely, and all that is worthy of praise."
>
> (Philippians 4:8, CEB)

Not everyone in our lives is capable or able to give us what we expect from them. We need to STOP holding grudges, forgive, enjoy life, and make those good positive memories. I promise reconciliation and forgiveness will change life's negative outlook!

LESSON † "Life is like a camera. Just focus on what's important. Capture the good times. Develop from the negatives, and if things don't work out, just take another shot." – Ziad K. Abdelnour [3]

Is there someone who you need to reconcile with or forgive so that you can focus on having positive memories?

The Rose and the Woman

God made women to be strong and unique. However, many of us struggle with finding our true identity, purpose, and worth.

> "You made all the delicate, inner parts of my body and knit them together in my mother's womb. Thank you for making me so wonderfully complex! It is amazing to think about. Your workmanship is marvelous—and how well I know it."
>
> (Psalm 139:13-14, TLB)

A comparison of the rose and a woman (Author Unknown)

"God Created the Rose
In the Likeness
Of A Woman.
The Rose Represents
Her Beauty.
The Stem Represents
Her Strength.
The Petals Are Soft
As Her Delicate Skin
The Fragrance
So Pure & So Sweet
The Leaves Represent
Her Arms Outstretched
Always Loving & Giving
And for Protection
He gives her thorns.
Thank You, God
For Making Me A Woman." [4]

LESSON † **Each time you look at a rose, remember that God made you unique.**

Are there times when you don't feel like you are enough?

Through the Fire

Praise God we have reached what we call "hump day," Wednesday. It is my prayer that your week is getting easier and not harder.

Living a life that is pleasing to God is not always easy. We make the mistake of thinking that if we serve God, somehow our lives will magically be easy and without trials. All we know is that in our lives, we seem to be going literally through "hell" fire.

If it is our desire to be used by God, we can expect at some point to go through the fire (trials). God has said when we walk through the fire, we will not be burned, nor will the flames hurt us. God will allow us to go through the fire as a process of purifying and refining our character so that we can indeed be fit for the kingdom. Going through trials and difficult times only serves to test our faith.

> "Bless our God, O peoples! Give him a thunderous welcome! Didn't he set us on the road to life? Didn't he keep us out of the ditch? He trained us first, passed us like silver through refining fires, brought us into hardscrabble country, pushed us to our very limit, road-tested us inside and out, took us to hell and back; Finally he brought us to this well-watered place." (Psalm 66:8-12, MSG)

LESSON † **When we feel like we are going through many unnecessary hard times, we should keep going! We will come out as pure gold, purified, tested, and fit for the kingdom.**

Think of a hard time in your life. How did God turn it into something beautiful?

Cup Overflowing

It's another day's journey in which we can rejoice and be glad. I pray that each of us will start today with grateful hearts, thanking the Lord for all that He has done and continues to do for us.

I pray that the Lord continues to bless us beyond measure with His Word each day! Dave Ramsey is an American radio show host, author, and businessman, and whenever I hear his callers ask him how he's doing, he says: "Better than I deserve." His response reminds me so much of how our heavenly Father blesses us each day with His grace and mercy.

He gives so much to our loved ones and us, and by His mercies, He withholds much more than what we deserve.

> "The Lord remembers us and will bless us. He will bless the people of Israel and bless the priests, the descendants of Aaron. He will bless those who fear the Lord, both great and lowly. May the Lord richly bless both you and your children. May you be blessed by the Lord, who made heaven and earth. The heavens belong to the Lord, but he has given the earth to all humanity. The dead cannot sing praises to the Lord, for they have gone into the silence of the grave. But we can praise the Lord both now and forever! Praise the Lord!" (Psalm 115:12-18, NLT)

LESSON † We serve a God who is worthy of our praise every day because He is so good to us! And He desires to bless abundantly those of us who trust in Him. Let us give Him the highest praise, hallelujah, the Hebrew word for "praise the Lord."

Has there been a time in your life you felt that you didn't deserve the blessings of God?

Hey, You!

Let us thank God for His grace and strength that has seen us through another long and busy week. Let us forget about all the troubles and hard times that are behind us.

So many times, we can't wait until Friday because Friday is usually the end of our work week. Instead of thanking God that it's Friday, let's thank God for giving us "this" day!

Because our lives can change at any moment, let's learn to be happy and welcome each new day as an opportunity to be who God has called us to be. Let us smile and cherish every moment, every hour, and every day because we know that we have placed them in God's hand.

> "Desperate, I throw myself on you: you are my God! Hour by hour I place my days in your hand, safe from the hands out to get me. Warm me, your servant, with a smile; save me because you love me." (Psalm 31:14-16, MSG)

LESSON † **When we put God's love first, it makes every day special!**

When God wakes you up to a new day, what is your greeting to Him?

Life Options

Thank God, we have made it to the weekend. I pray that each of us will be able to, at last, get some much-needed rest. I pray that as we rest, reflect, or even work, that we will each choose to make the most of every opportunity, being not as the unwise but as the wise.

Our lives are full of options and choices. Being foolish and having wisdom are two moral issues that are often written about in scripture. Psalms 14:1 (NIV) says, "The fool says in his heart, 'There is no God.'" Our scripture today lets us know that we are wise when we make the most of our time learning and doing God's will. As believers, we don't want to be unwise, wasting our spiritual opportunities. We want to live a life of wisdom, making the most of our time and understanding God's will for our lives.

> "So be very careful how you live. Do not live like those who are not wise, but live wisely. Use every chance you have for doing good, because these are evil times. So do not be foolish but learn what the Lord wants you to do."
>
> (Ephesians 5:15-17, NCV)

LESSON † **If we're going to be able to know God better and to serve Him more, we must choose carefully how live!**

> "We can't rewind the past, nor fast-forward the future, so today, all we can do is play, record, and keep moving until something should press the stop button."
>
> – Anthony Liccione [5]

Can you choose to be a light for Christ, intentionally witnessing of His love to those in you encounter today?

Now

It's a good thing to be among the living today. Let's give God the honor and praise because we know that without Him, we could not be here.

There's still a lot of uncertainty in our world today, and people expect to somehow return to what was. Many are talking about getting back to normal, whatever that may be. Unfortunately, we just can't know what the future holds, but thankfully we know that Jesus holds the future and all power in His Hands.

We're not promised tomorrow, next week, or even next month. There are no guarantees in this life, and there is a great move of God going on right NOW, and what God has for us is right NOW! I don't know what each of you is expecting or waiting for, but if there's ever been a time for us to be ready for a change, it is NOW. The time for being or doing what God has for us, having a break-through, being ready to receive what it is God has for us, or having deliverance and being set free—that time is NOW!

> "Now to Him who is able to do exceedingly abundantly above all that we ask or think, according to the power that works in us, to Him be glory in the church by Christ Jesus to all generations, forever and ever. Amen." (Ephesians 3:20-21, NKJV)

LESSON † With a NOW faith, we have the assurance that everything is all right. We can rejoice and be glad, taking no thought for tomorrow, because God is who He says He is and does what He says.

What one thing would you do today if you were sure you wouldn't fail at it?

There's No Place Like Home

Let us thank God for a new day and a week ahead with promise and possibilities. May each of us be a source of comfort, hope, and encouragement for those in or out of our homes.

Home is that place of safety and relief that we long for after a hard day's work. I thought about Dorothy from the *Wizard of Oz*, when she says, "There's no place like home."

As it turns out, Dorothy was only dreaming of being back home with her family in Kansas. The movie ends with her waking up in her bed surrounded by her family and friends with her saying, "There's no place like home!"

> "Then I saw 'a new heaven and a new earth,' for the first heaven and the first earth had passed away, and there was no longer any sea. I saw the Holy City, the new Jerusalem, coming down out of heaven from God, prepared as a bride beautifully dressed for her husband. And I heard a loud voice from the throne saying, 'Look! God's dwelling place is now among the people, and he will dwell with them. They will be his people, and God himself will be with them and be their God. "He will wipe every tear from their eyes. There will be no more death" or mourning or crying or pain, for the old order of things has passed away.'"
>
> (Revelation 21:1-4, NIV)

While living in a happy home may not be the case for everyone, it's reassuring to know that we have an eternal home in heaven.

LESSON † We must allow God to have priority in our homes if there is going to be love and peace.

Do you allow Jesus to make your heart His home?

Kindness

Let us thank God for waking us up today, another blessed day. I ask Him to order our steps! I pray that the Lord will increase the love that He has given to each of us so that we will be able to reach out and share that love and kindness to those we encounter today—hopefully, making a positive impact in their life.

According to the Mental Health Association, "We have chosen kindness because of its singular ability to unlock our shared humanity. Kindness strengthens relationships, develops community, and deepens solidarity. It is a cornerstone of our individual and collective mental health. Wisdom from every culture across history recognizes that kindness is something that all human beings need to experience and practice to be fully alive."[6]

Genuine love and kindness, no matter the source, can improve feelings of confidence and help give someone a positive outlook on life.

> "'I tell you, love your enemies. Help and give without expecting a return. You'll never—I promise—regret it. Live out this God-created identity the way our Father lives toward us, generously and graciously, even when we're at our worst. Our Father is kind; you be kind.'"
>
> (Luke 6:35-36, MSG)

LESSON † There is this misconception that kindness shows weakness. That is not true! Kindness, more often than not, requires courage and strength. Let's be kind!

How do you think God is inviting you to see others with kindness?

God Uses Broken Vessels

Let us thank God for allowing us to make it halfway through another week. I hope that each of you is feeling energized, creative, and ready to take on the day, and that you will be able to leave all the broken pieces of yesterday behind.

The feeling of brokenness and pain is a common bond between all of us. Yet, although we are compared to fragile broken vessels of clay, God is calling us to carry the valuable message of salvation.

We must fellowship daily with Him, knowing that He shines the brightest through our brokenness when we allow Him—not ourselves—to be our source of power. Let us be motivated and encouraged, knowing that we are seen as worthy to the almighty God.

> "Our bodies are made of clay, yet we have the treasure of the Good News in them. This shows that the superior power of this treasure belongs to God and doesn't come from us. In every way we're troubled, but we aren't crushed by our troubles. We're frustrated, but we don't give up. We're persecuted, but we're not abandoned. We're captured, but we're not killed. We always carry around the death of Jesus in our bodies so that the life of Jesus is also shown in our bodies." (2 Corinthians 4:7-10)

LESSON † We may be broken vessels, but God's desire is for us to become a reflection of Him so that others can see Him in and through us. With His grace and power, He will use our broken life experiences to help comfort others who are broken.

Has there ever been a time when you used your brokenness to help others?

Gracefully and Beautifully Broken

It's another "grateful Thursday" for us to give God glory and praises for keeping us. I pray that everyone is comforted knowing that we serve an awesome God who wants only the best for us.

Because we belong to God, nothing is happening in our lives that He is not concerned about. It's His desire for us to be whole. If you're feeling broken, dealing with an issue, or just feeling down, yield and surrender them all to the Lord. Know that He can and will make you whole again.

> "Jesus said to her, 'Daughter, you took a risk of faith, and now you're healed and whole. Live well, live blessed! Be healed of your plague.'" (Mark 5:34, MSG)

Today's scripture reminds me of the ancient Japanese practice of re-pairing cracked or broken ceramics with gold or silver, called the art of kintsugi. Once repaired, the pieces become even more beautiful and unique.

LESSON † **Our brokenness and our repairs are part of who we are and should be embraced and not hidden. And like the kintsugi pieces, our brokenness and repairs will make us better than new. Once God fixes us, we are free to live a well and blessed life.**

Is there a brokenness about you that you initially wanted to hide but decided to embrace?

Keep Going—You've Got This

Let us thank God for bringing us to the end of another week. Let us thank Him for encouraging us when we felt like giving up, and most of all, let's thank Him for guiding us when we didn't know which way to turn.

We must know that we're not alone! More importantly, every day of our lives, we must understand that we serve a God who cares so deeply for each of us! He has promised in His Word that He will never leave us nor forsake us!

> "So, what do you think? With God on our side like this, how can we lose? If God didn't hesitate to put everything on the line for us, embracing our condition and exposing himself to the worst by sending his own Son, is there anything else he wouldn't gladly and freely do for us? And who would dare tangle with God by messing with one of God's chosen? Who would dare even to point a finger? The One who died for us—who was raised to life for us!—is in the presence of God at this very moment sticking up for us. Do you think anyone is going to be able to drive a wedge between us and Christ's love for us? There is no way! Not trouble, not hard times, not hatred, not hunger, not homelessness, not bullying threats, not backstabbing, not even the worst sins listed in Scripture."
>
> (Romans 8:31-35, MSG)

LESSON † **We have an enemy who wants us to think that we are not good enough for our God and that He does not care for us. We can never be separated from God's love.**

How can you experience a more intimate fellowship with God?

OMG

I pray that this weekend will be all that each of you has been waiting for.

When we find ourselves experiencing a season of weakness and struggling, it's crucial for us to emotionally check in with how we feel and sometimes even seek medical help.

Seeking help for our mental health as Christians does not mean that our faith in God is weak. If we want to change how we feel later, we should start by measuring how we feel now, and yes, we still need to accept God's love and compassion for us because, ultimately, He's in control.

> "Surely you know. Surely you have heard. The LORD is the God who lives forever, who created all the world. He does not become tired or need to rest. No one can understand how great his wisdom is. He gives strength to those who are tired and more power to those who are weak. Even children become tired and need to rest, and young people trip and fall. But the people who trust the LORD will become strong again. They will rise up as an eagle in the sky; they will run and not need rest; they will walk and not become tired."
> (Isaiah 40:28-31, NCV)

LESSON † There are benefits in waiting. As we pause and wait for God to do what He promises to do in our lives, we have time to examine the things we value in life and discover happiness where we are. Waiting also allows us to develop a sense of appreciation as we learn that God's unbelievable strength is our source of strength that helps us to rise above difficulties in our lives.

Has there ever been a time when you did not want to wait on God?

A Tried and Tested Faith

Let us thank God for loving us unconditionally and giving us another day to start over. I pray today that God blesses the person deep within each of us and the person we are striving to be.

Let us be encouraged to know that none of us are perfect, but God still hears our cries, and He hears every one of our prayers.

Just like the refining of gold removes its impurities, the undesirable things in our lives that are not according to the will of God will be removed.

> "'But he knows every detail of what is happening to me; and when he has examined me, he will pronounce me completely innocent—as pure as solid gold! I have stayed in God's paths, following his steps. I have not turned aside. I have not refused his commandments but have enjoyed them more than my daily food. Nevertheless, his mind concerning me remains unchanged, and who can turn him from his purposes? Whatever he wants to do, he does. So, he will do to me all he has planned, and there is more ahead.'" (Job 23:10-14, TLB)

LESSON † We can enjoy the experience of having a closer relationship with God through our tried and tested faith, a faith that is worth more than any precious stone, including pure gold. As children of God, we are like gold. We go through the fire, and we come out like pure gold.

"We cannot learn some of the lessons in the Word of God just by studying them. They are learned by experience", says J. Vernon McGee. [7]

Have you ever come through a trial, and then you were able to see God's purpose for it?

Let Us Remember Them

Pausing to remember those who have give their lives so that we are able to enjoy our freedom is honorable. May their example of sacrifice inspire in each of us the selfless love of our Lord and Savior Jesus Christ, who laid down His life for us.

> "Greater love hath no man than this, that a man lay down his life for his friends." (John 15:13, KJV)

We live in a very self-centered society where it's every man, woman, and child for themselves.

> "When you do things, do not let selfishness or pride be your guide. Instead, be humble and give more honor to others than to yourselves. Do not be interested only in your own life, but be interested in the lives of others. In your lives you must think and act like Christ Jesus. Christ himself was like God in everything. But he did not think that being equal with God was something to be used for his own benefit. But he gave up his place with God and made himself nothing. He was born to be a man and became like a servant. And when he was living as a man, he humbled himself and was fully obedient to God, even when that caused his death—death on a cross." (Philippians 2:3-8, NCV)

LESSON † For those of us who are blessed to live in America, let us also be grateful for the gift of freedom that we ultimately have in Jesus who gave His life so that we may live eternally.

Have you ever had to give up a freedom for the sake of other believers in Jesus?

Serenity Prayers

I pray that each of us feels comfortable, at peace, and has a sense of self-acceptance with who we are today. Too many times, we let the opinions of others dictate how or what we think about ourselves.

Today I'd like to share a familiar prayer. "God grant me the serenity to accept the things I cannot change; courage to change the things I can; and the wisdom to know the difference." This prayer helps to keep me grounded and focused in my thinking. It's called the "Serenity Prayer." Although this prayer is not in the Bible, it encourages us with three truths from the Bible: peace, courage, and wisdom.

When we focus on these three truths, they will help us focus on who we are and what God calls us to. In the early 40s, the group Alcoholics Anonymous started using the shorter version of the prayer in their twelve-step program. There is also another variation of this prayer by Eleanor Brownn: "God, grant me the serenity to stop beating myself up for not doing things perfectly, the courage to forgive myself because I'm working on doing better, and the wisdom to know that You already love me just the way I am." [8]

> "Actually, I don't have a sense of needing anything personally. I've learned by now to be quite content whatever my circumstances. I'm just as happy with little as with much, with much as with little. I've found the recipe for being happy whether full or hungry, hands full or hands empty. Whatever I have, wherever I am, I can make it through anything in the One who makes me who I am." (Philippians 4:11-13, MSG)

LESSON † We may not always know God's plans. We must appreciate where we are on our life's journey, even if we're where we don't want to be.

What do you need from the Holy Spirit today—peace, courage, or wisdom?

Advice from a Tree

We are halfway through the week, and I pray that each of us will have the faith to trust that God will see us through it. Let's keep going and don't give up, no matter what comes up against us.

We must not let the struggles in life break us. Some days are going to be better than others, and some days will be worse than others. We will have to decide to be weak or to be strong. We should always look for blessings and not curses in each day, and wisdom from the Lord to make it through life.

> "'This is what the LORD says: Cursed is the person who trusts humans, who makes flesh and blood his strength and whose heart turns away from the LORD. He will be like a bush in the wilderness. He will not see when something good comes. He will live in the dry places in the desert, in a salty land where no one can live. Blessed is the person who trusts the LORD. The LORD will be his confidence. He will be like a tree that is planted by water. It will send its roots down to a stream. It will not be afraid in the heat of summer. Its leaves will turn green. It will not be anxious during droughts. It will not stop producing fruit."
>
> (Jeremiah 17:5-8)

This scripture asks us to look at ourselves and decide who we trust.

LESSON † Let us be like a well-watered tree that is blessed and that has strength for hard times and even some to share as we bear fruit for the Lord!

Is there someone in your life who you tend to put all your trust in? Why?

Plant in Tears, Weep in Joy

What an excellent time to be grateful for what God is doing for us. Today I pray for victory in each of our lives.

There will be those times when pain, suffering, isolation, and death will occur at any time. We can be assured that God has the ability to restore our lives beyond our greatest imagination. The tears that we shed can be the seeds that will grow into our harvest of joy tomorrow.

> "And we know that all that happens to us is working for our good if we love God and are fitting into his plans."
>
> (Romans 8:28, TLB)

God can restore and bring good out of ALL the tragic situations or anything that we will experience.

> "When the LORD brought back his exiles to Jerusalem, it was like a dream! We were filled with laughter, and we sang for joy. And the other nations said, 'What amazing things the LORD has done for them.' Yes, the LORD has done amazing things for us! What joy! Restore our fortunes, LORD, as streams renew the desert. Those who plant in tears will harvest with shouts of joy. They weep as they go to plant their seed, but they sing as they return with the harvest."
>
> (Psalm 126:1-6, NLT)

LESSON † We must be patient as we wait and look for our blessings to come because God's great harvest of joy is coming!

Are you ready for a harvest? What are you expecting in your season of harvest?

Divided Nation

Let us thank the Lord for allowing us to make it through another week. We know that He is in control and that He knows all about it. As we go through this weekend, let's ask that He give us the strength to make it through safe from all dangers, seen and unseen.

Our country sadly has its experience with riots and violence because of racial and ethnic inequalities. Because of sin and evil, the world is in a fallen state. It will never be free of violence until Satan is fully restrained. We must individually and collectively continue to use the weapon of prayer, education, and our right to vote for change to fight for justice and peace.

As humans, we have a desire for justice because it is in our nature. However, retaliation and revenge belong to God, not to man. God is fully aware of our struggles, and the day of His anger is coming, and it will be inescapable!

> "Knowing their thoughts, He told them: 'Every kingdom divided against itself is headed for destruction, and no city or house divided against itself will stand.'"
>
> (Matthew 12:25, HCSB)

LESSON † According to Jesus, division and infighting can only lead to collapse and destruction! United We Stand—Divided We Fall!

Are you always willing to show godly love toward others who are different from you in order to live united?

God Has the Most Amazing Plan

Let us thank God for hearing our unspoken thoughts and understanding everything we can't explain during troubled times.

The Word encourages us to trust God during difficult times of our life because He is with us even during those times. Sometimes, it may be hard for us to believe, but we serve an awesome God who has had a plan for all humanity since the beginning of time.

> "'For just as the heavens are higher than the earth, so my ways are higher than your ways and my thoughts higher than your thoughts.'" (Isaiah 55:9, NLT)

How reassuring it is to know that God can turn things around, even during times of crisis.

> "This is what the LORD says: When Babylon's 70 years are over, I will come to you. I will keep my promise to you and bring you back to this place. I know the plans that I have for you, declares the LORD. They are plans for peace and not disaster, plans to give you a future filled with hope."
> (Jeremiah 29:10-11)

LESSON † In this life, there are no guarantees that we will not have any pain, suffering, or hardships. But as long as God's mission is our focus, we can have an endless hope that He will see us through our situations.

How does knowing that God has a plan for your life help you?

Pentecost

Thank God for the coming of the Holy Spirit's gift, the church's birth, and the amazing plan and fulfilled promise made by Jesus and predicted by the prophets.

God has given us the most powerful and unifying gift—the presence of His Son's Spirit, which is His very own life, breath, and energy that connects every believer to Him.

The Lord will pour out His Spirit on all people:

> "'After this, I will pour my Spirit on everyone. Your sons and daughters will prophesy. Your old men will dream dreams. Your young men will see visions. In those days I will pour my Spirit on servants, on both men and women." (Joel 2:28-29)

The coming of the Holy Spirit:

> "When the day of Pentecost came, they were all together in one place. Suddenly a noise like a strong, blowing wind came from heaven and filled the whole house where they were sitting. They saw something like flames of fire that were separated and stood over each person there. They were all filled with the Holy Spirit, and they began to speak different languages by the power the Holy Spirit was giving them."
> (Acts 2:1-4, NCV)

LESSON † He, the Spirit, came to comfort us, lead us, guide us, teach us His truth, and empower us to live a life that's a witness of the successful things of God in our lives.

Do you feel that God is still active and moving in your life and the lives of others today?

The Roll Call

On this morning's roll call, who's here grateful that God woke you up this morning? Say amen if you are grateful!

Each of us must focus on getting our hearts right, renewing our minds and our thinking. We are encouraged to keep building a relationship with God and commit to understanding the purpose for which we are called.

We should not let anything take our eyes off our goal of knowing Christ.

> "I'm not saying that I have this all together, that I have it made. But I am well on my way, reaching out for Christ, who has so wondrously reached out for me. Friends, don't get me wrong: By no means do I count myself an expert in all of this, but I've got my eye on the goal, where God is beckoning us onward—to Jesus. I'm off and running, and I'm not turning back. So let's keep focused on that goal, those of us who want everything God has for us. If any of you have something else in mind, something less than total commitment, God will clear your blurred vision—you'll see it yet! Now that we're on the right track, let's stay on it."
>
> (Philippians 3:12-16, MSG)

LESSON † Let us be grateful for each new day, set goals, and make commitments that can change our lives.

Name one goal that you have set for yourself today to help you keep your focus on knowing Christ.

Upgraded with the Word of God

Let's incline our ears to hear what the Lord is saying to us during our days of trouble.

We're in a time when we need an upgrade of the Holy Spirit's power! With it, we will have more wisdom, more strength, and clearer direction. We serve a God who is still working things out. He desires to give us the best that life has to offer, and He will perfect all that concerns each of us.

No matter where we find ourselves in life at this moment in time, if we listen and commit to the Word of God, we will be elevated or upgraded not only spiritually but emotionally, physically, and financially. Our whole life will be better!

> "My child, pay attention to what I say. Listen carefully to my words. Don't lose sight of them. Let them penetrate deep into your heart, for they bring life to those who find them, and healing to their whole body. Guard your heart above all else, for it determines the course of your life."
>
> (Proverbs 4:20-23, NLT)

LESSON † We can, with confidence, entrust our lives to the Word of God. It will keep us, heal us, build us up, deliver us, and it will elevate and upgrade us from one level of victory and success to another level.

What one thing would make your life better if you had it?

Help is On the Way

Welcome to this "hump day"! I thank God that He's our way-maker and that He has helped us to make it halfway through another week.

Sometimes life can and will get hard! But the truth is, we serve a mighty and powerful God who can turn our pain into HOPE. As individuals and also as a nation, we must continue to trust God! God's Word lets us know that no matter what may come our way, He's got it handled.

> "'Don't be afraid, because I am with you. Don't be intimidated; I am your God. I will strengthen you. I will help you. I will support you with my victorious right hand. Everyone who is angry with you will be ashamed and disgraced. Those who oppose you will be reduced to nothing and disappear. You will search for your enemies, but you will not find them. Those who are at war with you will be reduced to nothing and no longer exist. I, the LORD your God, hold your right hand and say to you, "Don't be afraid; I will help you."'"
>
> (Isaiah 41:10-13)

LESSON ✝ The Lord, our God, is always watching and waiting for us to give Him all the impossible things that we experience in our lives. When we give them to Him, He delights in it because it shows that we trust in Him. He can handle them!

Has there been a time when you felt you were all alone and you didn't even trust God to help you? How do you reach out to those who are lonely?

We Shall Overcome

Let us thank God for another day to give Him praises. Today is "grateful Thursday," and although we continue to face some scary, troubled, and painful times, we still have so much to be thankful for.

Many are exhausted, expecting change and trying to change things. As believers, we should continue to expect that there will be trouble in an unbelieving world that is not connected with Christ, His Word, and the love that He has for His people. At the same time, we can expect our relationship with Christ to provide us with hope, peace, and comfort because we are connected to Him.

> "'The time is coming, and is already here, when all of you will be scattered. Each of you will go your own way and leave me all alone. Yet, I'm not all alone, because the Father is with me. I've told you this so that my peace will be with you. In the world you'll have trouble. But cheer up! I have overcome the world." (John 16:32-33)

LESSON † We shall overcome! Knowing that the final victory has already been won reassures us that we can hold on to the hope, peace, and comfort of Christ in our most trying and difficult times.

Think of a time when you felt that someone had a role in taking your joy away. Did you communicate it to them, or did you wait for them to come to you?

Weekend Loading

Thank God that we've made it to the end of another week. My prayer is that God will grant each of us a break from the stresses of our past week. May this coming weekend be filled with rest and peace, and let it be the beginning of a fresh start.

No matter how hard or stressful the week has been, we must continue to trust the Lord. Sometimes, the hard things that we experience put us on the path whereby our life changes will come through. In scripture, Jesus says to Simon Peter, "'You do not realize now what I am doing, but later you will understand'" (John 13:7, NIV).

We may not understand why we experience the hard and stressful things in our lives. But we can always ask God to help us let go of our concerns.

> "Come and see what the LORD has done, the desolations he has brought on the earth. He makes wars cease to the ends of the earth. He breaks the bow and shatters the spear; he burns the shields with fire. He says, 'Be still, and know that I am God; I will be exalted among the nations, I will be exalted in the earth.' The LORD Almighty is with us; the God of Jacob is our fortress." (Psalm 46:8-11, NIV)

LESSON † **Sometimes, when our life feels like it is falling apart, it may be hard for us to be still and trust God. As we approach this weekend, let's slow down, stay calm, and lean on God to get us through.**

How do you find rest from your labor? And do you invite God into your labors?

Healing the Wounds

I pray that God will remove the blindness and the coldness from the hearts of the people. I'm asking that we join together in unity and pray for personal healing in our lives and the land.

While our country is considered the greatest, we are still in need of healing! Together, we are strong! Unity is our Lord and Savior's goal, but it is the dread of Satan, and he will use any evil means necessary to break the bonds of unity. Thankfully, we serve a God who has a plan for evil and the troubles in our lives and the world.

> "The LORD appeared to him at night and said: 'I have heard your prayer and have chosen this place for myself as a temple for sacrifices. When I shut up the heavens so that there is no rain, or command locusts to devour the land or send a plague among my people, if my people, who are called by my name, will humble themselves and pray and seek my face and turn from their wicked ways, then will I hear from heaven, and I will forgive their sin and will heal their land.'"
>
> (2 Chronicles 7:12-14, NIV)

LESSON † Today, God has given us in His Word and by the power of His Holy Spirit the assurance of answers to our prayers. The place God chose then for sacrifices was the physical temple that He instructed Solomon to build. Today, He chooses each of us!

I'll close with this quote from Iyanla Vanzant: "**Until you heal the wounds** of your **past, you** are going to bleed into the future." [9]

Are you feeling that there is a sure path to restoration and healing for our lives and nation?

Feelings

Thank God for bringing us to another day to worship Him in spirit, truth, and faith. I pray that every decision that we make today will come from the guidance of the Holy Spirit and not from our emotions.

Our feelings and emotions are very important in our lives, and they most often reveal our level of spiritual maturity. Because our feelings and emotions come and go, we must ask God to help us to check them. Time after time, we are misled and make big mistakes when we base life decisions and thoughts on how we feel rather than obeying God's Word.

The Holy Spirit's power will help us live beyond our emotions and feelings so that we can live a more balanced life based on faith and the truth of God's Word.

> "Woe to those addicted to feeling good—life without pain! those obsessed with looking good—life without wrinkles! They could not care less about their country going to ruin."
>
> (Amos 6:6, MSG)

LESSON † God did not send His Spirit just to make us look or feel good about ourselves. The Holy Spirit is the power that makes it possible for us to reach the world for Christ by showing His love to others. We should stop believing everything we think and check our feelings through the Holy Spirit.

Do you see yourself as a part of God's plan to tell others about His love?

Get in Position

As we take up our positions on this Monday, let us thank God for allowing us to see the start of a new week! I believe in blessings of love and peace for the coming week for each of us.

I want to remind you that God's mercies are new every day. God is doing a new thing! He's opening and closing new doors, giving new breaks and new blessings! We just need to prepare our minds and get into a position to receive.

You may be asking, what position and how do I know if I'm in it? Scripture lets us know the answer: "If we are living in the light, as God is in the light..." (1 John 1:7, NLT). Some translations say, "walking in the light."

Did you see it? In the light is the position that we need to be in. When we live or walk in the light, we will recognize and receive what God has for us. Let us get in position, be unified with the light, stay connected to the source, and live in it constantly.

> "Arise, my people! Let your light shine for all the nations to see! For the glory of the Lord is streaming from you. Darkness as black as night shall cover all the peoples of the earth, but the glory of the Lord will shine from you. All nations will come to your light; mighty kings will come to see the glory of the Lord upon you." (Isaiah 60:1-3, TLB)

LESSON † We are told that Satan disguises or changes himself as an angel of light, so we must study God's Word if we're going to know that we are in the true light of Jesus.

What are some practical ways you can renew your mind to the Word of God so that you silence the voice of the enemy?

Change Takes Time

Let us thank God for another day! I pray that each of us realizes that we are fearfully and wonderfully made, no matter what we may be facing today.

Our life is a process, and we can't expect every day to be perfect. Each day will have its ups and downs. At times it may be difficult to see or understand what God is doing in and through us. It's during those times of uncertainty that we must trust God. We're like the clay on the potter's wheel, and each of us will find ourselves in different stages of the process. Some of us will be working to fulfill our life's purpose, and some of us will see ourselves shaped and strengthened as we experience what seems like the worst pain and most challenging time of our life.

> "My brothers and sisters, be very happy when you are tested in different ways. You know that such testing of your faith produces endurance. Endure until your testing is over. Then you will be mature and complete, and you won't need anything." (James 1:2-4)

> "And I am certain that God, who began the good work within you, will continue his work until it is finally finished on the day when Christ Jesus returns."
>
> (Philippians 1:6, NLT)

LESSON † It won't always make sense, and it will never feel good, but during our times of process, we must turn to God, trust Him, and keep the faith because there is a promise on the other side of the process. He's not finished with us yet!

During times of hardships today, how does the biblical truth that God's promises are true comfort you?

Wait for It

Let us start this "hump day" Wednesday with comfort, knowing that God is in control and that everything will be all right.

Life has a way of serving us vulnerable and uncertain times. Although it appears that sickness, death, evil, and injustice prevail in the world, we can rest assured knowing that God sees the bigger picture even when we don't understand why things occur as they do. We serve the one and only true God who is the ruler over everything, good or evil, and we will experience both in our life. When we do, if we learn from them, they will help us to grow spiritually.

We know God works things out for us, so we must be patient and wait for God to reveal what He is doing. Nothing is what it looks like with God, and everything happens at the right time and the right moment. In the scripture today, we see Habakkuk, the prophet of God, complaining to God because his prayers for God to punish wickedness and evil in the land were going unanswered. God's response to Habakkuk is the same answer He would give to each of us today.

> "The LORD answered me: Write down this vision; clearly inscribe it on tablets so one may easily read it. For the vision is yet for the appointed time; it testifies about the end and will not lie. Though it delays, wait for it, since it will certainly come and not be late." (Habakkuk 2:2-3, HCSB)

LESSON † We shouldn't make the mistake of thinking, just because we live for God, that He will automatically answer our prayers when and how we want Him to.

Is there anything that you are expecting or waiting for God to do in your life?

Blessed

Let us thank God that He has brought us to another "grateful Thursday." I pray that God will bless each of us above measure today, far more than we can think or ask.

Who among us doesn't want to live a blessed life? I firmly believe that everyone wants to live a blessed life—a life without bad health, a life where all of our financial needs are met, and a life where love, peace, and joy abide. Many times, we struggle with how to receive the blessings and promises when God's Word makes it clear what is required if we're going to experience them.

> "Blessed is the person who does not follow the advice of wicked people, take the path of sinners, or join the company of mockers. Rather, he delights in the teachings of the LORD and reflects on his teachings day and night. He is like a tree planted beside streams—a tree that produces fruit in season and whose leaves do not wither. He succeeds in everything he does." (Psalm 1:1-3)

LESSON † The choice to be blessed is ours! Blessings follow our obedience to God's Word, and if we're going to live a blessed life, we must acknowledge that God is the source of ALL blessings.

Knowing that we must choose to live a blessed life, have you made up your mind to live a blessed life?

Payday is Coming

We've made it to another Friday—a day that for many average working people is known as payday. Let us thank Jehovah Jireh, "the Lord will provide," for the daily provisions that He provides for each of us. I pray that He blesses our bodies for His service and that He blesses the work that we've done with our hands. May our labor be not in vain.

For those who are working, paydays are perhaps the most anticipated days of the month. I'm sure that all of us expect to get paid for the work that we do on our jobs, and we look forward to receiving what we've earned or what we feel that we are deserving of for the job done.

The same principle that applies to getting paid in the world today applies in God's kingdom, too. If we do the work of the enemy, there will be a payment in the form of judgment, and if we do the work of God, there will be rewards.

> "The Son of Man will come with his angels in his Father's glory. Then he will pay back each person based on what that person has done." (Matthew 16:27)

LESSON † Jesus Christ has the authority to judge all the earth, Christians and non-believers. Yes, payday is coming for each of us. Will you be ready?

We know that the payment for sin is death. Are there still areas in your life where Satan has a foothold?

Encouraging Words at the Well

Self-Care Day

Most of us have waited all week for the weekend, looking for relaxation, relief, and escape from the worries and stresses of life. Today is another day that we can thank God for our life, health, and strength. I pray that God blesses each of us today with peace and rest from the chaos of a busy week.

Many of us take great pride in taking care of our physical health, but how many are committed and disciplined enough to focus on our spiritual health? When we take time to nourish and take care of our souls, it's called spiritual self-care. We look to find and develop a deeper connection to God by reading His Word and looking for the meaning of our lives. We must always stay on our spiritual paths.

I have desired to use Women @ the Well on Facebook and namiejeanministeries.com as ways of providing spiritual support systems where we can soak up God's Word to replenish our souls daily.

> "Return to your rest, my soul, for the LORD has been good to you." (Psalm 116:7, NIV)

> "Truly my soul finds rest in God; my salvation comes from him." (Psalm 62:1, NIV)

LESSON † No matter what difficulties or challenging times we may face, whenever we need spiritual rest, we can always turn to God's Word. If we read and apply it to our lives, it has the power to soothe, revive, and replenish us. Make this a self-care day, and let's relax and let go of our stress and worries today!

Do you notice a change in your life when you read the Bible regularly? How do you make sure you don't lose focus of God's care and spiritual support in your daily life?

Red, White, and Blue

Let us thank God for another day to be thankful for His sovereignty and protection. In America, the trio colors of red, white, and blue are synonymous with the American flag. Let's thank God for the men and women who have stood together and fought for the freedom of our great nation under the flag.

Flags and banners are used to commemorate and celebrate victories and freedom. They are also used to indicate the identity and power of a specific individual, family, organization, and country. In the Old Testament, flags and banners were generally used to rally and to gather troops for war.

Throughout scripture, God instructed individuals to erect a banner or a flag as a reminder of how He helped them be victorious.

> "After the victory, the LORD instructed Moses, 'Write this down on a scroll as a permanent reminder, and read it aloud to Joshua: I will erase the memory of Amalek from under heaven.' Moses built an altar there and named it Yahweh-Nissi (which means 'the LORD is my banner')."
>
> (Exodus 17:14-15, NLT)

LESSON † We must never forget that our country's greatness and freedom are because of God's sovereignty and protection.

Are you in the habit of declaring independence from God? How do you declare your dependence on Him?

Tired

Today is a new day and the beginning of a new week. Let us ask God to open the eyes of our hearts that we may see the possibilities and promises that are before us this coming week, and that we stay on the path that He has for each of us.

It would appear that living life can often feel like running a race. That's why Paul uses the analogy of life as a race in his writings. It's not a sprint but a marathon! He's encouraging believers then and today that life will be difficult at times, and if we're going to finish strong, we will need not to get tripped up, and we must run with endurance.

Although we may face some worrisome and tough times, we are encouraged not to give up!

> "Keep your eyes on Jesus, our leader and instructor. He was willing to die a shameful death on the cross because of the joy he knew would be his afterwards; and now he sits in the place of honor by the throne of God. If you want to keep from becoming fainthearted and weary, think about his patience as sinful men did such terrible things to him. After all, you have never yet struggled against sin and temptation until you sweat great drops of blood." (Hebrews 12:2-4, TLB)

> "We can't allow ourselves to get tired of living the right way."
> (Galatians 6:9a-10)

LESSON † To live effectively as Christians, we must understand that life involves hard work, and we will need the help of the Holy Spirit.

During your times of weariness, do you use it as a time to remind you that you have limitations and God is the One who can help you?

Good Old Days

Let us thank God for another day to experience all that He has for us. Let's thank God for promising to be with us when we have troubles and for being with us through the good and the bad times in our lives.

When we look in the rearview mirror of life (our past), what do we see? Are we embracing our present life? Or are we stuck in our past? In times of hardship, tragedy, or stress, we may long for the past and look back because we don't want to deal with our current pain and situations. According to the *Merriam-Webster Dictionary, the good old days* refers to "a period of time in the past that a person thinks were pleasant and better than the present time." [10] But if we're going to experience the peace that surpasses all understanding in our lives and all that God has for us, we need to start by making sure we are not stuck in the past.

> "Don't always be asking, 'Where are the good old days?' Wise folks don't ask questions like that." (Ecclesiastes 7:10, MSG)

LESSON † There is nothing wrong with looking back into one's past. The past can be a great teacher. The problem is that when we spend our time in the past, we miss being effective in the present. God wants to do a new thing in each of us! Don't you see it?

Is there something from your past that you cannot let go of, and it's blocking you from receiving the new things that God has for you?

The Struggle is Real

Let us thank God for helping us make it to another "hump day" Wednesday. I pray that each of us will be able to finish this week strong, feeling God's comfort and His reassurance to be with us always and especially during our time of struggles.

By the time we reach Wednesday, we may have had an uphill struggle working through and overcoming several challenges that often cause us to look at the coming days with dread. Even though things may not go well for us, we must take every opportunity to see each day as a new and wonderful day. We don't need to be anxious about what challenges tomorrow may bring. The Word tells us that we only have this day and that we should rejoice and be glad.

> "This is the day the LORD has made. Let's rejoice and be glad today!" (Psalm 118:24)

Whatever struggles each day may bring, we can be ready to face them because we have a divine Warrior and a Commander-in-Chief who knows what's best for us. He promises that He will not leave us nor forsake us.

LESSON † Lord knows that we've gone through so much already this year. Each of us has our struggles, but we cannot quit, even though sometimes it feels like it's easier to quit than to keep going. Yes, the struggle is real, but our God is, too!

Do you find yourself constantly worrying or concerned in your struggles, or are you trusting that the Almighty God is with you?

Born for a Purpose

Let us use today's new breath to give God the highest praise on this "grateful Thursday"! Say it out loud: HALLELUJAH! I pray that God gives each of us the strength and energy to make it through this blessed day, knowing that we are His children and that He will take care of our every need.

Each of us born into this world has a God-given purpose! We are made for a purpose that is only found when we look to God. As children of God, knowing our purpose will help us understand that everything that happens to us is not always about us but is only a means or the path to us fulfilling God's purpose for our lives.

Jesus, being our example of living a life that pleases God, showed us when He stood before Pilate that even He knew why He was born and what He was called to do.

> "Pilate asked him, 'So you are a king?' Jesus replied, 'You're correct in saying that I'm a king. I have been born and have come into the world for this reason: to testify to the truth. Everyone who belongs to the truth listens to me.'"
>
> (John 18:37)

LESSON ✝ I'm sure that we are all living lives that we hope will give us meaning. When we look to God to learn our purpose, He will lead us to know Him, worship Him, and live our lives for Him!

Do you know your life's purpose? And do you feel that you are able to fulfill it?

Freedom Delayed

Let's thank God for a change! Let us join together in unity and pray for continued change, peace, and liberty for all!

While the Bible has many stories of slavery and captivity, freedom, and deliverance, we need to know what God's intention was for humanity in the beginning.

> "Then God said, 'Let us make humans in our image, in our likeness. Let them rule the fish in the sea, the birds in the sky, the domestic animals all over the earth, and all the animals that crawl on the earth.' So, God created humans in his image. In the image of God, he created them. He created them male and female." (Genesis 1:26-27)

Regardless of race, gender, or situation in life, we are all created in the image of God. Scripture also clarifies that each of us is very valuable to Him and that each of us is deserving of fair treatment and justice and should be treated with dignity.

> "This Lord is the Spirit. Wherever the Lord's Spirit is, there is freedom." (2 Corinthians 3:17)

LESSON † **The Christian faith is about removing enslavement. Paul makes it known that the new covenant is better than the old because it is a ministry of freedom. Christ's death on the cross secures freedom for anyone who believes.**

Have you received and are you living in your freedom through Christ Jesus?

Fun in the Son

Let us thank God for another blessed day and weekend. I pray that the light of Christ shines bright in each of our lives today.

While many people look forward to the summertime for the much-awaited fun to be had in the sun. God created, and He controls all seasons of the year.

> "You determined all the boundaries of the earth. You created summer and winter." (Psalm 74:17)

Every season is necessary and important. Summer is the time when many of us take vacations. Because there is no such thing as a spiritual vacation, believers have the opportunity to make their summer a time of spiritual renewal by drawing closer to the Son.

> "Those who believe in the Son of God have the testimony of God in them. Those who don't believe God have made God a liar. They haven't believed the testimony that God has given about his Son." (1 John 5:10)

LESSON † **It is never God's desire for us to take a vacation from Him. He doesn't want us to become complacent during the summer. He doesn't want us to turn our backs on Him, but He does want us to have some summer fun in the SON!**

How do you find ways to include Jesus and the Word of God into your summer?

Dance with My Father Again

What a blessing it is to have the unwavering love of a father who loves you and the Lord! Unfortunately, not everyone feels that they have a reason to honor their earthly fathers. The enemy would have us focus only on our pain and hurt. If you're reading this and you have been hurt or disappointed by the man you call Dad, please know that people, no matter who they are, can only give us what they have.

Whether we're young or old, we can forgive for the things that we've missed from the man we call Dad. Our loved ones often pass on, and we are left with regrets and wishing for just one more (fill in the blank). Whether it's long or short, there is a road to reconciliation!

> "His preaching will turn the hearts of fathers to their children, and the hearts of children to their fathers. Otherwise I will come and strike the land with a curse."
>
> (Malachi 4:6, NLT)

LESSON † Just because bad things happen in our relationships with our dads, we should not just give up on them. We are not told to obey our parents because they are good or perfect, but because it is the right thing to do!

Many times, our earthly fathers fall short of God's characteristics as Father. What are some of God's characteristics as Father that you have longed for from your earthly father?

Walking with Confidence, Courage, and Style

Let us thank God for another Monday morning! I pray that each of us feels that we are awesome and that we're ready to walk confidently, courageously, and with style into another amazing and productive week.

It's a new morning and a new week filled with new mercies. Sometimes, just the start of a new week can cause some apprehensions in our lives. We find it hard, or we just don't know where to find the confidence to keep moving forward. We can find the confidence to start this new week by looking to the Lord. He will give us the confidence we need if we're feeling uncertain. On this new day, the Lord wants each of us to:

> "Lean on, trust in, *and* be confident in the Lord with all your heart *and* mind and do not rely on your own insight *or* understanding. In all your ways know, recognize, *and* acknowledge Him, *and* He will direct *and* make straight *and* plain your paths." (Proverbs 3:5-6, AMPC)

Too often, to live right, we try to please other people and not God.

> **LESSON** † It's impossible to follow God consistently without His life-changing love in our hearts. However, with confidence, we can change the outlook on our new week one small step at a time.

In your efforts to live right, do you try to please people or God? If you please people, how has that benefited you?

Show Me Where to Walk

As we continue to walk confidently, courageously, and with style, let us thank God for bringing us to the beginning of a new day. I pray that each of us will connect with God today and seek His guidance for today as we go about our way and that He will help us through any decisions and choices that we may need to make.

As Christians, we're taught to connect with God at the start of every morning by praying, meditating, reading the Bible, and through other quiet time activities so that we will be mindful of His presence with us throughout the day. The psalmist says:

> "Let the morning bring me word of your unfailing love, for I have put my trust in you. Show me the way I should go, for to you I entrust my life." (Psalm 143:8, NIV)

How many of you know that the enemy will attempt to confuse us, and he will set traps for us as we walk with God? We must remember that God's mercies are new every morning, and we don't have to wait until we're in trouble to seek Him. If the only time we seek Him is when we're in a situation, we are in trouble.

> "That the LORD your God may tell us the way we should walk and the thing we should do." (Jeremiah 42:3, HCSB)

LESSON † Each of us will come to a crossroad at some point in our lives, and we will have to choose which way to go. For some, the decision may be more challenging than for others.

What benefits of walking in the Spirit have you experienced?

Living Water

I pray that as we step into this "hump day" Wednesday that we will continue to trust, follow, and depend on God. We've got to keep moving and praying for strength so that we don't get weary.

We're on a journey with the Lord, and we must not take our eyes off of Him. There will be those days when our week gets to be a little painful and challenging. We must remember to continue to stand on the promises of God's Word during those times because when we read His Word in the Bible, it's like we're drinking life-sustaining living water! One thing that is certain to us as God's people is that He's forever working to assure us that we can trust in Him.

Throughout the pages of the Bible, there's a history of God's life-giving truths and His eternal gift of running water that quenches the souls of His people in the most barren of places.

> "You in Your great mercy forsook them not in the wilderness; the pillar of the cloud departed not from them by day to lead them in the way, nor the pillar of fire by night to light the way they should go. You also gave Your good Spirit to instruct them, and withheld not Your manna from them, and gave water for their thirst." (Nehemiah 9:19-20, AMPC)

> "They did not thirst when He led them through the deserts; He made water flow for them from the rock; He split the rock, and water gushed out." (Isaiah 48:21, HCSB)

LESSON † We serve the God whose Word is like a powerful rushing stream of water that will never run dry.

What will help you stay on track with reading scripture and drinking from the steam of Living Water?

Bridge Over Troubled Water

Let us thank God for waking us up this "grateful Thursday." Let us thank Him for all that He does for us, for the strength He gives us that helps us make it through and survive all the troubles that life brings.

We're surrounded by many intensified and visible troubles these days. The world seems to be drowning, and we are all doing our best not to be washed away by the rough waves of its sins, illnesses, poverty, racism, and politics. When we find ourselves at a point in our lives when we are approaching or are in troubled waters and we need help moving forward, God will be that bridge over our troubled waters that will set our feet back on solid ground.

> "When you go through deep waters, I will be with you. When you go through rivers of difficulty, you will not drown."
>
> (Isaiah 43:2a, NLT)

LESSON † Yes, there are many troubled waters in this world, but we don't have to drown in them. God promises always to be with us! He's like a bridge over troubled waters that's there to make our paths easy and to give us safe passage over our troubled waters.

How are you on your journey today? Are you facing troubled waters and in need of a bridge?

Walking in Darkness

Let us thank God for allowing us to make it to another Friday morning. Let each of us ask God for His discerning spirit of wisdom so that we can know right from wrong and so that we can see the light from the darkness as we walk with Him today.

The darkness that we experience most of the time has nothing to do with sin or the devil but is usually an empty, lost, lonely feeling of being abandoned by God.

Remember Job? Unfortunately, when we as God's people come face to face with dark times, we don't always recognize what it is, and it in some ways almost always nearly takes us out. During these times of darkness, we often want to quit walking with God and return to our familiar ways that are not good instead of staying the course and remembering what it is that He has already done for us.

> "Who among you fears the LORD and obeys his servant? If you are walking in darkness, without a ray of light, trust in the LORD and rely on your God. But watch out, you who live in your own light and warm yourselves by your own fires. This is the reward you will receive from me: You will soon fall down in great torment." (Isaiah 50:10-11, NLT)

LESSON † We must keep walking with the Lord even when we don't feel His presence. It is far better for us to walk on the path in darkness with faith while trusting and following God than to walk by our light of self-sufficiency, which always burns out.

When going through dark times, do you seek God's help in providing His light or do you trust in your own?

Feet Slipping

The Lord has brought us to another weekend. I pray that each of us continues to trust that He will strengthen us and grant us what we need to keep moving forward. May we use this weekend to get some much-needed rest, relaxation, and replenishing.

How many of us have cried out, "Lord, have mercy," or, "Lord, help me"? I would be willing to say many of us, if not all of us. There are times we will all call on the Lord for help. We must continue to look to God because He is the same yesterday, today, and forever. When we face unwelcome situations and instabilities in our lives, they can make us feel weak and lost.

I'm reminded of David in the scripture today. He uses the analogy of his feet slipping as a way to say he is feeling weak. He knew, and he wants us to know today, that the Lord will be with us when we feel that our spiritual footing is slipping.

> "The Lord will not forsake his people, for they are his prize. Judgment will again be just, and all the upright will rejoice. Who will protect me from the wicked? Who will be my shield? I would have died unless the Lord had helped me. I screamed, 'I'm slipping, Lord!' and he was kind and saved me." (Psalm 94:14-18, TLB)

LESSON ✝ Are you slipping? No matter how we call on the Lord, He's got us, even when we don't know it! We need to hold on to the fact that His love is enough to save, support, hold, and keep us!

Have you ever been in distress and called on the Lord? How did He help you?

God is Able to Keep Us

Let us thank God for covering us this week with His favor and for shielding us from dangers seen and unseen. Let us continue to give Him all the glory, for He is and has indeed kept us safe and from falling.

You may have noticed that we've had a "theme of walking" this week that went like this:

As long as we walk with God:

> "The LORD directs the steps of the godly. He delights in every detail of their lives. Though they stumble, they will never fall, for the LORD holds them by the hand."
> (Psalm 37:23-24, NLT)

God can keep us:

> "He will not allow your foot to slip *or* to be moved; He Who keeps you will not slumber." (Psalm 121:3, AMPC)

LESSON † God is so powerful that He can keep us from stumbling or falling into sin. He can keep us from falling away from the faith so that He can, with joy, present us faultless or blameless before the presence of His glory.

Have there been times when you wanted to give up on your faith, but instead you sought the help of God?

Dusting Off Our Bibles

Let us thank God for the beginning of another week whereby we can give ourselves entirely to His work. May He give us wisdom and revelation as we read His Word this week, and let us grow in the grace and the knowledge of His truths.

Whether young or old, every believer needs to read the Word of God. Unfortunately, the Bible has little or no priority in the lives of many. King Josiah began a project to rebuild the temple that had been run down and deserted under the evil King Manasseh's leadership. As they were working, the high priest found a copy of the Book of the Law of Moses.

> "'On behalf of those who are left in Israel and Judah and me, ask the LORD about the words in this book that was found. The LORD's fierce anger has been poured on us because our ancestors did not obey the Lord's word by doing everything written in this book.'"
>
> (2 Chronicles 34:21)

LESSON † When we don't have access to God's Word, we can't live in obedience to Him. We need to be looking to God for His instructions. We need to be dusting off our Bibles so that it can provide us with the basics of God's truth and show us how we are to be living.

Do you live your life as a child of God? What will help you stay on track with reading the Bible?

Knock, Knock, Who's There?

Let us thank God for another day to give Him praise and to worship Him. I pray that God visits each of our homes, jobs, churches, cities, states, and the world with His love, healing, blessings, and miracles.

Life presents us with many challenging things, causing our lives to be full of stress. There may not be many knocks on our physical doors at times, but Jesus continues to knock on the doors of our hearts.

Jesus knocks at the door of each of our hearts because He wants to save us and have fellowship with us. The Laodicea church's problem was that they thought they were rich toward God, but they were spiritually dead. They had become lukewarm.

> "'Look! I have been standing at the door, and I am constantly knocking. If anyone hears me calling him and opens the door, I will come in and fellowship with him and he with me. I will let everyone who conquers sit beside me on my throne, just as I took my place with my Father on his throne when I had conquered.'"
>
> (Revelation 3:20-21, TLB)

LESSON † We must not knowingly keep Christ's life-altering presence and power on the other side of the door. He waits for us to respond to His presence and His love, and He wants us to open our lives to Him.

Jesus stands at the door of our hearts. If you haven't let Him in, will you let Him in today?

A New Thing

Let's give God thanks for allowing us to make it to another "hump day" Wednesday. Let us not enter this new day with any doubt or fear, but let us pray that God gives us the strength and the hope that will lead us to the things we need to finish strong.

We are told to forget or not to focus on our past situations, not because they are bad or wrong, but because we serve the only true and living God who wants to impact our lives by making a way out of no way every day. We need to always be ready for what God is doing.

> "The LORD says, 'Forget what happened before, and do not think about the past. Look at the new thing I am going to do. It is already happening. Don't you see it? I will make a road in the desert and rivers in the dry land.'"
>
> (Isaiah 43:18-19, NCV)

The Enduring Word Bible Commentary explains it this way: "Do not remember the former things, nor consider the things of old. This shows us there is a sense in which we must not forget the past in terms of God's great work on our behalf. There is also a sense in which we must forsake and forget the past, with all its discouragement and defeat, and move on to what God has for us in the future." [11]

LESSON † **God doesn't want us to get stuck by focusing on our past difficulties, mistakes, and sins.**

The wage of sin is death. Do you ask God to release you from the consequences of your past sins through Jesus's death on the cross?

Unshakeable Kingdom

I know that we praise God every morning for waking us up. However, today, let's stop and pause on this "grateful Thursday" morning and give Him another thank you for answering our prayers, providing for our needs, giving His blessings, and more importantly, for who He is.

May we be able to stand firm and not be shaken by things that happen around us. Yes, our world at times appears to be shaken as we face culture crisis, injustice, sickness, death, political unrest, judgment, and you name it, we experience it.

Although the world gets shaken, we must not think of it as strange, for the Word tells us that there is nothing new under the sun.

> "What was will be again, what happened will happen again. There's nothing new on this earth. Year after year it's the same old thing." (Ecclesiastes 1:9, MSG)

Despite everything that we go through, we must not give up on our God, who is the Creator of heaven and earth.

> "Therefore, since we are receiving a kingdom that cannot be shaken, let us hold on to grace. By it, we may serve God acceptably, with reverence and awe, for our God is a consuming fire." (Hebrews 12:28-29, HCSB)

LESSON † I believe that the world is shaking now because God is cleaning the house. Eventually, it will crumble, and only the unshakable kingdom of God will stand.

On what foundation do you put your faith? How are you putting it on Jesus the Solid Rock?

Hope in a World That's Not Our Home

We've made it to another Friday. Instead of just thanking God that it's Friday, let us give Him the glory for our life, health, and strength that has allowed us to make it here today. We never know from day to day what we'll be doing or where we will be. No matter what, no matter where, God remains the same today, yesterday, and forever! God continues to be the only constant in our lives as we live in this world today.

The Apostle Peter lets us know in this scripture today that as Christians, we live as "pilgrims and strangers" in this world as he shares with us what our relationship with this world is supposed to look like.

> "Dear friends, since you are foreigners and temporary residents {in the world}, I'm encouraging you to keep away from the desires of your corrupt nature. These desires constantly attack you. Live decent lives among unbelievers."
>
> (1 Peter 2:11)

Ever since the fall of man in Genesis chapter three, when sin first entered this world, the world became such a colossal battleground where the angels under Satan's power and those under God's authority are at war.

> **LESSON** † Because of what God has done through Christ Jesus and the fact that He is with us in this world, we can remain hopeful and live in a place that we know is not our home.

As we live here on earth, how do you keep from focusing on your circumstances and instead put your hope in our eternal home to come?

God Has a Plan – Do You Trust Him?

May God's peace and love be with each of us on this beautiful day. I pray that as we go about our way today, we will be safe. I pray that the Spirit of God guides us and unites us as one nation. May He continue to bless us and keep us!

By trusting in God, He's made it possible for us to endure and survive as a powerful and influential nation for over 200 years. Unfortunately, one of man's greatest temptations is not to trust God, and another is to live outside of His will. No one should want to be out of God's will or His hands, and rightfully so. Since the beginning of time, God the Lord of creation, our mighty God, has always had a plan for ALL humanity and desires that not one of us perish.

> "And God saw everything that he had made and that it was very good." (Genesis 1:31a)

The Lord's plans stand firm forever. He is entirely trustworthy, and His intentions never change.

> "The LORD blocks the plans of the nations. He frustrates the schemes of the people of the world. The LORD's plan stands firm forever. His thoughts stand firm in every generation. Blessed is the nation whose God is the LORD. Blessed are the people he has chosen as his own." (Psalm 33:10-12)

LESSON † Whenever we find ourselves doubting that we don't have anyone or anything to trust in, we should remember that God is consistent, and He has included every one of us in His plan. "In God We Trust"!

Are there areas in your life where you haven't surrendered to God? What's stopping you?

Reset the World

Let us thank God for the blessing of seeing another day. Let us continue to trust in His unfailing love as we lift our families and everything that concerns us into His hands. His grace is sufficient for each of us today.

In this world, we will face many difficult times, but our compassionate and just God generously renews His grace in every situation we face. Sometimes waiting on God can seem like an eternity. We want the easy button or the reset button of life pushed immediately.

God pushed the reset button on the earth before because of sin. He told Noah, "It's all over. It's the end of the human race. The violence is everywhere. I'm making a clean sweep." We are fortunate He promised not to do that again and that He would establish a covenant with Noah, which includes each of us today.

> "'Then I saw a new heaven and a new earth, for the old heaven and the old earth had disappeared. And the sea was also gone. And I saw the holy city, the new Jerusalem, coming down from God out of heaven like a bride beautifully dressed for her husband. I heard a loud shout from the throne, saying, 'Look, God's home is now among his people! He will live with them, and they will be his people. God himself will be with them.'" (Revelation 21:1-3, NLT)

LESSON † God's ultimate desire for a renewal or a resetting of this world is because He wants to become entirely reunited with us. He wants the earth's condition to reset back to the way things were before sin crept in.

Has there been a time when your life was interrupted and you didn't see it as God's way of renewing your mind and resetting your life?

Moving Forward

I venture to say, God says that He wants us to make this thing personal. What thing? This Christian walk (our relationship) with Him.

Today, let's declare and decree victory this week by believing, praying, and meditating on the following scripture:

> "But now, O Jacob, listen to the LORD who created you. O Israel, the one who formed you says, 'Do not be afraid, for I have ransomed you. I have called you by name; you are mine. When you go through deep waters, I will be with you. When you go through rivers of difficulty, you will not drown. When you walk through the fire of oppression, you will not be burned up; the flames will not consume you.'"
>
> (Isaiah 43:1-2, NLT)

The scripture clarifies that God created the people of Israel, and they were unique to him. It also lets us know God redeemed them and called them by name to belong to Him and that He protected them whenever they found themselves "between a rock and a hard place" (in trouble).

> **LESSON** † We will, at some point in our life, go through rivers of difficulty. They will either cause us to drown or force us to grow stronger. When we go through in our strength, we are more likely to drown.

We, too, are unique to God! What thing has He saved you from that makes you feel special and unique to God?

Let Go of Pressure to Prove Yourself

Let us thank God for bringing us to another day. He's giving us yet another chance to know Him and to follow Him. May each of us experience Him in a new way by being better than we were yesterday.

Everyone desires to be a good person. Unfortunately, in trying to be good or even better, we tend to rely on others' opinions about who or what we should be, thus causing us to work at proving ourselves as worthy by them or by their standards. Don't get me wrong—I don't think that there is anything wrong with getting or giving the viewpoint or assessing others in our life.

I believe it becomes a problem when we rely solely on what others think about us or assume that others should live up to our standards rather than what our Heavenly Father says about each of us.

> "So encourage each other and build each other up, just as you are already doing." (1 Thessalonians 5:11, NLT)

> "See that no one pays back evil for evil, but always try to do good to each other and to all people."
> (1 Thessalonians 5:15, NLT)

LESSON ✝ Since we all need to be made right with God, we don't need to pressure ourselves to prove ourselves to each other. We will only be made right and free from sin by the grace of God, which is a gift to us through Jesus.

What is it that you think makes each of us a good person?

Medicine for Your Soul

May God continue to bless each of our hearts and homes on this "hump day" Wednesday. May He give us the strength to make it through this week.

We need God's strength and power to survive each day. There will not always be one clear plan. We can thank God that Jesus is our Great Physician, and He has the best-prescribed medicine for our wounded bodies and souls. The truth of God's Word is the prescription for whatever troubles, worries, or pains us, but like medicine, it can only work if it is applied to the affected areas.

We see Jesus being that Great Physician, that expert doctor giving a medical prescription. He is prescribing the most potent medicine, the truth of who He is, only to have it rejected like bad medicine.

> "Jesus answered, Is it not written in your Law, I said, You are gods? So men are called gods [by the Law], men to whom God's message came—and the Scripture cannot be set aside *or* cancelled *or* broken *or* annulled—[If that is true] do you say of the One Whom the Father consecrated *and* dedicated *and* set apart for Himself and sent into the world, You are blaspheming, because I said, I am the Son of God? If I am not doing the works [performing the deeds] of My Father, then do not believe Me [do not adhere to Me and trust Me and rely on Me]" (John 10:34-37, AMPC)

LESSON † **The truth will save our life. If we're going to receive God's prescribed healing, we need faith that enables us to know Him and to believe in Him.**

Can you think of a time you refused to accept discipline or something that you knew was for your good?

Praise God from Whom All Blessings Flow

Let us praise God from whom all of our blessings flow on this "grateful Thursday." Let each of us continue to expect God's favor in our lives. May He show us His love, His strength, His protection, and His guidance this day.

Whatever we need, how many of you know that Jesus is truly our ride or die friend. He promises to be with each of us even unto the end of time. Now that's a friend who is worthy of being praised! Every day, each of us can choose whether we live our lives with joy and peace, believing God's promise to pour us out an abundance of blessings, or we can show doubt and disbelief in the way that we live by what we think or what we say.

> "Everything comes from him; Everything happens through him; Everything ends up in him. Always glory! Always praise! Yes. Yes. Yes." (Romans 11:36, MSG)

LESSON † Let us choose this day to be grateful with an open heart, no matter our situation. Let us praise Him on the mountain top and praise Him in the valley!

What do you need from God? Do you believe He's going to give it to you?

The Pursuit of Happiness

Welcome to this blessed Friday. Let us remember that God's promises still apply to each of us, and thank God for getting us to the end of another week. May our weekend be a happy one.

Speaking of happiness, most of us, deep down, want to be happy. As Christians, we prefer to use the word "blessed," which according to the *Holman Study Bible,* is a Hebrew word (*'ashrey*) that expresses happiness, joy, and satisfaction in one's state or circumstances. [12]

> "Blessed (happy, fortunate, prosperous, and enviable) is the man who walks *and* lives not in the counsel of the ungodly [following their advice, their plans and purposes], nor stands [submissive and inactive] in the path where sinners walk, nor sits down [to relax and rest] where the scornful [and the mockers] gather. But his delight and desire are in the law of the Lord, and on His law (the precepts, the instructions, the teachings of God) he habitually meditates (ponders and studies) by day and by night. And he shall be like a tree firmly planted [and tended] by the streams of water, ready to bring forth its fruit in its season; its leaf also shall not fade or wither; and everything he does shall prosper [and come to maturity]." (Psalm 1:1-3, AMPC)

LESSON † **If we're going to achieve happiness worth having, we must have God's Word in our hearts. The only place we can find real, lasting happiness is in a relationship with God.**

Using an emoji, how would you describe your feelings about your relationship with God today?

Everything is Going to Be All Right

We've made it to the weekend. This means that we didn't quit, and we didn't give up! May the Lord continue to strengthen each of us in our weakness and faith when we're fearful. Because the Lord hears our prayers, we can rest assured that everything is going to be all right.

Living through everything that life throws at us, we can't help but find ourselves worrying. We can't help but worry about things like our health, money, and family issues. We tend to worry even when there is little or no reason to worry. The Bible has a lot to say about worrying. Not to spoil the ending, but everything will be all right!

> "So don't ever worry about tomorrow. After all, tomorrow will worry about itself. Each day has enough trouble of its own."
> (Matthew 6:34)

> "Don't worry about anything; instead, pray about everything; tell God your needs, and don't forget to thank him for his answers." (Philippians 4:6, TLB)

LESSON † **Worry weighs a person down. The Word doesn't discourage us from planning for the future, but it does prohibit us from worrying about it.**

Do you recognize God's comforting presence when the weight of worry presents itself in your life?

We Shall Wear a Crown

It is my prayer that each of you feels content in knowing that you are treasured and loved by God on this blessed Sunday morning.

We must continue to hold on, knowing that every blessing promised to us and ordained by God is on the way. We may not know when or how, but we must trust and believe that our best is yet to come.

As Christians living in this world, we should keep our minds clear and be alert that we have an enemy, the devil, who is prowling around like a roaring lion as he looks for someone to devour. We, however, can stand firm and don't have to let anybody or anything change who we are. If we cave into the trials of life because we don't have the faith and self-assurance of God's presence and care, we won't experience being blessed or have the confidence that we can have eternal life.

> "Blessed are those who endure when they are tested. When they pass the test, they will receive the crown of life that God has promised to those who love him." (James 1:12)

LESSON † **We must love God, seek wisdom, and persevere to the end to be saved and inherit the crown of life.**

What one thing is testing your faith in God? Are you willing to endure to the end?

Spiritual GPS

Let us thank God for this new day and the beginning of this new week. May He guide our steps in the ways that we should go throughout this week.

No matter if we begin a new week stuck or feeling like we're in darkness and in need of direction, there is help when we trust what God's Word says about being guided. God is interested in every part of our life, physically and emotionally—not just the spiritual aspect. He has promised to provide us with the Holy Spirit to lead, guide, and teach us when we submit every part of our life to Him. The Holy Spirit is not only the spiritual GPS to our soul, but He, the Holy Spirit, along with the Word of God, will lead and guide us in the right direction in our daily lives. The Spirit is the voice that warns us when we are heading down the wrong path, but it is up to us to hear Him and follow Him.

> "The LORD says, 'I will make you wise and show you where to go. I will guide you and watch over you.'" (Psalm 32:8, NCV)

> "Since we live by the Spirit, we must also follow the Spirit." (Galatians 5:25, HCSB)

LESSON ✝ God desires to guide us with His love and wisdom and teach us the best way to live each day as mature children of God, equipped for any task.

When driving, we put our trust in our navigation systems by following the directions given. How might we show God we're trusting in Him?

The Burning Bush

Let us thank God for waking us up this day, another day to experience His presence and His loving care. May He give us the patience today to wait as He continues to make a way when we can't see a way.

Today's focus will be on Moses first seeing God in the burning bush. He wondered why the fire wasn't consuming the bush. It was after going to check it out that Moses heard God's voice through the burning bush.

> "Meanwhile, Moses was shepherding the flock of his father-in-law Jethro, the priest of Midian. He led the flock to the far side of the wilderness and came to Horeb, the mountain of God. Then the Angel of the LORD appeared to him in a flame of fire within a bush. As Moses looked, he saw that the bush was on fire but was not consumed. So Moses thought: I must go over and look at this remarkable sight. Why isn't the bush burning up? When the LORD saw that he had gone over to look, God called out to him from the bush, 'Moses, Moses!' 'Here I am,' he answered. 'Do not come closer,' He said. 'Remove the sandals from your feet, for the place where you are standing is holy ground.'"
>
> (Exodus 3:1-5, HCSB)

God uses whatever means necessary to get our attention.

> **LESSON** † There will be many burning bush moments in each of our lives to encounter God's presence. I'll close with the following quote from Elizabeth Barrett Browning: "Earth is crammed with heaven, And every common bush afire with God: But only he who sees takes off his shoes." [13]

Are you hearing from God? And does it help you to see what He does for you more clearly?

Owe No Man Anything but Love

I pray that everyone's week is going well on this "hump day" Wednesday. May we all have the confidence to continue moving forward this week, no matter our circumstances. Let us thank God for the gift of life and those He has placed in our lives to make it more productive.

There is a saying, "In this world nothing is certain but taxes and death." Wouldn't it be helpful for the government to let us off the hook with our taxes?

> "Fulfill your obligations as a citizen. Pay your taxes, pay your bills, respect your leaders. Don't run up debts, except for the huge debt of love you owe each other. When you love others, you complete what the law has been after all along." (Romans 13:7-8, MSG)

> "Why is love for others called an obligation? We are forever in debt to Christ for the love he has poured out on us. We can begin to repay this debt by fulfilling our obligation to love others in turn. Because Christ's love will always be infinitely higher than ours, we will always have a duty to love our neighbors."—Life Application Study Bible [14]

LESSON † Tax time can be exhausting. We must never put the gospel to shame by failing to give Christ the honor due to His name or Caesar (the government).

Do you agree that when Christians love others and obey the ruling governing authority, it is a mission to help build God's kingdom?

A Gratitude Check-In

We know that every day is a day of thanksgiving! May God rain down blessing after blessing on each of us on this "grateful Thursday."

Sometimes we may have to adjust and get used to the season of being still.

The attitude that we have in our heart and our thinking will determine our life and how high it will go with God. God wants to bless His people and doesn't want us only checking the boxes of religious acts.

> "Let the people give thanks to you, O God. Let all the people give thanks to you. The earth has yielded its harvest. May God, our God, bless us. May God bless us, and may all the ends of the earth worship him." (Psalm 67:5-7)

LESSON † **We have an enemy who wants to wear us down so that we will lose interest in worshiping our good God.**

Today we are encouraged to do a gratitude check! What are you grateful for and how is your attitude toward worship?

Joy on the Way

As we encounter any problems and the busyness of today, let us ask God to give us the grace and wisdom to serve Him as we come to the end of this week and that we will be a blessing to those who He sends our way.

Sometimes it can get hard on this journey we call life. With so much chaos, pain, and grief going on, many are asking that age-old question: *W.I.G.I.A.T.* (where is God in all this?). The answer remains the same! He is with us, and He is fully aware of all the upheaval in this world. We live in a fallen world where bad things happen ever since sin entered it. Because God's ways are not like our ways, we cannot understand what He is doing. Our almighty, all-knowing God knows what He is doing and continues to have a plan. He only asks that we depend on Him for what we need.

> "The sufferings we have now are nothing compared to the great glory that will be shown to us. Everything God made is waiting with excitement for God to show his children's glory completely." (Romans 8:18-19, NCV)

LESSON † **God has given us His best: His Son, His Holy Spirit, forgiveness, and the promise of eternal life. God has promised us that *JOY* is on the way!**

In what situations in your life might you be missing out on experiencing joy?

Entrusting Our Children to the Lord

Let us thank God for bringing us to another blessed weekend. Today, let us pray for the children and the educators around.

Regardless of our children's ages, we all want our children to be safe and desperately want to protect them from harm.

As Christian parents, we desire that our children be saved and covered by the blood of Jesus and that they will grow up knowing, loving, and obeying God's Word. We must teach our children while they are young to be aware of and responsive to the Holy Spirit's work in their lives as they grow.

> "Parents will tell their children what you have done. They will retell your mighty acts." (Psalm 145:4, NCV)

LESSON † We must pray for those making decisions that pertain to our children and their education. We must pray for our children's emotional, physical, and spiritual protection as they leave home to get their education.

Has there ever been a time when you didn't trust your child or children with others?

My Sheep Hear My Voice

It is my prayer that each of us feels God's presence this day. I pray that each of us hears His voice guiding and directing our steps. As we study God's Word with each passing day, I pray that each of us feels like we are growing closer and closer to Him.

It can be hard to hear what the Lord is trying to say to us when we are so occupied with the cares of life. When we grow closer to God, we will be able to hear and recognize His voice. God sent Jesus to show us the most realistic path to know Him and welcome His (the Lord Jesus's) return. Unfortunately, when he began His work, only a few recognized and followed Him as the coming Messiah, the One with the authority and power.

> "'Oh, there is so much more I want to tell you, but you can't understand it now. When the Holy Spirit, who is truth, comes, he shall guide you into all truth, for he will not be presenting his own ideas, but will be passing on to you what he has heard. He will tell you about the future. He shall praise me and bring me great honor by showing you my glory. All the Father's glory is mine; this is what I mean when I say that he will show you my glory. In just a little while I will be gone, and you will see me no more; but just a little while after that, and you will see me again!'"
>
> (John 16:12-16, TLB)

LESSON † We must not allow the world's noise to keep us from hearing the voice of God.

Is there an area of your life where you are humbly listening to hear God's voice for guidance?

Coming Out of a Storm – Don't Judge Me

Let us pause and thank God for the beginning of a new week. Let us use this day as the beginning of an opportunity to obtain our highest potential during this week. May it be peaceful and calm, no matter what situations we find ourselves facing.

Most of us know that life can get stressful quickly and without notice. It can happen in many different and unexpected ways. It may be that our health fails us unexpectedly, our financial status abruptly changes, or death may even come knocking. It's like a storm that blows into our midst, bringing strong winds, heavy rains, thunder, lightning, and sometimes hail.

> "A great windstorm arose, and the waves beat into the boat so that the boat was already being swamped. But he was in the stern, asleep on the cushion; and they woke him up and said to him, 'Teacher, do you not care that we are perishing?' He woke up and rebuked the wind and said to the sea, 'Peace! Be still!' Then the wind ceased, and there was a dead calm."
>
> (Mark 4:37-39, NRSV)

LESSON † Regardless of judgment or the fact that we may not understand why the storms and trials come into our life, we must not give up or quit.

> "Don't judge. You don't know what storms someone has just walked through." – Kristen Butler [15]

What experiences have you had of negatively and wrongfully judging someone?

Don't Miss an Opportunity of a Lifetime

Let us pray for God's divine direction as we face making decisions today, and let us not push God aside. He knows every decision and every challenge that we face.

As this week progresses, many of us will find ourselves having to make at least one decision, if not many. Unfortunately, many of us will probably not see it as an opportunity of a lifetime because we often have other priorities and things in our lives that we would much rather keep. It may be our jobs, families, and relationships that we desire to have.

In our scripture today, we have a young man who asked Jesus what he must do to have eternal life but did not like the answer that Jesus gave. He walked away sad and missed the opportunity of a lifetime to follow Jesus!

> "The young man replied, 'I have obeyed all these command-ments. What else do I need to do?' Jesus said to him, 'If you want to be perfect, sell what you own. Give the money to the poor, and you will have treasure in heaven. Then follow me!' When the young man heard this, he went away sad because he owned a lot of property." (Matthew 19:20-22)

LESSON † When it comes to our spiritual walk, there will be risks, but ultimately it will be rewarding.

Would you see it as an opportunity of a lifetime, an interruption, or something impossible if asked to be who God wanted you to be? To do what He wanted you to do? Or to go where He wanted you to go?

S.P.A.M. – Satan Persistently Attacking Me

It is my prayer that the Lord guide our thoughts and continue to give us the endurance to continue to move forward through this week on this "hump day" Wednesday.

Ever since Satan got kicked out of heaven (Ezekiel 28:12-19 and Isaiah 14:12-14), he has been persistently trying to persuade us who are God's people to do everything against God and what He desires for our lives. Satan works full time to bombard evil thoughts in our minds. It's like those annoying spam emails that we all receive that are irritating, dangerous, and time-consuming.

The spammers and Satan both use the same tricks and tactics. Thomas Adams says they both are "like fishers who bait their hooks according to the fish's appetite they are trying to catch." [16] The Word lets us know that we must be ready to pray without ceasing because Satan and His armies persistently work at attacking us.

> "'So be ready all the time. Pray that you will be strong enough to escape all these things that will happen and that you will be able to stand before the Son of Man.'"
>
> (Luke 21:36, NCV)

It would be foolish for us to be part-time, half-dressed Christians and think that we can defeat a full-time devil.

> **LESSON** † The same way technology uses a firewall to protect our devices, we must also let God's Word be the firewall against the enemy's attacks in our lives.

What real temptations are you facing today? How does knowing that Jesus is with you help you to withstand them?

Chosen by God

Let us thank God for waking us up on this "grateful Thursday" morning. We can be thankful for many things this day, but the most important thing is to awaken as a child of God.

God wants you to know this day that before the creation of the world, He chose you through Christ to be holy and perfect in His presence. The tragedy of life is that it takes some of us longer than others to realize that, whether it's brokenness, being ignored, or rejection, when we look around, we are not alone, and none of these afflictions are solely for us. Some are blessings, and some are lessons so that we can help each other. We are called for a purpose that is unique to our situations in life.

> "Take a good look, friends, at who you were when you got called into this life. I don't see many of 'the brightest and the best' among you, not many influential, not many from high-society families. Isn't it obvious that God deliberately chose men and women that the culture overlooks and exploits and abuses, chose these 'nobodies' to expose the hollow pretensions of the 'somebodies'?"
>
> (1 Corinthians 1:26-28, MSG)

Charles Spurgeon said, "Whenever God means to make a man great, He always breaks him in pieces first." [17]

LESSON † God's infinite power to choose the most ordinary of us is never based on anything we can do or accomplish.

Have you ever felt insignificant, broken, ignored, or rejected? If so, how did you overcome?

We are Stronger Together

Let us thank God for seeing us through another week with the help of the Lord. I pray that each of us continues to feel His presence and that He gives us the strength and others to help us make it through whatever difficulties we may face.

Having a strong faith will help us make it through when we find ourselves in the harshest circumstances in our lives.

Having pride has also put undue pressure on us to hide our weaknesses and not rely on others' support and help. Ever since creation, God did not intend for humanity to be alone.

> "Two people are better off than one, for they can help each other succeed. If one person falls, the other can reach out and help. But someone who falls alone is in real trouble. Likewise, two people lying close together can keep each other warm. But how can one be warm alone? A person standing alone can be attacked and defeated, but two can stand back-to-back and conquer. Three are even better, for a triple-braided cord is not easily broken."
>
> (Ecclesiastes 4:9-12, NLT)

LESSON † When everything in our lives is good, it's easy to be strong. The real test of strength shows when we face our struggles. Remember, we are stronger together!

What has God equipped you to do for those in need around you? And how do you use it to strengthen and encourage them?

Don't Drown in Sorrow – Cry Out to God

Let us ask the Lord for the strength not to get weary during this weekend.

In this life, we are going to have difficulties that we will have to go through. More times than not, we won't understand why. We should also thank God for having a relationship with Him and the right people that He has allowed to come into our lives. The enemy, Satan, would like nothing more than for us to cry and to give up! It's all right to cry, but if we want God to move on our behalf, we must stop crying and complaining about our sorrows and start crying out to God.

Unfortunately, too many reliable people are trying to be strong. They are the ones who have cried all night, and they don't recognize that they are drowning, trying to be the anchor for everyone else. Thank God, we have a friend in Jesus! As the hymn says, "What a privilege to carry everything to God in prayer! O, what peace we forfeit... because we do not carry everything to God in prayer." [18]

> "The LORD is waiting to be kind to you. He rises to have compassion on you. The LORD is a God of justice. Blessed are all those who wait for him. You will live in Zion, in Jerusalem. You won't cry anymore. The LORD will certainly have pity on you when you cry for help. As soon as he hears you, he will answer you." (Isaiah 30:18-19)

LESSON † The prophet Jeremiah writes: "The LORD says: Cursed is the person who trusts humans, who makes flesh and blood his strength and whose heart turns away from the Lord'" (Jeremiah 17:5).

Who are the friends that you surround yourself with? When you are burdened, who or what do you consider your anchor?

Here I Am – Send Me

Let us thank God for the Holy Spirit that He has sent to the church to lead, guide, and teach us the way to Him.

As Christians, our lives are to be used to influence the world to bring glory to God. God used prophets of old to deliver His Word. God still today has a desire for us to spread His Word—the Good News—around the world today.

In our scripture today, in a vision on a day of atonement, God took Isaiah's sins away. Isaiah heard the Lord speak indirectly to him of a need he had.

> "'Then I heard the voice of the Lord, saying, 'Whom will I send? Who will go for us?' I said, 'Here I am. Send me!' And he said, 'Go and tell these people, "No matter how closely you listen, you'll never understand. No matter how closely you look, you'll never see." '" (Isaiah 6:6-9)

LESSON † Despite our sinful condition in life, God wants to use each of us, just as He used Isaiah.

How are you living out your faith so that others might be influenced to choose a life with Christ?

Each New Day is a Fresh Start

As we began this new day, let us do our best to stay on the right path that God has for us. May this week be the beginning of something bigger and better.

Many of us are familiar with the saying, "It's never too late to change." We serve a God who gives us many opportunities, and He always provides us with a way to become who or what He is calling us to be. Change, although it can be painful, is the thing that helps us to develop and grow. Once we make up our minds to embrace change, we are one step closer to improving with each right decision we make.

> "The godly may trip seven times, but they will get up again. But one disaster is enough to overthrow the wicked."
>
> (Proverbs 24:16, NLT)

We should not let our past failures determine if we decide to change or stay the same. We must choose to be who or what God wants us to be.

LESSON † We must not allow the enemy's voice to convince us that we are not strong enough to start over, because we have the assurance that we can have the strength to start over in life.

Are you in the habit of daily asking God to help you rid yourself of personal sins and wrongdoings?

Surrendering All to God

As we continue to travel throughout this week, I pray that God will be our source of strength and shield and that our hearts will trust in Him completely.

We often talk about a fresh start or starting over in life. We understand that God is the giver of chances and that changes on our behalf would have to occur. Today we want to have a new experience by walking in our fresh start whereby we must surrender.

As children of God, when we begin our new Christian walk on this journey of life with God, our knowledge in Him is unclear, and we are uncertain about our trust in Him. But, as our relationship with Him grows, so does our daily confidence in Him.

> "O taste and see that the Lord [our God] is good! Blessed (happy, fortunate, to be envied) is the man who trusts *and* takes refuge in Him." (Psalm 34:8, AMPC)

When we acknowledge that God is the giver of life, we can walk in obedience and surrender our all by following Him, and we will discover His goodness.

LESSON † To begin or maintain our walk with God, we must surrender our all to Him.

Are you struggling when it comes to trusting God with all your heart? If so, what are you holding on to?

Standing Strong During Life Challenges

Let us thank God for waking us up on this "hump day" Wednesday. I pray that each of us is blessed with the Lord's strength and His guidance to lead us.

No matter how strong or secure we think we are in life, there will be times when we will face challenges that will weaken us and test our faith. Regardless of the source of our challenges, we must learn to rejoice and be patient as we endure them while maintaining hope as we deal with them.

> "We can rejoice, too, when we run into problems and trials, for we know that they are good for us—they help us learn to be patient. And patience develops strength of character in us and helps us trust God more each time we use it until finally our hope and faith are strong and steady. Then, when that happens, we are able to hold our heads high no matter what happens and know that all is well, for we know how dearly God loves us, and we feel this warm love everywhere within us because God has given us the Holy Spirit to fill our hearts with his love." (Romans 5:3-5, TLB)

LESSON † We must ask the Lord to teach us to be patient during our challenges in life because we know that He is working things out. The Lord says that He will instruct and guide us down the best pathway for our lives.

Are you known to be patient and stay firmly anchored in God's truth and grace when experiencing life challenges?

Laying to Rest the Old Me

Let us thank God for allowing us to make it to this "grateful Thursday." Let us come before our good God with grateful and humble hearts, not being anxious for anything.

With so many distractions in the world, we must keep our minds and our eyes on the Lord. As God's people, we must discern what is right from that which is evil.

God has a plan for each of us to become new creations, and we must do our part by making changes in our life by renewing our minds to live as Christ did.

> "So I tell you and encourage you in the Lord's name not to live any longer like other people in the world. Their minds are set on worthless things. They can't understand because they are in the dark. They are excluded from the life that God approves of because of their ignorance and stubbornness."
> (Ephesians 4:17-18)

LESSON † Once we lay the old me to rest, we will no longer desire our past ways that do not line up with the will of God, but we will want to live a life that glorifies God.

What old habits or ways have you put to rest in order to honor God?

Encouraging Words at the Well

He Restores My Soul

As we move through the months, let us thank the Lord for giving us the strength to make it through another and for being our defense and protecting us from all hurt, harm, and dangers. We may not know what the future holds for us, but we can have hope because we know who holds the future.

> "Comparing believers to sheep is a common practice because sheep are known to need constant care, and when left alone, they can fall into various dangers. Like sheep, we all have gone astray, only to find ourselves in need of protection and the Shepherd's tender loving care. We have a Shepherd who tends the needs of His flock at any cost. He says, "'I am the good shepherd. The good shepherd gives his life for the sheep'" (John 10:11).

When we find ourselves feeling weary and our spirits low, we must do like the psalmist and remind ourselves of all the Lord's goodness and know that we can be back in His presence.

> "The LORD is my Shepherd; I shall not want. He makes me lie down in green pastures; he leads me beside still waters; he restores my soul." (Psalm 23:1-3a, NRSV)

LESSON † As Christians, when we stay in the care of the Shepherd, we don't have to worry about what we have or don't have for today or tomorrow because He knows what we need more than we do. Jesus, as our Good Shepherd, cares for our every need as He guides us. He's the one who can and will take pleasure in restoring our tired and exhausted bodies and souls.

In what ways has God been your Shepherd?

Washing Machine-Like Faith

As we start this new day, may we trust the Lord with our whole hearts as we walk with Him and have a new desire to seek His face.

Many of us know that life is uncertain and that we can never predict when hard times, problems, or difficulties will come.

I remember this saying that goes something like this: Problems, troubles, and difficulties are like washing machines. They twist us, spin us, and knock us around. But we come out brighter, cleaner, and better than before.

It can sometimes feel like those troubles, problems, and difficult times are never going to end.

> "God, who shows you his kindness and who has called you through Christ Jesus to his eternal glory, will restore you, strengthen you, make you strong, and support you as you suffer for a little while. Power belongs to him forever. Amen."
> (1 Peter 5:10-11)

LESSON † One thing for sure, we are all guaranteed eternal life with Christ, where there will be no suffering.

Reflect on a time when the Lord delivered you from some type of trouble that felt like it was never going to end. Did you come out better for it?

Tears of Repentance

Let us start this Sunday out with prayer and praise as we remember our Lord and Savior Jesus Christ.

As God's people, we serve an awesome God who continues to prove His love for us, and we, as always, keep going astray. Not everyone likes to talk about repentance because it somehow implies that one is broken and imperfect.

To repent is to turn away from our desires and turn in another direction toward the ways of God. We have an enemy, Satan, who is banking on us to delay our repentance to continue to follow him in sin.

> "'Repent, then, and turn to God, so that your sins may be wiped out, that times of refreshing may come from the Lord, and that he may send the Messiah, who has been appointed for you—even Jesus. Heaven must receive him until the time comes for God to restore everything, as he promised long ago through his holy prophets." (Acts 3:19-21, NIV)

LESSON ✝ God doesn't want us to feel sorry and only cry tears. He wants us to confess, repent, and be baptized.

Are you willing to do what is required of us to be made acceptable unto God?

Stay Strong and Courageous

May each of us be given a reasonable portion of health and strength to overcome every stronghold trying to interrupt the plans set before us.

For many, a new week means new challenges and new possibilities for continued success. However, for others, a new week brings with it the feelings of heavy burdens and responsibilities for them. As we move forward this week, no matter what situations we may find ourselves in, we must prepare to move forward with confidence and faith.

Having confidence and faith doesn't mean that we won't have fear or mixed feelings. It means that we will have to possess the courage to trust that we can handle whatever happens.

> "'No one will be able to defeat you all your life. Just as I was with Moses, so I will be with you. I will not leave you or forget you. Joshua, be strong and brave! You must lead these people so they can take the land that I promised their fathers I would give them. Be strong and brave. Be sure to obey all the teachings my servant Moses gave you. If you follow them exactly, you will be successful in everything you do.'"
>
> (Joshua 1:5-7, NCV)

LESSON † As Christians, trusting God is not an option.

Has there been a time when you were afraid, but couldn't show it because others were depending on you?

A Time to Shine

May each of us have a beautiful, blessed Tuesday. Today, I pray that when we feel like worrying, we will seek God in prayer, and when we feel like complaining, we will let our light shine.

During dark times in life, we have every reason to want to look down; however, the reality is that we each carry a purpose. As children of God, we are chosen for the darkness. It is in the dark times that God brings out the awesomeness in us. We must see our lives as our time to shine.

Too often, we ask God to remove us from people and places that He intends for us to be witnesses to and be a strong influence.

> "'You are the light that gives light to the world. A city that is built on a hill cannot be hidden. And people don't hide a light under a bowl. They put it on a lampstand so the light shines for all the people in the house. In the same way, you should be a light for other people. Live so that they will see the good things you do and will praise your Father in heaven.'" (Matthew 5:14-16, NCV)

LESSON † Jesus wants us to allow His light to overflow and shine in a dark world for those who do not know Him, making a difference in others' lives.

Do you see your life as a bright beacon or light that has lost its glow? Why?

Don't Worry

We've made it halfway through this week. Thank God for giving us the strength to make it to this "hump day" Wednesday. If you're feeling tired, you need to know that God's love will give us the necessary strength to finish strong. May each of us receive His comfort today and be filled with His peace.

The Bible tells us not to worry about anything. Jesus commanded us not to fear, yet we find ourselves worrying about so many things in our lives. To worry is to dwell on our circumstances and situations.

In his devotional *One Day at a Time,* William MacDonald says worry is a sin: "It doubts the wisdom of God; it implies He doesn't know what He is doing. It doubts the love of God; it says He doesn't care. It doubts the power of God; it says He is not able to overcome the circumstances that cause us to worry." [19]

> "Never worry about anything. But in every situation let God know what you need in prayers and requests while giving thanks." (Philippians 4:6)

LESSON † Worrying is the opposite of trusting God. So let us not worry by dwelling and focusing on our situations and circumstances, taking our eyes off Christ and His ability to take care of us.

If you could give to God one thing that you are worrying about, what would it be?

The God Who Rescues

Let us thank God on this "grateful Thursday" for waking us up and hearing our prayers. Let us thank Him for the hope that this new day brings.

To live during a time when it's hard to trust those who we look to lead us can be hard. That mistrust can bring on a heightened level of anxiety and stress. It can cause us to feel like there is no hope or no end to the suffering that we face. There's some good news for those who trust, believe, and obey the Lord! We serve a God who is in the business of loving, protecting, and rescuing His people.

As believers, we have a Savior who came to save us. That's why King David, when he was in distress, would always call on Him for help. He said that God would reach down from heaven and rescue him from deep waters and from his enemies' power.

> "Help, GOD—I've hit rock bottom! Master, hear my cry for help! Listen hard! Open your ears! Listen to my cries for mercy." (Psalm 130:1-2, MSG)

LESSON † In this life, we will face many problems that will make us feel hopeless. We must keep looking to God and pray. Through Jesus, we have never-ending freedom that enables us to have the power to be rescued from anything that can hold us back. God hears our prayers, and He will rescue us!

Reflect on a time when you felt the bottom had fallen out of your life. Who did you turn to for help?

God Looks at the Heart

Thank God that we have made it through another week with the help of the Lord. As we enter the weekend, may we all show the love of God to those whom we encounter.

Despite what others may think of us, we must never think of ourselves as unqualified to serve God and those He places in our lives. When we judge ourselves and others, we most times will get it wrong.

And when it came to David, certainly little ruddy David was not the one. So they thought!

> "But Samuel said, 'No, the LORD has not chosen this one.' Jesse had seven of his sons pass by Samuel. But Samuel said to him, 'The LORD has not chosen any of these.' Then he asked Jesse, 'Are these all the sons you have?' Jesse answered, 'I still have the youngest son. He is out taking care of the sheep.' Samuel said, 'Send for him. We will not sit down to eat until he arrives.' So Jesse sent and had his youngest son brought in. He was a fine boy, tanned, and handsome. The LORD said to Samuel, 'Go, appoint him, because he is the one.'"
>
> (1 Samuel 16:11-12, NCV)

LESSON † **We must not be so quick to misjudge others.**

Has there been a time when someone you thought was insignificant turned out to be someone you respected and loved?

Keep on Dreaming

Let us thank God for giving us the strength to make it to the week-end. I pray that our faith will continue to guide us and that as we rest from this week's labor, we have enough strength and courage to finish strong, achieving what God has set before us.

Many times, we dare to dream. Those of us who believe can dream and dream big because "'nothing is impossible for God'" (Luke 1:37). We can be confident that our God can render powerless the limitations we put on ourselves and allow others to put on us. Our God will give us the desires of our hearts!

> "Trust in the LORD and do good. Then you will live safely in the land and prosper. Take delight in the LORD, and he will give you your heart's desires. Commit everything you do to the LORD. Trust him, and he will help you."
>
> (Psalm 37:3-5, NLT)

LESSON † We can do all things through Christ because our God can give us the strength for each new day, and He can make all the good, bad, and ugly things work together for our good if we only believe.

What dream has God put in your heart that you feel powerless to achieve?

Lion of the Tribe of Judah

Let us thank God for seeing another blessed Sunday morning. It is my prayer that as we pause to worship Him on this day, we will thank Him for being our great Creator and generous God who guides us each day in making wise decisions.

Despite the things we face, we still must choose to live by choice and not by chance. We have an enemy who is scheming and desires to keep us from having a relationship with God. We must continually ask God for enough wisdom and strength to allow us not to give in to the enemy's deception.

We must be able to know the genuine Lion from the counterfeit lion. The difference between the two lions is Satan. The roaring lion of destruction is roaming around causing pain, delusions, and confusion.

> "But one of the elders said to me, 'Do not cry! The Lion from the tribe of Judah, David's descendant, has won the victory so that he is able to open the scroll and its seven seals.'"
> (Revelation 5:5, NCV)

LESSON † **We should not side with the lion Satan because we will lose our souls. The Lion Jesus, has proven Himself worthy of our praise and is not to be feared.**

Are you easily confused in choosing which lion to follow? How do you know the difference?

We're All in This Together

As we begin this new week, let us ask God to cover our loved ones and us with His protecting wings from all hurt and harm.

When living through adverse times, many of us find ourselves asking, "Is there any hope for us?" Many people take on the ideology of "us vs. them" and are not living according to God's Word, which says, "Love must be sincere. Hate what is evil; cling to what is good. Be devoted to one another in love. Honor one another above yourselves" (Romans 12:9-10, NIV). Like the John Donne poem says, "No man is an island." [20]

> "Well, then, are we Jews *better* than others? No, not at all, for we have already shown that all men alike are sinners, whether Jews or Gentiles. As the Scriptures say, 'No one is good—no one in all the world is innocent.' No one has ever really followed God's paths or even truly wanted to. Everyone has turned away; all have gone wrong. No one anywhere has kept on doing what is right; not one."
>
> (Romans 3:9-12, TLB)

LESSON † **We must hold on to what is right, pure, and divine during difficult times.**

Each of us must live right. Who are you depending on to help you do it?

Live Right in an Upside-Down World

Let us start this day by walking in righteousness as we are given this new day for new opportunities, and let's ask God to help us not to fear but that we may rise above every situation that comes up against us.

We live in times of transition and change with each passing day. What we experience each year will be written in history, whether good or bad. Our morals are being challenged at every turn because we live in an ever-changing world that has a habit of being turned upside down. We must learn how to be a change agent in this world without allowing this world to change us.

We must not become insensitive to the things going on in our world.

> "Don't become like the people of this world. Instead, change the way you think. Then you will always be able to determine what God really wants—what is good, pleasing, and perfect."
> (Romans 12:2)

LESSON † We will never have a perfect world until Jesus returns, but as long as we have breath in our bodies, we should try to live right and strive to make a difference in the world.

With each new day we are given a chance to make a difference. What difference do you want to make in the world today?

Feeling Down? Look Above

Thank God we have made it to another "hump day" Wednesday. I pray and trust the days behind us are just that and that each of us feels the loving and caring presence of God in our lives. If anyone is feeling down, we bind that spirit and ask God to restore us with whatever we may need to finish this week strong.

During uncertain times, many of us will face many different situations and circumstances. It may be our finances, our marriages, our ministries, and maybe our children. These times can be painful and troubling, leaving us not feeling upbeat and causing our spirits to be downcast.

Some people believe that we won't or don't experience challenging times or painful circumstances once we become believers. That's not true, but what is true is that we serve the God who is the Restorer and the Repairer of our lives. For anyone who's feeling down and unsure where your help will come from, look above and glorify, magnify, and give the Lord praise. He is with us. He's the lifter of our head!

> "But You, LORD, are a shield around me, my glory, and the One who lifts up my head." (Psalm 3:3, HCSB)

LESSON † Praise the Lord! When we seek the Lord, we will lack for nothing good. We must continually seek His strength and His face because He is powerful and gives victory to us as His chosen people.

God asks us to give Him praises. Is there a praise on your tongue today? And are you willing to praise Him with it?

The Lord is Our Light and Salvation

Let us thank God for waking us up on this "grateful Thursday" and for the countless blessings that He has given to us this week. May the joy of the Lord shine through each of us today!

In this life, we can expect to have our ups and downs and dark times, yet we still have much to be grateful for despite what we may be going through. As children of God, we can have the confidence that the light of the Lord is present, even when the darkness seems unbearable.

> "The LORD is my light and my salvation—so why should I be afraid? The LORD is my fortress, protecting me from danger, so why should I tremble? When evil people come to devour me, when my enemies and foes attack me, they will stumble and fall. Though a mighty army surrounds me, my heart will not be afraid. Even if I am attacked, I will remain confident."
>
> (Psalm 27:1-3, NLT)

LESSON † We can be grateful because, like the psalmist, we are always in God's presence.

Has there been a time in your life when you were fearful? And how did you overcome it?

We Serve a Big God

Let us thank God for making it to the end of another week. I pray that each of us remains lifted in spirits and secure in the Lord. May we continue to be hopeful and be still knowing that we are loved and thought about by an awesome God.

Sometimes the way things are in life, we can find ourselves being tired and overwhelmed. We tend to forget that we serve a God who is so much bigger than any circumstance that we can have.

It is easy for us to become overwhelmed by the problems we encounter. As God's children, He has provided us with the answers to whatever situation or circumstances we might experience during our lifetime.

> "You, dear children, are from God and have overcome them, because the one who is in you is greater than the one in the world." (1 John 4:4, NIV)

LESSON † Our current situation or circumstances may seem overwhelming to us, but we must know this: Our God promises never to leave us, and He is bigger than any problem. We must never allow our pain or circumstances to become more than we can bear and lose our connection with God.

How do you relate with a big God you cannot see?

Be Happy

Thank God we have made it to Saturday. May it bring with it much joy and happiness.

Most of us only want to be free to follow our hearts and do what we want to do, if only for one day. There is not a person who does not want to be happy. Everybody is looking for happiness in this life. The problem with that is we think that happiness will find us. The reality is that we must find it. Each of us is responsible for our happiness, and we are the makers of our happiness.

Our day-to-day happiness has much more to do with our mindset than it does with what's happening around us. We must choose to be happy despite our circumstances.

> "Happy are the people whose God is the LORD."
> (Psalm 144:15b, NCV)

LESSON † We can only find true happiness in God! The fact that we believe in God doesn't mean that everything in our lives will go well and that we will be happy all the time. There will be circumstances in our life that will make feeling happy very hard. When we find ourselves struggling to have happiness, we shouldn't hesitate to get help from therapists and counselors.

Many people wait all week for the weekend to be happy. What do you do to make yourself happy?

A Living Hope in Christ

Let us thank God for His new mercies each day and a life full of promises. May He continue to take care of our every need through the blessings of His Son Jesus.

The cares of this life can often make us feel emotionally and physically drained. However, we can and we must keep going. God promises to be with us and to see us through. He has promised us a living hope in Jesus Christ.

As Christians, our hope begins and ends with our belief and confession that Jesus is the Son of God resurrected from the dead. Any hope that does not include Christ is meaningless and temporary at best.

> "Praise the God and Father of our Lord Jesus Christ. According to His great mercy, He has given us a new birth into a living hope through the resurrection of Jesus Christ from the dead and into an inheritance that is imperishable, uncorrupted, and unfading, kept in heaven for you." (1 Peter 1:3-4, HCSB)

LESSON † We must not make the mistake of thinking that our hope comes from our possessions or what we do. Our hope comes from who we are in Christ!

Are there times in your life when the cares of this world leave you feeling hopeless?

Well Done

As we begin this new week, let us thank God in advance for every opportunity and responsibility that comes our way. Let us use them to bring glory and honor to Him.

Since each of us has many roles and positions that we are expected to manage or get done, I suspect some of us would think twice or be reluctant to say that we wanted more responsibilities. On the other hand, some will take pride in taking on more. Since the beginning of time, we've been expected to work.

We are all deserving of recognition and appreciation for what we do. However, whether it's on our job or building God's kingdom, we should desire to give our best and be committed to serving with integrity and honor despite the absence of awards or accolades.

> "His lord said unto him, Well done, thou good and faithful servant: thou hast been faithful over a few things, I will make thee ruler over many things: enter thou into the joy of thy lord." (Matthew 25:21, KJV)

LESSON † **We are blessed to be chosen to be God's faithful and trustworthy servants. Man is the giver of *awards* for what we do, but God is the giver of *rewards* for what we do.**

Do you perform your job well for the award or for the reward?

Peace of God

Let us thank God for a new day. I pray that when faced with chaos, each of us will seek to be at peace and have a calm heart as we allow God to use us to bring about peace even when we don't fully understand. May He grant us peace as we wait patiently for His plan.

At some point in our lives, we will all face some unpleasant cir-cum-stances that will worsen and move us out of our level of comfort. We may be met with some of life's most significant decisions, have a challenging conversation with our loved ones and friends, or get un-wanted test results from the doctor. We can go through some divisive and troubling times and face many challenges. Some people will continue doing good things. However, many hearts will be filled with hatred, chaos, and confusion.

Most are troubled because of a lack of inner peace. Peace comes from being mentally and spiritually at ease and with enough knowledge and understanding to be strong in the face of division, strife, and anxiety.

> "'Glory to God in highest heaven, and peace on earth to those with whom God is pleased.'" (Luke 2:14, NLT)

LESSON † Being at peace is not the absence of having trouble in our lives. There will never be total peace until Jesus comes back. Having a peaceful mindset can help us find our strength and comfort and deal with any confusion and anxiety. The only way to have real peace is to live a life with God's glory in view.

Have there been times when, faced with challenges, you continued to have peace?

You've Got This!

As we go from day to day, it doesn't take long for our enthusiasm to fade and for us to become discouraged, especially when we encounter criticism and opposition from others.

> "Yet, the strength of those who wait with hope in the LORD will be renewed. They will soar on wings like eagles. They will run and won't become weary. They will walk and won't grow tired." (Isaiah 40:31)

LESSON ✝ Keep going, and don't give up! You have what it takes. God's got you, and you've got this.

Do you ask God to help you to look for others who need an encouraging word or help from you?

Enough

Thank God for another "grateful Thursday." Let us allow our gratitude to make us truly thankful for what we have and who we are.

In our human condition's frailty, we often allow our hearts to forget the blessings and the promises of God. Throughout the history of humanity, we also tend to underestimate His providence. We can look at the Israelites when God freed them from Egypt and provided manna every morning. Instead of thanking God for where He had brought them from and what He was doing, they complained to and frustrated Moses as though they had a sense of entitlement.

> "'Where am I supposed to get meat for all these people who are whining to me, "Give us meat; we want meat." I can't do this by myself—it's too much, all these people. If this is how you intend to treat me, do me a favor and kill me. I've seen enough; I've had enough. Let me out of here.'"
>
> (Numbers 11:13-15, MSG)

LESSON † God wants to stretch our faith and desires that we depend upon Him because He is sufficient and enough. We must be grateful, continually praising God, and keeping our focus on who we are and what we have and not what we don't have.

What will you thank God for today? How can you remind yourself to thank Him more often for who He is and what He's done?

Balancing Life & Work

As we come to the end of another week and the beginning of the weekend, let's pray that God continues blessing the work of our hands today and forever.

There's a saying that says: "You can't have everything." But that doesn't stop us from trying. We must all decide what we value in life. Although today is Friday, and the weekend is right around the corner, let us work gladly today working as unto the Lord, doing His will.

I know that we're all committed to doing good in all areas of our lives. And no matter how we look at it, we all only get twenty-four hours in our day and seven days a week. When our focus is solely on productivity, it can only carry us so far. Let us love and live the life we have right now by balancing our work with our lives.

> "It's useless to rise early and go to bed late, and work your worried fingers to the bone. Don't you know he enjoys giving rest to those he loves?" (Psalm 127:2, MSG)

LESSON † Each week, we struggle to provide for our family's needs, and we work hard to have enough. We serve the God who rested when He created the world. He provides us with rest, and He blesses the work of the godly. Thank God, we've made it through another week!

At the end of a busy and hard work week, are you more concerned about your productivity or getting some well-deserved rest?

Your Unique Self

Thank God that we made it to the weekend. Let us continue to trust God on this blessed Saturday. Let us accept as truth that we are uniquely created and ask Him to show us His plan for our lives this day and every day going forward.

How many of us struggle with our self-image? Do you find yourself constantly asking the question, "Why am I here?" The Word tells us that we are here because God has uniquely created us. Not one of us is here by chance or accident, but we are here for a purpose.

> "'Before I made you in your mother's womb, I chose you. Before you were born, I set you apart for a special work. I appointed you as a prophet to the nations.'"
>
> (Jeremiah 1:5, NCV)

God knew every one of us, just like He knew Jeremiah, long before we were born or even conceived. He thought about each of us and planned for us.

LESSON † The next time we find ourselves doubting who we are and questioning why we are here, we need to know that we are God's priceless masterpiece, and He was willing to pay any amount to acquire us.

How does the image you have for yourself compare to the image that God has for you?

Patience is a Virtue

Good morning, good afternoon, or good evening on this blessed Sunday. May God grant each of us the virtue of patience as we wait to see and understand the timing of His plans as they unfold for our lives.

God has nothing but good plans for our lives, and that's why we are told to carry everything to Him in prayer. Many of us have something in our lives that we are longing to have. However, we fail to seek peace and the patience that will help us to wait as the answers to our prayers manifest.

At the right time, He will make everything happen.

> "But do not forget this one thing, dear friends: To the Lord one day is as a thousand years, and a thousand years is as one day. The Lord is not slow in doing what he promised—the way some people understand slowness. But God is being patient with you. He does not want anyone to be lost, but he wants all people to change their hearts and lives."
>
> (2 Peter 3:8-9, NCV)

LESSON † God is a God of patience, and His timing is everything, always perfect, always on time, and never too late. We, too, must be patient and not give up hope and should always do the Lord's will in our lives. More importantly, He is coming soon.

Are you patiently waiting for the Lord's return? What are you doing to prepare yourself spiritually while you are waiting?

The Audacity to Hope

As we start this new week, let us thank God in advance for the hope and possibilities that will come our way this week.

For many people living during difficult and challenging times, it's easy to lose hope and give up when faced with uncertainty. God will help us to overcome, even when things are at their lowest.

> "Blessed is the man that trusteth in the LORD, and whose hope the LORD is." (Jeremiah 17:7, KJV)

LESSON † There is an 1885 painting by George Frederic Watts called "Hope." This is how the painting was described in a 1913 book called *Famous Paintings*.

"'Hope' illustrates the power of this picture to make people think. The blinded figure, seated on the sphere with her broken lyre, is bending her ear to catch what music she may from the last remaining string. She cannot see the star shining above her; one by one the sweet notes of music have been taken from her, but still she sits, bowed but not broken, plucking with tender fingers whatever melody she may from the last string of those that gave her the full harmonies of beauty.

She has no vision either of the star above or of the world of darkness and gloom below. Her attitude of dejection almost rejects the conventional idea that there is happiness to be found when everything seems lost, but the picture suggests the larger hope of the world that there is peace and light above the turmoil and sorrow of the earth." [21]

When was a time you faced a difficult time and felt hopeless? Who did you turn to for help first?

Trusting God One Step at a Time

Let us thank God for a new day to show up and do our part. Let us thank Him for everything that comes our way, and let us trust Him to direct our paths.

As we navigate and survive life's journey, trust is something that we must learn very early. As individuals on a personal level, we tend to trust those who are most like us. We trust our families, and we trust our best friends, to name a few. When we take a closer look at life, there are many opportunities to trust everywhere we look.

Of all our trusting relationships, our relationship with God provides us with the most significant opportunity to trust.

> "Trust in the LORD with all your heart; do not depend on your own understanding. Seek his will in all you do, and he will show you which path to take." (Proverbs 3:5-6, NLT)

There's a Chinese proverb that says: "The journey of a thousand miles begins with one step." [22]

Martin Luther King, Jr., said, "Faith is taking the first step even when you don't see the whole staircase." [23]

LESSON † Things will happen in each of our lives that no one, not even ourselves, will understand. However, we must have the faith to trust the Lord to lead us to continue taking the steps needed to make it through and meet and complete our goals.

Does your faith allow you to trust God completely even when you can't see what He's doing? Are there times you get ahead of Him?

A Storm is Coming - Are You Prepared?

I pray that each of us will continue to stand firm on this "hump day" Wednesday. I pray the Lord will take away all our worries, sicknesses, addictions, and sadness. May we be anchored in God's Word and prayer no matter what we face.

Storms will happen in our lives and we should always be prepared.

They come out of nowhere, usually unexpected, life-altering, and often halting our plans. When we find ourselves distressed or troubled by our storms of life, we can turn to God for comfort and help.

> "Immediately after this, Jesus insisted that his disciples get back into the boat and cross to the other side of the lake, while he sent the people home. After sending them home, he went up into the hills by himself to pray. Night fell while he was there alone. Meanwhile, the disciples were in trouble far away from land, for a strong wind had risen, and they were fighting heavy waves." (Matthew 14:22-24, NLT2)

LESSON † At any given time, each of us can find ourselves in a storm, coming out of a storm, or getting ready to enter a storm.

What does preparing for a storm look like for you? How can you be sure you are ready?

He's Intentional

Let us thank God for His mercy and grace on this "grateful Thursday." May we feel safe knowing that He knows all about us, all about our needs, and He promises to provide. Let's thank God for creating each of us with a divine plan and purpose.

As Christians, we are to live for Jesus. This doesn't mean that we will always have an easy life, but we can live a life where we know that our lives are in the best hands. Whatever God does or allows in our lives will always be for our good because He is intentional, and He never fails us.

> "For I know the plans I have for you, says the Lord. They are plans for good and not for evil, to give you a future and a hope." (Jeremiah 29:11, TLB)

Jeremiah 29 is a message of hope to the Jewish exiles in Babylon, telling them to make the best of their seventy years of captivity because God had a plan to allow it. We, too, knowing that we are in the best hands, can live our lives effectively and intentionally.

LESSON † **When we live a life that is intentional about our relationship with the Lord, with His help, we will survive the less desirable situations and conditions, and we will be able to make the best of them.**

Has there been a time when God worked a bad situation out for your good in your life? Did it help to strengthen your fellowship with Him?

Keep Going - The Best is Yet to Come

Let us thank God for seeing us to the end of another week. It's my prayer that we release everything that has tried to hold us back so that we can boldly move forward with God's strength to finish strong and not give in nor give up.

We are all determined and motivated to do well in life, until we feel the pain of the setbacks in life that make us feel sad and empty and keep us stuck. When we prioritize and focus on these setbacks, they have the power to drain and exhaust us!

> "Forget what happened in the past, and do not dwell on events from long ago. I am going to do something new. It is already happening. Don't you recognize it? I will clear away in the desert. I will make rivers on dry land."
>
> (Isaiah 43:18-19)

At some point, each of us will face the temptation to sit down on God and not to trust Him in our lives. But He is faithful! He will not allow our temptations or our setbacks to be more than we can stand. When we face them, He will show us a way out and a way to endure.

LESSON † Our eyes will only be open to new possibilities when we keep them lifted to the hills from where our help comes. Our help comes from the Lord, who made heaven and earth (Psalm 121:2).

What one thing in life helps you remember to persevere?

As a Man Thinketh

Let us thank God for another blessed Saturday. We have made it to the weekend. Let us praise God for the past week, and let us choose not to think about any negative situations that we may have faced this week. May this day bring us more wisdom, strength, peace, and joy as we continue to keep our minds on God.

Each day we must choose where we will place our thoughts because they control our lives. The Lord has promised to keep us in perfect peace when our minds and hearts stay on Him.

> "My child, pay attention to my words; listen closely to what I say. Don't ever forget my words; keep them always in mind. They are the key to life for those who find them; they bring health to the whole body. Be careful what you think, because your thoughts run your life." (Proverbs 4:20-23, NCV)

LESSON † Our minds are our greatest asset, and more than anything, Satan desires to have them!

Have you noticed in your life that reading God's Word daily will help to transform your mind from negative to positive thoughts?

Power in Prayer

Thank God for waking us up on this blessed Sunday morning. Let us thank Him for allowing us to come before His throne with praise to worship Him boldly. On this day that we set aside to honor God, let us lay our burdens aside and offer up our most sincere prayers and praise like never before.

We should never underestimate the power of prayer.

> "And we are sure of this, that he will listen to us whenever we ask him for anything in line with his will. And if we really know he is listening when we talk to him and make our requests, then we can be sure that he will answer us."
>
> (1 John 5:14-15, TLB)

Praying for God's will is not always easy for us to do, especially when the things we want are not according to His will. In the model prayer (Matthew 6:9-13), Jesus teaches the disciples and us to pray for God's will to be done on earth as it is in heaven. When we pray for God's will to be done, we acknowledge that He knows what's best and that we surrender our will to His will. Almost always, we look for immediate answers to our prayers and wonder if God has heard us when we don't see results.

LESSON † God will respond to our prayers in four ways: Yes, no, wait, and "My grace is sufficient."

What is something you are praying for/about? Are you prepared for His answer to be yes, no, wait, or "My grace is sufficient"?

Unshakable Hope

May we have a good Monday morning, afternoon, or evening. We have a lot to thank God for. May our faith remain strong in the Lord, and may each of us find the strength we need today.

With each new day, many unexpected struggles can fill our lives. As believers, we are not immune to having struggles.

As believers, though, we must always be ready and willing to share the hope that we have in Christ Jesus. A hope that is unshakable when we're rooted in Him. Today's scripture is written by King David when his son Absalom was trying to take the kingdom and kill his dad. We know David is known as a man after God's heart, yet he faced many struggles.

> "I stand silently before the Lord, waiting for him to rescue me. For salvation comes from him alone. Yes, he alone is my Rock, my rescuer, defense, and fortress. Why then should I be tense with fear when troubles come? But what is this? They pick on me at a time when my throne is tottering; they plot my death and use lies and deceit to try to force me from the throne. They are so friendly to my face while cursing in their hearts! But I stand silently before the Lord, waiting for him to rescue me. For salvation comes from him alone."
>
> (Psalm 62:1-5, TLB)

LESSON † **To have that unshakable hope, like King David, we must choose to trust God even during the darkest and most uncertain times in our lives.**

Reflect on a time when your hope was shaken and how it built your faith.

Moving on to the New

As we dawn a new day, may we grow closer to God and allow Him to lead and guide us as we move through this new chapter of our lives.

With each passing day, God makes us new and unique. With Christ, every moment of every day brings a fresh and new beginning and the chance for a new start. We don't have to fret over or be consumed by what we consider to be our failures because God renews His grace every day and in every situation that we may face.

> "Because of the LORD's great love we are not consumed, for his compassions never fail. They are new every morning; great is your faithfulness. I say to myself, 'The LORD is my portion; therefore, I will wait for him.'"
>
> (Lamentations 3:22-24, NIV)

LESSON † For us not to be discouraged and to be able to keep up with the newness that life brings to us, we must understand that life is sometimes hard, and the world can be a cruel, mean, and lonely place.

Knowing that this life is temporary, how does that change the way you are currently living?

God Can Do It Just Like That

We have made it halfway through to another "hump day" Wednesday, and some of us may be feeling exhausted or can't see our way through. Let us look to God for the strength we need to finish strong, knowing that He has us in His sight and will never leave us alone.

We serve an all-powerful God who continuously wows us. He proves and demonstrates as He gives substance to His love for all. He gets our attention in creation, in relationships, and by heaven and earth declaring His glory.

We sometimes have to wait to see God's magnificent glory. We must keep the faith. There is hope, and a change is also coming! God can do it just like that! Our limited imagination does not limit God's love nor His power. God can do anything, far more than we can ever imagine, guess, or request in our wildest dreams. In God's timing:

> "No longer will you hear about violence in your land or desolation and destruction within your borders. You will call your walls Salvation and your gates Praise. The sun will no longer be your light during the day, nor will the brightness of the moon give you light, But the LORD will be your everlasting light. Your God will be your glory. Your sun will no longer go down, nor will your moon disappear. The LORD will be your everlasting light, and your days of sadness will be over. Then all your people will be righteous, and they will possess the land permanently."
>
> (Isaiah 60:18-21)

LESSON † We don't have peaceful permanent lives or cities here on earth, but we are looking for the life and city that we will have in the future.

What is something that seems impossible in your life that you are hoping God will do, just like that?

God is Blessing You!

Happy "grateful Thursday." Today is a gift to us from God, so let us enjoy it. May God shower us with His most incredible blessings, and I pray that they will flow through us to those we encounter.

God will never tempt us. However, He will use the most challenging things and situations in our lives to shape us and to bless us. Since the beginning of time, God, the Father of lights, has been the giver of all good things. He floods the light of His love on us. He blesses us with the gifts of His goodness and grace.

> "Don't let anyone under pressure to give in to evil say, 'God is trying to trip me up.' God is impervious to evil, and puts evil in no one's way. The temptation to give in to evil comes from us and only us. We have no one to blame but the leering, seducing flare-up of our own lust. Lust gets pregnant, and has a baby: sin! Sin grows up to adulthood, and becomes a real killer. So, my very dear friends, don't get thrown off course. Every desirable and beneficial gift comes out of heaven. The gifts are rivers of light cascading down from the Father of Light. There is nothing deceitful in God, nothing two-faced, nothing fickle. He brought us to life using the true Word, showing us off as the crown of all his creatures." (James 1:13-18, MSG)

LESSON † God has blessed us with a measure of faith. We don't have to be fed up or discouraged about what is happening and what will happen next. Our faith will see us through!

Blessings are not always tangible things. What has God blessed you with this week?

The Power of Persuasion

This Friday, let us thank the Lord for being our Shepherd leading and guiding us as we continue to lean and depend on Him for direction in our lives.

Every day we are being pushed and pulled in many different directions. It seems like everyone is trying to persuade us to help them, give to them, or do what they want us to do. There is nothing wrong with persuasion. Our ability to persuade and influence people can be one of our most critical and valuable skills. But when we underestimate people's power to persuade and convince others to see things their way, we have a problem. Especially the things that go against what we know to be correct and against our faith.

> "'King Agrippa, do you believe the prophets? I know that you do believe.' Then Agrippa said to Paul, 'You almost persuade me to become a Christian.' And Paul said, 'I would to God that not only you, but also all who hear me today, might become both almost and altogether such as I am, except for these chains.'" (Acts 26:27-29, NKJV)

Sharing God's Word can sometimes feel like the proverb that says: "You can lead a horse to water, but you can't make him drink." [24] We can give someone a chance or an opportunity, but we can't force them to take it.

> **LESSON** † We are to be patient with ourselves and those we share with because God ultimately has the power of persuasion and will give the increase.

How are you leading non-believers to Christ?

Jesus on the Mainline

Praise God, for we know that Jesus is on the mainline, and we can reach Him at any time. Lord God, we ask that You please help us all and our plans for the weekend. Continue to lead and protect each of us and those whom we love.

We can all relate to being able to pick up the phone to call our parents, best friend, or pastor when the going gets tough, and sometimes we don't get an answer. But what an excellent assurance. Talking to Jesus is just like being a phone call away because He is on the mainline. It's reassuring to know that God wants us to call Him in our times of trouble. It's a great privilege and honor knowing that we can talk to our God anytime, anywhere, and concerning anything. He already knows everything about us.

> "While Jeremiah was still locked up in jail, a second Message from GOD was given to him: This is GOD's Message, the God who made earth, made it livable and lasting, known everywhere as GOD: 'Call to me and I will answer you. I'll tell you marvelous and wondrous things that you could never figure out on your own.'" (Jeremiah 33:1-3, MSG)

LESSON † Unlike when we sometimes call on man and can't get an answer, God always answers. It may not be what we want to hear, but He still hears our prayers, and He always answers them.

We serve a big God, and all we need to do is call on Him!

What is something you need to call out to the Lord about? He is waiting and listening.

Revive Us Again

Let us thank God for allowing us to see another blessed Sunday and experience and enjoy His blessings and favor upon us today. Let us ask God to search our hearts and remove anything ungodly in us.

No matter how bad times get, they can always get worse. When the times get so bad, we need a revival in the land, and it should begin in each of us. God's Word warns that there are some difficult times ahead.

> "But know this: Difficult times will come in the last days. For people will be lovers of self, lovers of money, boastful, proud, blasphemers, disobedient to parents, ungrateful, unholy, unloving, irreconcilable, slanderers, without self-control, brutal, without love for what is good, traitors, reckless, conceited, lovers of pleasure rather than lovers of God, holding to the form of godliness but denying its power. Avoid these people!" (2 Timothy 3:1-5, HCSB)

We need to be more aware of our need for more of God's LOVE for each other.

> **LESSON** ✝ **Every Christian is a member of God's universal church and we all belong to Him.**

As we offer our whole being to God, a change will happen in our hearts, from the inside out.

What areas of your life have you not offered up to Christ?

Our Labor is Not in Vain

Let us thank God for this new day. We thank Him for the blessing of working and His strength to complete each day. We pray for all the essential and frontline workers who place their lives on the line for us. We pray for their safety, pay increases, and that those who need work will find a job.

Ever since creation, God has given us work to do. God demonstrates that He loves us and that He has created each of us for a purpose by allowing us to see each new day. No day has to be wasted because He gives us the strength to accomplish our day-to-day tasks in our lives.

> "Whatever you do, do it enthusiastically, as something done for the Lord and not for men." (Colossians 3:23, HCSB)

LESSON † Certainly, serving God matters. As Christians, we work hard and struggle to live a godly life because we place our confidence in God. He is the Savior of all people, especially those who believe.

Are you enthusiastically serving God with your work here on earth?

Faithfully Committed

Let us thank God for this Tuesday, which He has made. May we continue to be committed to His will as we go through this week. I pray that He gives us the grace to be committed to Him in prayer, worship, and the study of His Word this week.

We serve a good God who is faithful to do what He has committed to us. He has also called for us to commit ourselves to Him.

Because our affections reveal our faith, we are tempted to measure, examine, or judge our and others' Christian walk based on the things we do.

> "Test yourselves to see if you are in the faith. Examine yourselves. Or do you yourselves not recognize that Jesus Christ is in you?—unless you fail the test. And I hope you will recognize that we do not fail the test. Now we pray to God that you do nothing wrong—not that we may appear to pass the test, but that you may do what is right, even though we may appear to fail. For we are not able to do anything against the truth, but only for the truth."
>
> (2 Corinthians 13:5-8, HCSB)

LESSON † As Christians, God has called us to holiness and not religion. The challenge that Paul laid out for them to do a spiritual self-examination is excellent for each of us today.

Would you pass the spiritual test Paul gave to the church of Corinth?

Encouraging Words at the Well

Overloaded

Let us humbly thank God for allowing us to make it halfway through this week to this "hump day" Wednesday. May God continue to guide us and strengthen us to overcome any obstacles we may face.

I once saw a picture of an overloaded donkey. That picture showed how we look when we don't carry everything to God in prayer. It is also a reminder that many of us are carrying around heavy burdens that are hurting and weighing us down. Jesus has promised us rest from carrying heavy loads. However, we tend to have too much going on in our lives, or we tend to surround ourselves with those who overload us with their burdens.

> "Then Jesus said, 'Come to me, all of you who are weary and carry heavy burdens, and I will give you rest.'"
>
> (Matthew 11:28, NLT)

Donkeys are known as the beasts of burden. They are generally used to carry heavy loads or perform other heavy work. As Christians, we are told that God won't put more on us than we can bear and that we should get rid of everything that slows us down, especially sin that distracts us.

LESSON † We need to know that we are not created to be a beast of burden, but we are promised through Christ Jesus to be able to carry whatever is placed on us. We can release to God whatever burdens or situations weigh us down. God wants to help us carry them, and He always sends someone willing to help us.

In what ways can you help or assist those around you feeling overloaded and weighed down by life's burdens?

Blessings in Disguise

Let us thank God for allowing us to see this "grateful Thursday." Thank God for all the many blessings, hope, and the strength we need not to lose heart.

When we find ourselves in tight places or with our backs up against the wall and it appears that we have no way out, God assures and reassures us that He is in control and that He'll be with us.

> "The Spirit of the Sovereign LORD is upon me, for the LORD has anointed me to bring good news to the poor. He has sent me to comfort the brokenhearted and to proclaim that captives will be released and prisoners will be freed. He has sent me to tell those who mourn that the time of the LORD's favor has come, and with it, the day of God's anger against their enemies. To all who mourn in Israel, he will give a crown of beauty for ashes, a joyous blessing instead of mourning, festive praise instead of despair. In their righteousness, they will be like great oaks that the LORD has planted for his own glory." (Isaiah 61:1-3, NLT)

LESSON † **Our God has a plan for our lives, and we must trust it, live it, and enjoy it because those seemingly hopeless situations and circumstances that feel like the end are the beginning. They are blessings in disguise!**

God, being all powerful, can do what He pleases, how He pleases. Has there been a time when God used someone or something you least expected to bless you? Or you to bless someone you least expected?

Nothing is Impossible with God

Thank God that we have made it to the end of this week. Let us remember the blessings that we have experienced so far this week.

As Christians, what a joy we have of sharing our life experiences. Each of us is allowed to share our God-given lessons.

We can thank God that we have each other to help us empathize and navigate so that we do not walk in circles, not understanding our seasons of life.

> "The angel answered her, 'The Holy Spirit will come to you, and the power of the Most High will overshadow you. Therefore, the holy child developing inside you will be called the Son of God. Elizabeth, your relative, is six months pregnant with a son in her old age. People said she couldn't have a child. But nothing is impossible for God.' Mary answered, 'I am the Lord's servant. Let everything you've said happen to me.' Then the angel left her."
>
> (Luke 1:35-38)

LESSON † In our praying and sharing of God's will, we must be mindful and aware of God's presence, knowing nothing is impossible with God whom we trust.

Has there been a time when you had given up on what looked like an impossible situation only to have God make it a possible situation?

God Gives Us Strength

This week may have been an emotional, long, and stressful week for some. May each of us find time to rest, relax, and unwind on this blessed Saturday.

Are you feeling weary and tired? With all the troubles in our world, it's no surprise that many people feel tired, exhausted, and weighed down.

> "Don't you know? Haven't you heard? The eternal God, the LORD, the Creator of the ends of the earth, doesn't grow tired or become weary. His understanding is beyond reach. He gives strength to those who grow tired and increases the strength of those who are weak. Even young people grow tired and become weary, and young men will stumble and fall. Yet, the strength of those who wait with hope in the LORD will be renewed. They will soar on wings like eagles. They will run and won't become weary. They will walk and won't grow tired." (Isaiah 40:28-31)

We find ourselves looking for hope, peace, and strength from many unfulfilled sources during challenging times.

LESSON † **Life can and will be challenging, full of worries. However, the Lord is waiting for us. He is ready to strengthen and renew us from our weariness. God gives us strength, so let's trade in our weariness for His rest in our lives!**

When life seems too much to bear, are you comfortable resting in the powerful presence of God?

Acceptable Life and Worship

Let us come before our holy God on this blessed Sunday with bowed heads and humble hearts as we worship Him.

There are so many things that we worship besides the Lord. We must not allow the things of the world to make us give up on God.

God is holy and has given us a standard for living and how we are to worship Him. According to the Law in the Old Testament, a sacrifice was necessary, but God made it plain that obedience from the heart was much more critical.

God wants us to live a good life where He gets the glory and we give Him acceptable worship!

> "'I can't stand your religious meetings. I'm fed up with your conferences and conventions. I want nothing to do with your religion projects, your pretentious slogans and goals. I'm sick of your fund-raising schemes, your public relations, and image making. I've had all I can take of your noisy ego-music. When was the last time you sang to *me*? Do you know what I want? I want justice—oceans of it. I want fairness—rivers of it. That's what I want. That's *all* I want.'"
>
> (Amos 5:21-24, MSG)

LESSON † Without hesitation, we must be mindful of the condition of our hearts and attitudes as we commit to worshiping God.

Are you mindful of the condition of your life and your heart before entering into worship to God?

Let Go and Let God

Let us enter this new week with the peace of God, and let's let go of all of our worries and the problems of last week and let God take care of them.

Although the world gets stressful, some live their best life while others need a little encouragement. More often than not, there are times when we allow the stressors of life to crowd our hearts and minds. We find ourselves or our loved ones desperately needing something to change in our lives. Those needs come in many forms. They may be healing, financial, peace, salvation, wisdom, or hope.

God is our protection and our strength. He always helps us in our times of trouble. For us to let go and let God, we must first acknowledge that in and of ourselves, we are not always able to change the circumstances in our own lives, not to mention the lives of others. We must trust God and have faith, allowing Him to do what only He can do.

> "If any of you needs wisdom to know what you should do, you should ask God, and he will give it to you. God is generous to everyone and doesn't find fault with them. When you ask for something, don't have any doubts. A person who has doubts is like a wave that is blown by the wind and tossed by the sea." (James 1:5-6)

LESSON † While we may not always know God's plan, He gives us the wisdom to know that we can let go and trust Him when we bring our concerns to Him. He assures us of His strength and willingness to help us.

Once you have taken your cares to God in prayer, do you take them back on?

Wisdom for a New Day

Thank God for this blessed Tuesday. May He provide everything that each of us needs and may every step that we take today to be ordered by Him.

Now that we are two days into this new week, do you find yourself staying on course with the plans and commitments you made for this new week? While making plans for the future is helpful and wise, we often fail to involve the Lord in our decision-making and planning for each new day.

We serve a good God who cares about us and the decisions that we make. We tend to pressure ourselves to achieve the goals and plans that we have devised in our hearts. As God's children, we should remember that the only real commitment we need to make and keep for each day is to ask the Lord where He desires us to go and what He wants us to do.

> "We can make our plans, but the LORD determines our steps."
> (Proverbs 16:9, NLT)

> "Put GOD in charge of your work, then what you've planned
> will take place." (Proverbs 16:3, MSG)

LESSON † Each of us has the free will to make choices in our lives. We have the assurance of knowing that we're not perfect nor alone because, through the Holy Spirit, the Lord leads and guides us along the best way and directs our steps in the way we should go.

When making plans, do you make it a habit of putting God first or do you invite Him after you have made them?

Watcha Lookin' 4

Thank God that we have made it to this "hump day" Wednesday, the middle of this week. We have awakened this morning with a loving God who is almighty.

Every day we go to God in prayer, seeking and asking for something. We should be looking to Him for everything because it is He who sustains us.

The inspiration for today's title comes from Kirk Franklin's CD "Whatcha Lookin' 4." When our faith is weak, and we are looking for fulfillment in this life, instead of digging deeper into God's Word, we tend to dig into the things of this world, as if we will find what our soul needs.

> "But even there, if you seek GOD, your God, you'll be able to find him if you're serious, looking for him with your whole heart and soul." (Deuteronomy 4:29, MSG)

LESSON † The song "Whatcha Lookin 4" ends with this biblical truth:

"(Jesus saying)
What you want
I've got it
What you need, I'm the One you're lookin' 4
It's yours
I'm the One you're lookin' 4" [25]

Do you always know what you are looking for from God? Do you find yourself digging deeper in the Word to find it?

God is Good

Let us count our many blessings on this "grateful Thursday" and praise God for all the things that He has already done, the things He's doing, and the things He's going to do.

Whether it's a natural disaster, or other chaos in the world, we can still confidently say that God is good! Each of us has been witness to this truth many times during our life. The fact that He woke us up today and has secured our salvation through His only begotten Son, Jesus, is a testament to His goodness.

Our lives can sometimes be difficult and challenging, causing us to struggle to maintain our faith. The word tells us that the Lord is good! He is a stronghold in the day of trouble, and He knows those who take refuge in Him. We must trust God completely and maintain the confidence that He knows us.

> "The LORD is good to everyone; he is merciful to all he has made." (Psalm 145:9, NCV)

LESSON † We don't ever have to doubt God's goodness because He has not and He never will stop being good. We sometimes stop being grateful.

Are there times when you have experienced the goodness of God? Did you share the ways God has been good to you with others?

God Sits High, Reaches Low

Let us approach God's throne this Friday with humility, realizing that we can't do anything without Him. I pray that He touches the lives of each of us who may be struggling where we need Him most.

We may all have experienced painful, fearful, and heartbreaking times in our lives that were so uncomfortable it felt like we were drowning. Have you ever heard the saying, "God sits high and looks low?" Better yet, have you ever asked when you were going through something, "Where is God?" The Lord takes pleasure in protecting us. He may not come when we want Him to, but He's always on time. He reaches low too!

David, the psalmist, uses the imagery of drowning to let us know where his help came from when he was helpless, weak, and in distress. He says:

> "He reached down from high above and took hold of me. He pulled me out of the raging water." (Psalm 18:16)

LESSON ✝ During those times in our life when we feel like throwing in the towel, giving up, and struggling to take care of the things in our lives or the lives of those we love, God will do the same for us. He reaches down and rescues us!

Reflect on a time when you felt like giving up, only to have God reach down and rescue you.

Stay Focused

Thank God that we have made it to another blessed weekend! I pray that things have gone well for each of us this far and that we continue trusting God's timing in our lives.

Many of us spend a lot of time waiting for something. We are waiting for something to happen, something to change, or just waiting for our circumstances to get better. In our waiting, we must continue to pray, stay focused, and not give up.

Let us stay focused and not give in to the distractions and dis-cour-agements that will come to make us give up.

> "Jesus told his disciples, 'Situations that cause people to lose their faith are certain to arise. But how horrible it will be for the person who causes someone to lose his faith!'" (Luke 17:1)

LESSON † **God takes pleasure in helping His people. As God's people, we can stay focused and not give up when we live by faith.**

Do you allow your struggles to keep you from spiritually focusing? Where are you currently struggling in your life that keeps you from focusing on God's care for you?

Mirror, Mirror on the Wall

Let us thank God for allowing us to see this blessed Sunday. Let us serve Him with gladness, and may He help each of us not to see our worship and serving as unwanted responsibilities but as ways to reflect the Lord's image in all that we do.

"Mirror, mirror on the wall, do you see Christ in me at all?" [26]

We know that mirrors don't show an accurate reflection since everything in a mirror is backward. Yet, at least once every day, we look in a mirror to examine our outer selves to see if we're presentable enough to be seen by others. If there are any flaws, we correct them.

> "But don't just listen to God's word. You must do what it says. Otherwise, you are only fooling yourselves. For if you listen to the word and don't obey, it is like glancing at your face in a mirror. You see yourself, walk away, and forget what you look like." (James 1:22-24, NLT)

What good would a mirror be if we didn't do anything about the flaws we see in ourselves?

LESSON † **Having the confidence that God fearfully and wonderfully made us, we can take heart that He fully knows us and, through our faith, spend eternity getting to know Him fully one day.**

Ask yourself the question, "Mirror, mirror on the wall, do you see Christ in me at all?"

Do All Things without Complaining!

Let us thank God for this Monday morning. May each of us begin this week with a positive outlook knowing that complaining, grumbling, or whining won't change any situation's outcome.

One of our most significant challenges is to do everything without grumbling or complaining. It's more comfortable and easier to think about and complain about the things that are not right than to think about the things that are right in our lives. As children of God, we must realize that our complaints have more profound implications, whether we are complaining about others, our circumstances, or our situations.

When we complain, it shows that we don't trust God, His sovereignty, or the plans that He has for our lives that will allow us to be in unhappy, uncomfortable situations and circumstances that we are complaining about. Nothing happens in our lives that God isn't aware of. We know that all things work together for our good. God has promised never to leave us or forsake us, and He has the power to see us through every situation according to His purpose.

> "Do everything without complaining and arguing, so that no one can criticize you. Live clean, innocent lives as children of God, shining like bright lights in a world full of crooked and perverse people." (Philippians 2:14-15, NLT)

LESSON † If we're going to be an effective witness of the power of God's Word in this dark, crooked, and corrupt world, we must stop complaining and allow God to transform us into the stars that we are. We must shine among our families, co-workers, neighbors, and all we encounter like the bright light God says we are.

How are you shining your light for others to see?

Stay in the Bible

Let us thank God as we continue to move through this blessed week. May we seek His wisdom to strengthen and enlighten us about which way we should go and what we should do.

To live our lives declaring that we are children of the Most High God, we must have a clear picture and an understanding of what He wants us to believe, communicate, and do.

The problem with that is we have an adversary who goes around like a roaring lion looking to destroy us. He doesn't want us to know God's Word. He comes to kill, steal, and destroy all that God says is good.

Satan, our enemy, knows that his time is limited and his fate has already been sealed.

Satan does everything in his limited power to keep us away from the Word of God, even if it means distorting it, using his influences to distract us, even causing us to be discouraged because of a lack of understanding.

> "'This book of instruction must not depart from your mouth; you are to recite it day and night so that you may carefully observe everything written in it. For then you will prosper and succeed in whatever you do.'" (Joshua 1:8, HCSB)

LESSON † So let's not allow Satan and the seemingly innocent things of this world to keep us from God's Word.

In what ways does the enemy try to keep you away from God's Word?

Don't Give Up Under Pressure

Thank God for allowing us to make it to this "hump day" Wednesday! As we continue to journey through this week, let us continue to lean on and trust God when we are weak and find ourselves in uncertain, confusing, and hard-pressed times.

We can find ourselves facing many stressful feelings with each passing day, but we must not give up. I remember reading that some days are diamonds, and some are coal, but every day is a golden opportunity for us to grow and demonstrate God's love and gratefulness, impacting the world around us in every right way. God has never promised us a stress-free life, but He said:

> "'In the same way, I will not cause pain without allowing
> something new to be born,' says the LORD."
>
> (Isaiah 66:9a, NCV)

We are stronger than we think when we keep a positive outlook.

LESSON † In *Living by the Word*, Alice Walker says, "Some periods of our growth are so confusing that we don't even recognize that growth is happening...Those long periods when something inside ourselves seems to be waiting, holding its breath, unsure about what the next step should be, eventually become the periods we wait for, for it is in those periods that we realize that we are being prepared for the next phase of our life and that, in all probability, a new level of the personality is about to be revealed." [27]

Reflect on a time when you wanted to give up. How did you faith grow during that time, and how have you been able to help others in similar seasons of their lives?

God's Word - Our Most Powerful Weapon

On this "grateful Thursday," let us thank God for empowering us with the strength and wisdom to fight against and capture every stronghold that comes from every negative thought that tries to take root in our minds.

The world has always been opposed to God's Word. Satan, our biggest enemy, wants us to be ashamed of and ignorant of God's Word. He wants us to deny God's words and use our words to cause division and strife, hurt others, complain, and lie. When difficulties arise in our lives, we're able to use and proclaim God's Word over our situations. Likewise, when we know God's Word and receive blessings and breakthroughs, we can praise Him and proclaim His goodness.

Today, we can be grateful as children of God because He has given us His Word, which is our most powerful weapon in defeating our spiritual and physical enemies.

> "Never stop reciting these teachings. You must think about them night and day so that you will faithfully do everything written in them. Only then will you prosper and succeed."
>
> (Joshua 1:8)

LESSON † **None of us knows all of the Word. Start with one scripture, and eventually, one will turn into an arsenal.**

What is a scripture you have used to battle the enemy?

Living Worthy of the Gospel

Let us start this last day of the week with an attitude of praise and worship. God has blessed each of us to make it to the end of another week. He is truly worthy to be praised.

Many are struggling to find their God-given purpose in life! We often see our achievements in life as our identity. it can lead us to never realizing our real God-given purpose in life. According to God's Word, we are to live our lives every day by His Word, and we must yield to the Holy Spirit. Our life's purpose is to praise and please God by honoring Him—not people—with our words, actions, and thoughts. Whether it's in our personal lives or our public work, we should strive to be people of integrity by always doing what is right even when no one else is doing it.

> "Make every effort to give yourself to God as the kind of person he will approve. Be a worker who is not ashamed and who uses the true teaching in the right way."
>
> (2 Timothy 2:15, NCV)

The Life Application Study Bible says, "Because God will examine what kind of workers we have been for him, we should build our lives on his Word and build his Word into our lives. It alone tells us how to live for him and serve him." [28]

LESSON † As Christians, the right thing for us to do is bring glory to God because there is no one greater worthy of our praise and worship.

How can you bring glory to God today?

Power of Open Doors

Let us thank God for guiding our steps into another blessed weekend! May He continue to bless us with the wisdom and discernment to continue making wise decisions and only walking through the doors He opens.

There is power in open doors, and we serve a God who loves to open doors for us. What we need, God has it, but we must be aware of who has opened the door and must be careful who we let enter with us. Both the power of good and evil can open a door, and both will enter an open door.

As children of God, we are encouraged to be on the lookout, not leaving ourselves open and exposed and giving the enemy a foothold, whether it's the door to our homes, hearts, minds, earthly relationships, or our relationship with God.

> "'Keep asking, and it will be given to you. Keep searching, and you will find. Keep knocking, and the door will be opened to you. For everyone who asks receives, and the one who searches finds, and to the one who knocks, the door will be opened.'" (Matthew 7:7-8, HCSB)

LESSON † Because we serve a God of open doors, the enemy will try to enter them, and when we don't allow him in, he looks for ways to deceive us with doors that he opens. Those are the doors that God often times closes to protect us. The good news is that when God opens a door, no devil can shut it, and when God closes a door, no devil can open it.

Reflect on the door(s) God has opened and closed on your behalf.

Family Worship - Who Are You Serving?

Let us thank God for deciding to wake us up on this beautiful, blessed Sunday morning. May we continue to allow Him to reign in our hearts and our homes, helping us and giving us a choice in making the right decisions.

The truth is that nothing can take away the fact that we will be able to honor, worship, and serve God. We will need to make decisions that we will sometimes find challenging, and we may not always know the right choice to make.

> "'But if you don't want to serve the LORD, then choose today whom you will serve. Even if you choose the gods your ancestors served on the other side of the Euphrates or the gods of the Amorites in whose land you live, my family and I will still serve the LORD.'" (Joshua 24:15)

Just like the people in Joshua's days had to choose whether they would obey the Lord, who had proven His steadfast love, or follow the gods of that land, which were only handmade idols, we, too, must make a decision today whether we are going to serve the one and only true God or worship idols.

LESSON † Once we choose to serve God, we should reinforce our choice every day by making prayer and the Word of God the tools and weapons that we use in all of our decision making in every area of our lives.

Each day are you consulting with God and looking to Him for guidance?

Keep Your Head Up

On this blessed Monday morning, let us thank God in advance for the blessings that He has in store for each of us today and for those blessings that are just around the corner this week.

We can begin and finish this week strong if we keep our heads up and focus on Jesus! Let us approach and stay the course during this new week, knowing that through our faith, no matter what we may have to face, God is already there.

> "We do this by keeping our eyes on Jesus, the champion who initiates and perfects our faith. Because of the joy awaiting him, he endured the cross, disregarding its shame. Now he is seated in the place of honor beside God's throne. Think of all the hostility he endured from sinful people; then you won't become weary and give up." (Hebrews 12:2-3, NLT)

Although we may face hardships and discouragements today or this week, we must not lose sight of the fact that we are never alone in life and that there is help.

The *Life Application Study Bible* says, "Many have already made it through life, enduring far more difficult circumstances than we have experienced. Suffering is the training ground for Christian maturity. It develops our patience and makes our final victory sweet." [29].

LESSON † We can never avoid hardships and discouragements in this world. If we want to have successful days, we must keep our heads up, our thoughts and spiritual eyes stayed on the Lord. He will keep us in perfect peace and make our path straight every time.

Think of a time when difficult circumstances brought you closer to God.

Surrounded by Greatness

Let us thank God for waking us up this Tuesday morning, giving us life, a reasonable portion of health, and strength to endure. Let us also thank Him for our family and circle of friends He has placed in our lives to encourage and support us.

The people around us matter because they have the power to encourage, inspire, and uplift us. They also can hinder us and destroy our inner peace. As we go about our daily lives, we would be wise to thank God for those He has placed on our path and in our lives. Also, we must remember to be thankful for knowing Him.

> "Friends come and friends go, but a true friend sticks by you like family." (Proverbs 18:24, MSG)

> "As iron sharpens iron, so a friend sharpens a friend."
> (Proverbs 27:17, NLT)

> "Become wise by walking with the wise; hang out with fools and watch your life fall to pieces." (Proverbs 13:20, MSG)

LESSON † For all the loyal and faithful friends we have met during our lifetime who have helped to sharpen us, we have no one to thank but God. With godly wisdom and accountability, let us, without judgment, be reliable, respectful, and trustworthy in our relationships. Let us surround ourselves with greatness with no strings attached, and let's positively impact others.

Are you sitting among godly counsel and friends that you can share the ups and downs of life with?

Mission Possible

Let us thank God for allowing us to make it halfway through this week. On this "hump day" Wednesday, may He bless each of us with the spirit, desire, courage, and confidence to focus on the plans that He has for us and the things we want.

We have been given this new day. It's up to us to do whatever we choose with this new day. If we choose to accept it, our mission for today is to use it and do good. If we're feeling afraid for some reason, if things are not looking up for us today and we're thinking that we are not going to be able to make it through today, we can, with confidence, know that our God is working all things out for our good.

> "Do not fear, for I am with you; do not be afraid, for I am your God. I will strengthen you; I will help you; I will hold on to you with My righteous right hand."
>
> (Isaiah 41:10, HCSB)

LESSON † No matter what's happening in our lives, we are not limited by our situations and circumstances because there is nothing too big for God, and all things are possible with Him.

Do you have a limited view of God and put Him in a box?

195

God Has More for Us!

Let us thank God for seeing this "grateful Thursday." Let's thank Him for fresh starts and new beginnings whereby we have a chance to trust God to do more than what we have already asked or thought.

No matter if it's a new day or a new month, those of us who are faithful to God are looking for a wonder-working miracle or just an opportunity to start over.

> "But as Scripture says: 'No eye has seen, no ear has heard, and no mind has imagined the things that God has prepared for those who love him.'" (1 Corinthians 2:9)

> "God can do anything, you know—far more than you could ever imagine or guess or request in your wildest dreams! He does it not by pushing us around but by working within us, his Spirit deeply and gently within us."
> (Ephesians 3:20, MSG)

LESSON † Our prayers will be powerful and will come to pass when we allow God to change our hearts and our desires so that they perfectly line up with His will for us.

How are you allowing God to change your heart and fill you with Him?

Lessons from the Ants

Thank God for providing us with the strength and everything needed to complete the work set before us this week.

Today is the end of the work week for many, while for others, their work week continues. Whether working a job for ourselves or caring for loved ones, it's our ministry before God, and we should work at it by doing our very best. As Christians, we know that the Lord will reward our labors when we diligently and persistently persevere. So let's not get tired of doing what is good. We will receive a harvest of blessing at just the right time if we don't give up.

We are encouraged to live our lives to the fullest, and work is a part of it. The Word tells us that if we want to prosper, whatever we do, we should not be lazy.

The Word also tells us to watch the ants because they exhibit practical characteristics that we can benefit from and apply to prosper and be successful in our everyday lives. Ants work together in groups with no leader. Ants don't waste their time and are very productive.

> "Take a lesson from the ants, you lazybones. Learn from their ways and become wise!" (Proverbs 6:6, NLT)

LESSON † As Christians, we should be present, productive, and ready to work diligently in God's kingdom, our personal lives, and our jobs.

Are you using your talents and skills to help others and build God's kingdom?

Bought with a Price

Let us thank God for allowing us to reach this weekend. Let us start our day with Him, and let us appreciate everything and take nothing for granted.

There is so much confusion and evil in the world trying to destroy everything God has created. Not everyone on earth is a believer. There are believers and non-believers. While Jesus warned about false teachers, today we can apply the same warning for those whose words sound religious, but they are only interested in what benefits them. They minimize God and glorify themselves.

> "'You can identify them by their fruit, that is, by the way they act.'" (Matthew 7:16a, NLT)

Everyone has the choice not to perish or to have eternal life by following Christ. As believers, we can stand on that promise because God loves us so much that He would pay any price to possess us! We have been bought at a high price.

> "For ye are bought with a price: therefore glorify God in your body, and in your spirit, which are God's."
>
> (1 Corinthians 6:20, KJV)

LESSON † We should not be wasting our lives sinning or mistreating others, and we should be aware that God is real, and He finds value in each of us. God gave His only Son, Jesus, who came down from heaven and shed His blood to pay a debt that He did not owe and a debt we could not pay.

Are you pleasing and honoring God with your life and choices?

We Are What We Eat

Thank God for enabling us to see another blessed Sunday so that we can pause to magnify and worship Him in spirit and truth. May He allow the light of the Holy Spirit to shine in us today as we read and hear the Word. God, bless Your men and women with an on-time, life-changing word today.

While here on earth, we as human beings have bodies. Three critical elements make up our mortal bodies. We have flesh (the body), soul, and spirit. All of us are essentially spirits that live in bodies. I've heard it said that we are heavenly beings having an earthly experience.

> "'God is a spirit. Those who worship him must worship in spirit and truth.'" (John 4:24)

While taking care of our earthly bodies is critical and very important, we must focus more on our spiritual growth than our natural development as God's people. It's important to know that the way we relate and connect with God is with our spirit and not our bodies.

> "Jesus answered, 'Scripture says, "A person cannot live on bread alone but on every word that God speaks."'"
>
> (Matthew 4:4)

LESSON † Besides God's Word being life and health to us, we must feast on it daily, allowing it to nourish our spirits so that we can grow from infant Christians to mature Christians. "We are what we eat!"

Are you meditating on God's Word both day and night? How does your day change when you focus on God?

Can God Really Use Me?

Let us thank God for the start of this new week. May we surrender every area of our lives to Him and let us seek and use every opportunity to say yes to what God has for us this week.

Every day someone is asking the question, "Can God really use me?" There is no heavier weight to carry than the burden of us thinking that we are useless and unredeemable because of something that we have done. When we hold on to the thought of who we want to be or what we want to do, rather than surrendering to who God says we are and what He wants us to do; we leave room for the enemy to convince us that we are indeed not worthy or lack perfection for God's use.

God does not look for us to be perfect, but He is looking for obedience and a yes. We've all been given gifts by God so that we can serve. As God's people, we must rely on the Spirit's power to help us yield and be obedient each day. When we allow the Spirit, He will shape us into presentable and useful vessels.

> "If you keep yourself pure, you will be a special utensil for honorable use. Your life will be clean, and you will be ready for the Master to use you for every good work."
>
> (2 Timothy 2:21, NLT)

LESSON † Yes, God can, and He will use each of us. We must know and be willing to surrender to who we are in Christ. We must never allow the things that we've done to make us feel ashamed or guilty, thinking that God can no longer use us.

Have you allowed yourself to be fully used by God or are you allowing your past to hold you back?

What a Mighty God We Serve!

Let us give God the honor and praise for this new day. It's Tuesday, and we did not have the power to wake ourselves.

Waiting for God from day to day is not easy. While we don't know what to expect, we know for sure that we serve a mighty God who was, who is, and who is to come. It often feels like God isn't hearing or answering our prayers and that He doesn't understand the urgency of our situations and circumstances.

> "I pray that the glorious Father, the God of our Lord Jesus Christ, would give you a spirit of wisdom and revelation as you come to know Christ better. Then, you will have deeper insight. You will know the confidence that he calls you to have and the glorious wealth that God's people will inherit. You will also know the unlimited greatness of his power as it works with might and strength for us, the believers."
>
> (Ephesians 1:17-19)

LESSON † We must keep faith because God is caring, loving, and He is the creator of the universe and has promised never to leave us or forsake us!

Describe a time when God showed up for you in a mighty way. What did you learn about God in that time?

Burdens? Give Them to God

On this "hump day" Wednesday, let us thank God for giving us strength when we are weary, burdened, and discouraged. Thank Him for guiding and keeping us on the right path when we don't know which way to go or what to do.

Each day we face many challenges in our lives that we find too heavy to bear. We never know what weight or burden we will encounter. Not all burdens we carry are heavy. They can be light, and they are seldom new. Often, they are old things that we cannot let go of that we find ourselves carrying.

We needlessly carry things that we should not or don't have to. We serve a compassionate God who wants to carry our burdens. We can thank the Lord, who daily bears our burdens for us.

The word tells us to:

> "Give your burdens to the Lord. He will carry them. He will not permit the godly to slip or fall." (Psalm 55:22, TLB)

LESSON ✝ From day to day, month to month, and yes, sometimes over many years, we take on more than we need to carry because we often underestimate the weight of the burdens that we have. Each new day, let us take the opportunity to be willing to follow God and give Him all of our burdens, pains, sorrows, and fears of today, yesterday, and tomorrow.

Is there something that has weighed you down for some time? Have you given it over to the Lord?

Hold On – Help is on the Way

Let us thank God for another "grateful Thursday." Let us continue to show Him our gratitude by accepting everything in our lives with joy, even the complicated things.

We live in a dark and fallen world. No matter who we are, and especially if we're believers, we will find ourselves struggling and faced with uncertain situations at some point and time in our lives. Jesus lets us know that things may be dark now, but we should hold on to what we have because the Light is coming. Help is on the way!

> "'Because you have obeyed my command to endure, I will keep you safe during the time of testing which is coming to the whole world to test those living on earth. I am coming soon! Hold on to what you have so that no one takes your crown.'" (Revelation 3:10-11)

LESSON † We don't have to get worked up or discouraged because it looks like evil and injustice seem to be prevailing in the world. We should keep in mind what God said to Habakkuk, "Wait {patiently}" (Habakkuk 2:3, AMP). His mercies never end.

How can we stay encouraged when we see evil happening around us?

Mercies New Everyday

Yay, we made it to Friday! Let us thank God for another day, another chance to do His will in our lives, and another opportunity to become better at loving Him and each other.

The week has come to an end, and we have survived another week. What didn't take us out has probably strengthened us. Up until now, we may or may not have done everything according to God's plan, but we can thank God that there are no limits to His love and His grace and that there are no boundaries to His mercies.

> "'The reason I can {still} find hope is that I keep this one thing in mind: the LORD's mercy. We were not completely wiped out. His compassion is never limited. It is new every morning. His faithfulness is great. My soul can say, "The LORD is my lot {in life}. That is why I find hope in him.""'
>
> (Lamentations 3:21-24)

LESSON † Each of us makes mistakes and does unacceptable things from time to time, but we are not destroyed because we serve a merciful God of great love, whose compassions never fail! We shouldn't be hard on ourselves because God gives us many chances to get things right, and He also desires us to do the same for each other.

How did it make you feel when God showed you mercy for a wrong you committed?

Rest on Promises of God's Word

Thank God that we have made it to another weekend! May each of us get to rest and relax on this blessed Saturday from this week's stress, hardships, and labor.

For everyone who needs, seeks, and believes God's Word, may we rest, be safe, and be comforted this weekend, knowing that God's grace is sufficient and will bring us through whatever we may face. We must all keep in mind daily that none of us are immune from the temptations of the evil one. If it's peace and comfort that we need and want in our lives, then we must hide God's Word in our hearts.

> "I always keep the LORD in front of me. When he is by my side, I cannot be moved. That is why my heart is glad and my soul rejoices. My body rests securely." (Psalm 16:8-9)

LESSON † **We must continually ask God for the daily strength to keep our minds stayed on Him so that we will be kept secure in our faith and will have peace of mind and rest for our souls.**

Do you find that your life is more peaceful when you rest on the promises of God's Word? What is one of your favorite scriptures to rest on?

A Servant Leader

Thank God for another day. Let us boldly approach the throne of God on this Sunday.

While we know that we are to show appreciation throughout the year for our pastors and clergy, anytime is a good time to recognize and honor them for their work for the kingdom of God and the support they give to all as servant leaders. As the body of Christ, we must encourage and lift each other up—especially our pastors who have many responsibilities and carry the burdens of many.

Our desire should be to have a pastor who loves God, is a strong leader, and knows that their approval comes from God.

> "And I will give you shepherds after my own heart, who will guide you with knowledge and understanding."
> (Jeremiah 3:15, NLT)

One of the most extraordinary things we can do is recognize that pastors aren't perfect. They are not immune to the enemy's attacks and can also experience many of the same struggles that everyone else does.

In the *Life Application Study Bible,* it says, "Israel would not only reject the true shepherd; it would accept a worthless shepherd instead. This shepherd would serve his concerns rather than the concerns of his flock and would destroy rather than defend them." [30]

LESSON † Praise God for an excellent pastor, who will prepare, not fear preaching God's Word, and not only defend but teach the Bible and about Jesus so that we can relate.

Do you see yourself as a servant leader? What characteristics qualify you?

God is a Way Maker

Let us thank God for the beginning of a new week. We may not know what this week holds or what we will face, but the one thing we know is who holds the future.

None of us can expect to be successful in our lives without God's favor to us daily. As people of God, we don't need to know what the future holds because our faith allows us to trust God, the One who makes a way and who holds the future.

> "'I am the LORD, who opened a way through the waters, making a dry path through the sea.'" (Isaiah 43:16, NLT)

> "I will go before you and level the mountains [to make the crooked places straight]; I will break in pieces the doors of bronze and cut asunder the bars of iron."
> (Isaiah 45:2, AMPC)

> "In all your ways know, recognize, *and* acknowledge Him, and He will direct *and* make straight *and* plain your paths."
> (Proverbs 3:6, AMPC)

LESSON † As we walk and live as faithful believers, we don't have to worry or be held back because of our circumstances. No matter what we may face, we should pray to God, who has promised to make a way and always be with us.

Has there ever been a time when you couldn't see how you were going to make it, but God showed up and made a way?

Christ Our Foundation

Thank God for another blessed day. May it be productive as we trust and believe Him to work everything for our good.

Although living in a community is essential and has a lot to do with having a stable and reliable life, we must each day obey and build our lives on Jesus, the Solid Rock.

If we were to ask a house builder, what is the essential part of building a house, they would say the foundation—not just any foundation but a stable and solid foundation. We can use the metaphor of building a house when we live our lives, especially when it comes to sincerely and genuinely building up others and building God's kingdom.

> "'Therefore, everyone who hears what I say and obeys it will be like a wise person who built a house on rock. Rain poured, and floods came. Winds blew and beat against that house. But it did not collapse, because its foundation was on rock. Everyone who hears what I say but doesn't obey it will be like a foolish person who built a house on sand. Rain poured, and floods came. Winds blew and struck that house. It collapsed, and the result was a total disaster.'"
>
> (Matthew 7:24-27)

LESSON † Building on a firm foundation will help us to weather the storms of life. We must live and build our works on the foundation of Christ Jesus. For, in the end, He will judge our works to see if they have lasting value.

As you build and work in God's kingdom, are you doing what you do for His glory so that it may stand?

In My Shoes, It Gets Tough Sometimes

We have made it to another "hump day" Wednesday. Let us look to the future, forget the tragic past, and continue to remember God is our strength, and He is with us.

When we are experiencing difficult and challenging times, we may not understand why. As we continue to live, we should not try to figure it out. We must continue to keep walking out our lives and trust God.

Yes, there will be times when in our shoes, it gets tough, and life feels unfair sometimes. We may find it hard sometimes to understand why God will allow those who love Him to go through and endure seasons of hard times. We can learn a lesson from Job, who went through so much and lost everything, yet he never gave up on God. Job says:

> "'For I have stayed on God's paths; I have followed his ways and not turned aside.'" (Job 23:11, NLT)

LESSON † **When walking in our shoes gets tough, let us keep our integrity and the confidence of God's justice. Keep going, walking worthy of our calling that God has called us for!**

Are you aware of your calling to serve God? Do you find it hard to use your calling while walking the path laid out for you by God?

Unseen and Unexpected Blessings

On this "grateful Thursday," let us thank God for waking us up and for keeping us safe, for healing us, for all the many blessings that we cannot see, and most of all, for saving us.

As we approach each new day, many wake up with certain things that we expect to take place. Regardless of whether we can see them come to pass or not, we have much to be grateful for in our lives. We often focus on the stresses so much that we fail to see the many unseen and unexpected blessings flowing on and through us.

> "Why is everyone hungry for more? 'More, more,' they say. 'More, more.' I have God's more-than-enough, more joy in one ordinary day than they get in all their shopping sprees. At day's end I'm ready for sound sleep, for you, GOD, have put my life back together." (Psalm 4:6-8, MSG)

Once we pause and stop, we will have the most incredible experience of recognizing the many unseen and unexpected blessings.

LESSON † Once we've been on the receiving end of an unexpected blessing, we know how important it is to trust God when He says that He will provide. Let's always remember to be grateful and to thank God each day for the many unexpected blessings that He so freely and graciously gives to us, seen and unseen.

Have you ever experienced receiving an unexpected blessing? How did you feel?

The Lord Hears Our Cries

We've made it to this Friday morning, the end of another week. It is my prayer that everyone has had a blessed week thus far. I pray that no matter what has happened, we realize that God is in control.

No matter who we are, we all want to know that we matter. We want to know that we're seen and that we're heard. Each day that has passed, and each day to come, we will undoubtedly pray and cry out to God to help us make it through.

Why? Because as God's people, we know that God is an incredible listener, and nothing can separate us from Him. He doesn't change how He feels about us. God listens, and He hears our cries. We may sometimes feel that we are not worthy of being seen or heard, but the psalmist lets us know that God will listen to us even when we are not our best.

> "I have called on you because you answer me, O God. Turn your ear toward me. Hear what I have to say." (Psalm 17:6)

> "I took my troubles to the LORD; I cried out to him, and he answered my prayer." (Psalm 120:1, NLT)

> "As for me, I will call upon God; and the LORD shall save me. Evening, and morning, and at noon, will I pray, and cry aloud: and he shall hear my voice." (Psalm 55:16-17, KJV)

LESSON † We may sometimes find ourselves crying out to God and feeling like He's not listening or hearing our cries. He hears all of them. Just be patient. God answers them according to His will.

Reflect on a time when you took your problems to the Lord! In what ways did He comfort you?

It's Easy to Judge

Thank God for making it to the weekend. He has promised to keep us in perfect peace when we keep our hearts and minds on Him, so this weekend, let's choose to allow the peace of God to rule in our hearts.

There will always be opposition in our world trying to steal our peace. Many will feel torn and separated and will judge others. People will condemn and reject others simply because they are not in agreement. It is easy to judge and see the fault in others and not ourselves. We must pray to have eyes to see the best in each other.

> "'Do not judge, so that you won't be judged. For with the judgment you use, you will be judged, and with the measure you use, it will be measured to you.'"
>
> (Matthew 7:1-2, HCSB)

> "Do not say, 'I'll get even with you!' Wait for the LORD, and he will save you." (Proverbs 20:22)

LESSON † "It is easy to judge! It's more difficult to understand. Understanding requires compassion, patience, and a willingness to believe that good hearts sometimes choose poor methods. Through judging, we separate. Through understanding, we grow."—Doe Zantamata [31]

Do you find it easy contributing to and participating in negative judgments about others?

Think Pink

So many continue to struggle with breast cancer. Let's think pink as we worship today. Let us pause to support the fighters, admire the survivors, and honor the taken of breast cancer.

Although mammograms can be just a little uncomfortable for some, we know that early detection saves lives. They can reveal whether we are cancer-free or not.

No one would ever choose to have breast cancer, but those who get it say that they realize that they have no choice but to face it daily. When I've spoken with those who are fighting and those who are survivors, they say they've found hope along their journeys that help them never give up and that they hold on to their faith in God.

> "Praise the God and Father of our Lord Jesus Christ, the Father of mercies and the God of all comfort. He comforts us in all our affliction, so that we may be able to comfort those who are in any kind of affliction, through the comfort we ourselves receive from God." (2 Corinthians 1:3-4, HCSB)

LESSON † Only God's power can fill any of us with enough strength to endure the pain and suffering with a spirit of joyfulness.

Have you experienced the healing touch of Jesus? Is there someone you can comfort or offer a prayer of comfort for today?

Testing the Spirits

Let us thank God for this new morning and the beginning of this new week. Let us ask Him for wisdom and to guide our thinking process so that we will do well.

We are overwhelmed with so much noise in the form of news and social media. We can become so confused that we don't know what to believe. As God's children, with each new day or beginning, we trust in God for His unfailing love and His promises to be with us and protect us.

> "Dear friends, don't believe all people who say that they have the Spirit. Instead, test them. See whether the spirit they have is from God, because there are many false prophets in the world. This is how you can recognize God's Spirit: Every person who declares that Jesus Christ has come as a human has the Spirit that is from God. But every person who doesn't declare that Jesus Christ has come as a human has a spirit that isn't from God. This is the spirit of the antichrist that you have heard is coming. That spirit is already in the world."
>
> (1 John 4:1-3)

LESSON † It's okay if we don't believe everything that we see or hear. We can overcome this by using the gift of discerning to know what is real and false by walking with God and knowing His Word.

Do you depend on the Holy Spirit to help you recognize and avoid deception?

What Matters is How We See Ourselves!

Let us thank God for this new day. Let us ask Him to give us the confidence and the ability to do His will and believe in ourselves.

We often talk about testing the spirits of others. Today, let us put our focus on ourselves.

It is so crucial that, as Christians, we know our identity in Christ. We must understand who we are and whose we are. When others cause issues in our lives, and when situations out of our control happen, we must decide not to let them or the way others feel about them negatively impact us. We may or may not have the ability to change people, issues, and situations, but we can change how we think about them and respond to them.

> "Test yourselves to see if you are in the faith. Examine yourselves. Or do you yourselves not recognize that Jesus Christ is in you?—unless you fail the test. And I hope you will recognize that we do not fail the test. Now we pray to God that you do nothing wrong—not that we may appear to pass the test, but that you may do what is right, even though we may appear to fail. For we are not able to do anything against the truth, but only for the truth." (2 Corinthians 13:5-8, HCSB)

LESSON † When we are faithful and believe in ourselves, anything is possible. What matters is the way we see ourselves.

Do you stress about the things that other people think about you? Or are you more concerned about the things you do that bring glory to God?

No Turning Back

Let us thank God for seeing another "hump day" Wednesday. We are halfway through the week. Let's not look back but focus on finishing strong by committing every burden or concern weighing heavy on us to God.

If we're going to finish this week or anything in life strong, we must be dedicated and not make a habit of looking back on our past mistakes or sins or looking to do anything that will pull us away from following Jesus. Although, some past life experiences and lessons from our past are worth looking back on.

> "But Jesus told him, 'Anyone who lets himself be distracted from the work I plan for him is not fit for the Kingdom of God.'" (Luke 9:62, TLB)

I once read something that said: "The reason why we often give up so fast is that we tend to look at how far we have to go instead of how far we have gotten."

LESSON † Past mistakes, sins, and other distractions will hold many of us back, even after saying that we want to follow Jesus. Thank God that we are not our past mistakes nor our sins. Let us not be distracted, and in whatever we set out to do, let's give it all we got! Keep pressing on. There is no turning back!

Are you willing to use some of your past mistakes or problems to help others today?

The Lord is in Our Midst

Let us be grateful to the mighty God we serve for another day's journey! We are here today. Let us thank Him for His righteousness and His justice. Let us be thankful for all that He gives, withholds, and for His daily protection.

There's nothing in or on this earth that should take away the joy that God wants to give to us as His children. Unfortunately, we have an adversary who would do everything in his limited power to do just that if we allow him. One lesson that will serve us well as God's people is to know that there is joy in obedience! Ultimately, the end result of learning and experiencing God's complete and all-inclusive love is joy!

> "Sing happily, people of Zion! Shout loudly, Israel! Celebrate and rejoice with all your heart, people of Jerusalem. The LORD has reversed the judgments against you. He has forced out your enemies. The king of Israel, the LORD, is with you. You will never fear disaster again. On that day Jerusalem will be told, 'Do not be afraid, Zion! Do not lose courage!' The LORD, your God, is with you. He is a hero who saves you. He happily rejoices over you, renews you with his love, and celebrates over you with shouts of joy." (Zephaniah 3:14-17)

LESSON † **God wants to give us joy! He wants to restore us. He promises that we will fear no more. He will take away His judgment, scatter our enemies, and He will be with us. God's restoration is not half-hearted but holistic. Not only will He restore our social status, but He will repair us spiritually, emotionally, and mentally.**

Does the assurance of Jesus's forever presence with you give you a sense of security and joy?

Unchained Power of Praise and Worship

Let us give God all the praise because we have made it to the end of another week. I pray that each of us is finishing strong and not being held captive to anything that has occurred.

The Lord is worthy to be praised! However, so many times we find ourselves in situations and circumstances intended to break us. God never intended for us to be imprisoned or so bound that we lose our joy. Mother Teresa once said, "Don't let anything so sadden your heart that it takes away the joy of your heart." [32]

> "Always be joyful. Never stop praying. Be thankful in all circumstances, for this is God's will for you who belong to Christ Jesus." (1 Thessalonians 5:16-18, NLT)

Each of us has the same daily opportunity to pass the most powerful test as we interact with others.

> **LESSON** † **As we move through life, we can hold on, knowing that God has the power to keep us.**

So, whatever we go through, we serve the God of the universe, who is on our side and is worthy of our praise and worship. He can and He will do supernatural things to set us free!

Have you made praise and worship a daily part of your life?

Encouraging Words at the Well

A New Beginning

Good morning, afternoon, or good evening. Thank God that we have made it to the weekend. As we enjoy this well-awaited day of rest for most people, let us thank God for an opportunity of freshness in our life.

For many, the end of the week is the best. But every day starts with a new beginning or a fresh start, which comes with great promises and hope. No matter how wayward or off course our life is right now, each day God offers each of us a fresh start. We're given a chance to have a fresh start if we accept God's promises. We don't have to focus on what might have been. God will wash away our sins, and we can receive a new heart for Him and have His Spirit within us.

> """I will sprinkle clean water on you and make you clean instead of unclean. Then I will cleanse you from all your idols. I will give you a new heart and put a new spirit in you. I will remove your stubborn hearts and give you obedient hearts. I will put my Spirit in you. I will enable you to live by my laws, and you will obey my rules.""" (Ezekiel 36:25-27)

LESSON † **Just as God promised to restore and give a fresh start to the people of Israel, He will do the same for each of us. God has a desire to give us a new heart for following Him, and He wants to put His Spirit within each of us to provide us with a fresh start and enable us to do His will.**

Do you feel the freedom and the freshness of a new beginning that comes when you confess your sins to God?

A House Not Made by Hands

Let us thank God for another blessed Sunday. As we worship today, may our praises and God's Word lift us, and may our lives be renewed by the Holy Spirit that is within each of us.

Even though life in these temporary bodies today seems so challenging and uncertain, we don't have to despair because God is in control.

> "We know that our body—the tent we live in here on earth—will be destroyed. But when that happens, God will have a house for us. It will not be a house made by human hands; instead, it will be a home in heaven that will last forever. But now we groan in this tent. We want God to give us our heavenly home, because it will clothe us so we will not be naked. While we live in this body, we have burdens, and we groan. We do not want to be naked, but we want to be clothed with our heavenly home. Then this body that dies will be fully covered with life. This is what God made us for, and he has given us the Spirit to be a guarantee for this new life." (2 Corinthians 5:1-5, NCV)

LESSON † Each of us is called to live for God and allow Him to live through us. We must focus our praise on Him and not on our places of worship. As God's people, we are destined for much more. We are destined for permanent heavenly bodies and to dwell with God.

What's your understanding of this temporary earthly body? Are you willing to let go of it to experience eternity and your permanent heavenly body?

Tell Satan His Access is Denied

Thank God that we've made it to the beginning of this new week. Let us be of one accord and stand together in prayer for the strength to resist and to avoid any temptations or evil attacks.

Some people will speak ill and will do all manner of evil against us, and their primary purpose is to do us harm.

If we're going to live victoriously, we are encouraged to resist the enemy's attacks, who is at war with God. Such attacks are nothing but tests of our faith, and we don't have to open the door and give him access to our lives.

> "'Get out of here, Satan,' Jesus told him. 'The Scriptures say, "Worship only the Lord God. Obey only him."' Then Satan went away, and angels came and cared for Jesus."
> (Matthew 4:10-11, TLB)

> "So let God work his will in you. Yell a loud *no* to the Devil and watch him make himself scarce. Say a quiet *yes* to God and he'll be there in no time. Quit dabbling in sin. Purify your inner life. Quit playing the field." (James 4:7-8, MSG)

LESSON † While we await the return of Christ, Satan is here now and doing his best to win over as many of God's people as he can. We don't have to fear, and we can tell Satan that his access is denied in our lives. The Word lets us know that we can resist the devil with the Holy Spirit's power, and he will flee from us.

Did you know that if you fill your mind with God's powerful words, you will have no room left for Satan's lies and attacks?

Encouraging Words at the Well

Know the Value of Your Worth

Let us thank God for His everlasting presence in our lives and His daily provisions. May His Spirit give us the courage, wisdom, and strength to take back everything that the enemy has stolen from us.

Despite all of the world's troubles and chaos, we can rest assured that God sees us. Although we can, without thinking, become caught up in our cares and the fears in our lives, God still cares so much about every aspect of each of our lives. According to scripture, we are more valuable than the birds, and God takes care of them, so He will take care of us. He genuinely values and cares for us.

> "'Look at the birds! They don't worry about what to eat—they don't need to sow or reap or store up food—for your heavenly Father feeds them. And you are far more valuable to him than they are. Will all your worries add a single moment to your life?'" (Matthew 6:26-27, TLB)

As God's children, He has promised to take care of our every need.

> "You can be sure that God will take care of everything you need, his generosity exceeding even yours in the glory that pours from Jesus." (Philippians 4:19, MSG)

LESSON † To God, we are priceless, and we are much more valuable than the birds. Still, God provides for them. The best thing that we can do when we start to worry about our cares and fears is to pray! God sees our needs, and He will provide.

Do you feel that God is providing everything you need? If not, what will it take for you to feel satisfied?

It's Okay to Cry Out to God

Thank God that we have made it halfway through the week to another "hump day" Wednesday and that we have God with us. Let's continue to ask for His guidance and strength to carry us through our times of misunderstanding and weakness.

If you have reached the middle of the week or there have been times in your life you felt that you have reached your limit, you probably know something about crying out to God if you have to. We can be comforted in knowing that our God promises to be with us, strengthen us, and help us. We know from scripture that there is a time to cry and that everyone will cry at some point in their lives. Yes, everyone!

We also know that many relate crying to weakness, but in scripture, we know that some of the most confident and strongest people cried out to God.

Most are familiar with John 11:35 when Jesus cried/wept when His friend Lazarus died. But He cried on several occasions, and He is God in the flesh.

> "During his life on earth, Jesus prayed to God, who could save him from death. He prayed and pleaded with loud crying and tears, and he was heard because of his devotion to God." (Hebrews 5:7)

LESSON † When we feel that we have reached our limit and are struggling with anything, the best thing we can do is cry out to the Lord and pray. The Lord will clear our minds and energize us with the strength to finish strong.

Has there been a time in your life when you were so overwhelmed that you cried out to God? Do you feel that He heard your cry?

My Cup Overflows

On this "grateful Thursday," let us give God the glory for all of His blessings. May each of our cups continue to overflow with God's many blessings so that we can share with others.

There is nothing more encouraging or exciting in life than having one's daily life needs and purposes fulfilled and met. As God's children, we can expect to receive the many blessings that our God so generously gives to us. When we talk about having our cup overflowing, we refer to our lives and the spiritual and emotional needs that help us fulfill our purposes.

We must manage and maintain the level in our cup and not let it go below the depletion level. If we allow it to go to a depletion level, we won't have anything to encourage and inspire ourselves, let alone doing good for others and those in our lives.

> "Besides, God will give you his constantly overflowing kindness. Then, when you always have everything you need, you can do more and more good things." (2 Corinthians 9:8)

> "You prepare a table before me in the presence of my enemies; You anoint my head with oil; my cup overflows."
> (Psalm 23:5, HCSB)

LESSON † We serve a God who desires not only to bless us exceedingly and abundantly with what we need. He gives us much more so that we will always have a cup/life overflowing.

Do you see the overflows in your life as a way to offer to others and those in need? When was the last time you shared your overflow?

Where There is Faith, There is Victory

Thank God that we have made it to this Friday. Let us thank Him for the grace to stand firm and strong no matter what has come our way.

As God's children, we're blessed to be chosen to be living in such a unique and special time. Despite this, we must continue to keep our faith because where there is faith, there is victory.

We must keep praying, knowing that God is the author and the finisher of our faith, this world, and our lives. The enemy would like nothing more for us to do but give up and give in when facing adversities for his daily attempt is to steal, kill, and destroy us. Since our faith directs our lives, we must be determined to be victorious by keeping our faith stirred up.

> "For every child of God defeats this evil world, and we achieve this victory through our faith." (1 John 5:4, NLT)

LESSON † **We have never been promised an easy or comfortable life as children of God. However, we are encouraged to be faithful and obedient to the end knowing that our victory is in our faith.**

Does knowing that your victory rests in God help you to claim the victory when life becomes uncomfortable?

Christians Like a Pumpkin

Thank God that we have made it to the weekend. Life goes by so quickly, and that's why we must not take anything for granted. Let us thank God for taking care of us, even the most minor details of our lives.

Pumpkins are most popular during the fall season and are used for carving for Halloween. We often search to find the perfect pumpkins to decorate or carve. The search for the ideal pumpkin reminds me of how God searches for us, picks us out of the world, and then fills us with everything needed to allow the light of His glory to shine through us.

> "'And I will give them one heart and put a new spirit within them; I will remove their heart of stone from their bodies and give them a heart of flesh, so they may follow My statutes, keep My ordinances, and practice them. Then they will be My people, and I will be their God. But as for those whose hearts pursue their desire for detestable things and practices, I will bring their actions down on their own heads.' This is the declaration of the Lord GOD." (Ezekiel 11:19-21, HCSB)

LESSON † We sometimes have a hard time dealing with the yucky and inner messiness in our lives, causing us to become stubborn and hard-hearted. We have nothing to fear.

Are you glad to know that God doesn't require anyone who has a desire to become a Christian to be all cleaned up before He chooses them?

We Shall See the Goodness of the Lord

Let us thank God for waking us up on this morning. May we feel His presence as He continues to pour out His amazing goodness on us.

Despite what we may experience in our lives, we are told in scripture to "taste and see that the Lord is good" (Psalm 34:8). Why? Because we serve a good God, who is good all the time.

> "Gideon said to Him, 'Please Sir, if the LORD is with us, why has all this happened? And where are all His wonders that our fathers told us about? They said, "Hasn't the LORD brought us out of Egypt?" But now the LORD has abandoned us and handed us over to Midian.'" (Judges 6:13, HCSB)

Many times, for whatever reason, we fail to see the goodness of God in our lives. Each of us must realize that we are much more valuable than what we've been through or what others think of us.

> "I remain confident of this: I will see the goodness of the LORD in the land of the living. Wait for the LORD; be strong and take heart and wait for the LORD." (Psalm 27:13-14, NIV)

LESSON † **We also can be confident of seeing the goodness of God while here in our present life.**

Are there times in your life when you don't feel valuable? In what ways has God showed you His goodness?

Never Give Up Praying

This Monday morning, let us be reminded that we belong to God and that we were created for a purpose. Let us not let the fact that it is Monday make us waste it.

In life, we will face many challenges, but we must not give up or stop praying because those challenges will be the thing that will get us to the place in life God wants us to be. Besides, as children of God, we are always to give ourselves to the work of the Lord. Week after week, even day after day, it can sometimes become easy for us to get tired of praying for something or someone. When this happens, Paul encourages us to be devoted and to be alert with thankful hearts in our prayers:

> "Don't be weary in prayer; keep at it; watch for God's answers, and remember to be thankful when they come."
>
> (Colossians 4:2, TLB)

The scripture's truth is that when we devote ourselves and persist with thankful hearts in our prayers, it demonstrates our trust and faith that God is with us and that He will answer our prayers.

> "Do you not know? Have you not heard? The LORD is the everlasting God, the Creator of the ends of the earth. He will not grow tired or weary, and his understanding no one can fathom. He gives strength to the weary and increases the power of the weak." (Isaiah 40:28-29, NIV)

LESSON † Prayer is our means of survival when faced with challenging times in our lives.

Reflect on a time when you got weary in your prayer life. What did you do to regain motivation and strength in your prayer life?

Plan of Man the Sovereignty of God

Let us thank God for allowing us to see this Tuesday. May we be comforted today knowing that God knows and understands what we are going through individually and collectively.

As God's people, we are to depend on and put our lives in His mighty hands no matter what. Many people like to refrain from discussing politics.

Despite that, we must realize and acknowledge that we are responsible as Christians to exercise our right to vote when choosing political leaders. These people, none of them perfect, will only temporarily represent us in government.

> "For unto us a child is born; unto us, a son is given; and the government shall be upon his shoulder. These will be his royal titles: 'Wonderful,' 'Counselor,' 'The Mighty God,' 'The Everlasting Father,' 'The Prince of Peace.' His ever-expanding, peaceful government will never end. He will rule with perfect fairness and justice from the throne of his father David. He will bring true justice and peace to all the nations of the world. This is going to happen because the Lord of heaven's armies has dedicated himself to do it!"
>
> (Isaiah 9:6-7, TLB)

LESSON † The Word lets us know that we lose our way without good direction. As Christians, we must follow wise counsel in our lives. Let us unite and approach the throne of God with confidence in prayer for God's will to always prevail.

Does knowing that God has sovereignty over the universe and the plans of man strengthen your trust in His will to prevail?

The Lord Will Hold All Things Together

This "hump day" Wednesday is the day the Lord has made. Let us continue to look to Him to hold us together and comfort us with gladness and His peace that surpasses our understanding during our time of need.

With so much sickness, death, confusion, and distrust that we are facing, it can feel like everything is falling apart. By faith, let us ask the Lord to help us not lean on our understanding but acknowledge Him to direct our path in all things. As God's people, we know that God has promised to have all things work for our good. We must love Him, allow Him to be the center of our lives, and release the burdens we carry to Him. Christ is our sustainer. He is supreme, and He will hold our lives together.

> "The Son reflects the glory of God and shows exactly what God is like. He holds everything together with his powerful word. When the Son made people clean from their sins, he sat down at the right side of God, the Great One in heaven."
> (Hebrews 1:3, NCV)

> "He existed before everything and holds everything together."
> (Colossians 1:17)

LESSON † Because Christ is the sustainer of all life, we can trust Him to sustain us daily because, in Him, everything that concerns us is held together, protected, and prevented from falling apart.

In what ways has God sustained you in your life? Do you feel that having God's faithful love, mercy, and grace is enough to sustain you?

A Gratitude Check

Please know on this "grateful Thursday" that God, our Abba Father, knows the desires of every one of our hearts and the things that we want to happen in our lives. Let us continue to trust Him to give us what we need.

At this minute, this hour, or this day, we may not know the details of God's plans for our lives. But we must remain in Him, be grateful, and take Him at His word that even though life events may sometimes not be what we want, they will always be for our good. We should be so grateful because we serve a God who loves us so much that He will take what the enemy means for evil to harm us and make it work out for our good.

> "Keep company with GOD, get in on the best. Open up before GOD, keep nothing back; he'll do whatever needs to be done: He'll validate your life in the clear light of day and stamp you with approval at high noon. Quiet down before GOD, be prayerful before him. Don't bother with those who climb the ladder, who elbow their way to the top. Bridle your anger, trash your wrath, cool your pipes—it only makes things worse." (Psalm 37:4-8, MSG)

LESSON † With the knowledge that our Father's mercies endure forever, we can have patience and peace because our eternal reward will be greater than any of the earthly concerns we face now.

How do you express your gratitude to God who takes care of your every need?

Encouraging Words at the Well

More of Jesus, Less of Me

Thank God, we have made it to Friday. Let us thank Him for the privilege of being in His presence and for meeting us where we're at in life.

Despite being filled with the Holy Spirit, many hearts feel empty or filled with chaos and confusion, and souls feel abandoned and depleted. When we feel empty or full of doubt and confusion, we can get the strength and peace we need from choosing to rest in having more of Jesus and less of ourselves.

> "'He must increase, but I must decrease.' The One who comes from above is above all. The one who is from the earth is earthly and speaks in earthly terms. The One who comes from heaven is above all. He testifies to what He has seen and heard, yet no one accepts His testimony. The one who has accepted His testimony has affirmed that God is true."
> (John 3:30-33, HCSB)

LESSON † Jesus must increase in importance in our lives, and we must decrease in importance. Then we must allow the Holy Spirit to fill us. He, the Holy Spirit, will not allow room for worry, doubt, and negativity to get the better of us.

Have you ever experienced the power of being filled once you chose the humility to allow Christ to shine through you by decreasing and allowing the presence of Christ to increase in your life?

We Will Always Reap What We Sow

Let us thank God for another weekend. May He continue to strengthen us and keep us on the path of righteousness. Let us choose to sow good seeds and spiritually grow as we walk the path of righteousness.

In this life, there will be times when we will want different things. However, when we allow our way of thinking to be focused only on our efforts and their outcome and not on the fact that the increase comes from God, it can make us feel that our lives are unjust and unfair.

> "Don't be misled—you cannot mock the justice of God. You will always harvest what you plant. Those who live only to satisfy their own sinful nature will harvest decay and death from that sinful nature. But those who live to please the Spirit will harvest everlasting life from the Spirit."
>
> (Galatians 6:7-8, NLT)

There is no going around it; we will reap a harvest from what we sow. It will either be a good or a bad harvest.

LESSON † Because we live in a time where we expect instant gratification, we must believe in the process and not expect instant results for the efforts that we put in. We must be patient. God will take care of the harvest.

The consequences of our actions do come to us. What are you sowing? Are you sowing in love?

Wait on God – He has a Plan

Let us thank God for the renewed confidence of faith and hope for the things not yet seen that He gives to us for another day's journey.

In this life, everything can and will change. We are blessed that we serve an unchangeable God. He is the God of Abraham, Isaac, and Jacob, who changes for no one.

> "The Lord, the God of battle, has spoken—who can change his plans? When his hand moves, who can stop him?"
> (Isaiah 14:27, TLB)

During our lifetime, there will be those times when we will not understand God's plans, and they will not always be clear to us. It is during these times when we need to hold on to our faith and wait on the Lord.

> "Faith shows the reality of what we hope for; it is the evidence of things we cannot see. Through their faith, the people in days of old earned a good reputation. By faith we understand that the entire universe was formed at God's command, that what we now see did not come from anything that can be seen."
> (Hebrews 11:1-3, NLT)

LESSON † Jesus once told His disciple Peter, "'You don't understand now why I am doing it; someday you will'" (John 13:7, TLB). Our God has the best plans, and He never has a bad plan. Although sometimes the process He uses can be painful, it will be worth the wait.

Do you find it hard waiting on God? Reflect on a time when you didn't understand what God was doing and you tried to rush the situation.

Seeing the Bigger Picture

Let us thank God for a new day and the start of a new week. Let us pray that with the help of the Holy Spirit, we will see everything through the eyes of Christ.

If we don't want the problems and disappointments in life to get us down and out, we need to see them from God's perspective. We will not always be able to see the bigger picture because the Lord tells us His thoughts are not like our thoughts, and our ways are not like His ways (Isaiah 55:8).

> "Because of the extravagance of those revelations, and so I wouldn't get a big head, I was given the gift of a handicap to keep me in constant touch with my limitations. Satan's angel did his best to get me down; what he in fact did was push me to my knees. No danger then of walking around high and mighty! At first, I didn't think of it as a gift, and begged God to remove it. Three times I did that, and then he told me, My grace is enough; it's all you need. My strength comes into its own in your weakness. Once I heard that, I was glad to let it happen. I quit focusing on the handicap and began appreciating the gift. It was a case of Christ's strength moving in on my weakness. Now I take limitations in stride, and with good cheer, these limitations that cut me down to size—abuse, accidents, opposition, bad breaks. I just let Christ take over! And so, the weaker I get, the stronger I become." (2 Corinthians 12:7-10, MSG)

LESSON † **When we trust God and see things the way He looks at them, we can take our eyes off the painful and disappointing circumstances in our lives.**

Do you react immediately to situations or do you take time to see them through the eyes of God? Has there been a time when you've overreacted?

No Pain No Gain

Let us thank God for the gift of another day to magnify His name and offer sacrifices of praise to Him no matter where we may find ourselves on this Tuesday and throughout the week.

"No pain, no gain" is a famous saying in the athletic world when we try to get into shape. It implies or suggests that we can't build strength and the power to endure without going through some pain or discomfort.

It's hard to achieve glory in God's eyes without sacrifice. No matter how painful we think our lives are, we must continue to endure, keep the faith and never give up as we wait for the Lord to look upon us with His favor for a healing touch to our bodies, minds, and souls.

> "We know that everything God made has been waiting until now in pain, like a woman ready to give birth. Not only the world, but we also have been waiting with pain inside us. We have the Spirit as the first part of God's promise. So, we are waiting for God to finish making us his own children, which means our bodies will be made free."
>
> (Romans 8:22-23, NCV)

LESSON † Jesus came to make us His disciples and ultimately made the greatest sacrifice. He endured great pain so that each of us could have our greatest gain of having eternal life.

Have you ever benefited from the sacrifice that someone other than Jesus made? Have you made sacrifices that others benefited from?

Encouraging Words at the Well

We are All One in Christ

Let us thank God on this "hump day" Wednesday for His protection from all hurt, harm, and dangers, for He has promised us that no weapons formed against us will ever prosper (Isaiah 54:17).

When we look back through the corridors of time, it's evidence of the truth when Jesus said to His disciples that there would be "'wars and rumors of wars'" (Matthew 24:6, NIV). He said these wars and rumors would be a part of our human existence here on earth, and no one should be alarmed.

No racial, political, social, or gender differences should divide us as a nation, stop us from loving each other, or hinder us from serving in unity in our country.

> "We are no longer Jews or Greeks or slaves or free men or even merely men or women, but we are all the same—we are Christians; we are one in Christ Jesus. And now that we are Christ's we are the true descendants of Abraham, and all of God's promises to him belong to us."
>
> (Galatians 3:28-29, TLB)

LESSON † We must understand that Christianity is war. It's a war like no other, in the sense that we are not fighting against people. As believers, we are called to a life of righteousness, and our warfare is against sin and evil.

There is no division in God's kingdom! Do you make an effort to live in harmony with all people?

Pray at All Times

Let us thank God in our prayers on this "grateful Thursday" for who He is and for giving us all we have and all we need. May He continue to guide us in His truth and bless us with the wisdom and strength to make it through the week.

We serve a God who delights in giving His children good gifts. The Word tells us that we are to pray at all times, asking for what we need. As His children, at no time should we lose our discipline and commitment to pray and stand firm in the faith.

Despite the truth that prayer is powerful and makes anything possible, too many times we tend to find it easy to stop praying. We say that God is not listening to us, or our prayers are not being heard or answered.

> "Pray all the time." (1 Thessalonians 5:17, MSG)

> "'And so it is with prayer—keep on asking and you will keep on getting; keep on looking and you will keep on finding; knock and the door will be opened. Everyone who asks, receives; all who seek, find; and the door is opened to everyone who knocks.'" (Luke 11:9-10, TLB)

LESSON † Even when we don't see our prayers' manifestation, we must not give up. We are to pray cheerfully expectant. Don't quit in hard times but pray all the harder. We must remember prayer is not about getting what we want from God or changing God's mind.

Does knowing that God is accessible to you help encourage you to pray at all times? Or do you only access Him when times are hard?

Better is the End of a Thing

Let us thank God for His presence as this week comes to an end. May this Friday bring to each of us more of God's favor and His grace.

We've reached the end of another week! There are times when things happen around us that we do not understand as we move through each new day, but we must continue to look to the Lord and keep our hands in His hands because we do not know even what today holds, but the Lord does.

When we are humble and patient, finishing is better than starting, especially knowing that God has promised to be with us, even until the end of time.

> "The end of something is better than its beginning. It is better to be patient than arrogant." (Ecclesiastes 7:8)

LESSON † Let us rest in our prayers as we reach the end of this week with patience and reflect on the many blessings we have received this week. Let us work hard to finish what we have started and leave nothing unfinished.

How long has it been since you began your walk with Christ? How has your faith grown as you have been walking with Him?

The Next Chapter

Thank God for allowing us to see another weekend. After a long week of moving forward, let us seek to continue living out God's purpose for our lives.

Our destiny is up to us. Each of us is born with a purpose that will not always be easy to fulfill. However, what will make fulfilling our destiny difficult is when we are not mentally or spiritually capable of moving forward from our current and past pains and sufferings. We have the power to say, "This is not how my story will end." No matter where we find ourselves in life's book, we are where we are supposed to be, and we don't have to stop there. We must keep turning the pages even when we feel we can't go on.

I once read, "If we don't give up, God has a plan for our pain and a reason for our struggles and a gift for our faithfulness." Throughout the Bible, we are encouraged to move forward, always looking ahead.

> "It's not that I've already reached the goal or have already completed the course. But I run to win that which Jesus Christ has already won for me. Brothers and sisters, I can't consider myself a winner yet. This is what I do: I don't look back, I lengthen my stride, and I run straight toward the goal to win the prize that God's heavenly call offers in Christ Jesus." (Philippians 3:12-14)

LESSON † We cannot move forward and start our next chapter if we keep re-reading the last chapter or stop reading. We should thank God for the things that have ended in our lives and praise God for the new beginnings in our lives.

What changes are you looking forward to in life that will help you to move forward?

We've Got Mail

Let us thank God for today and be receptive to what He has to say to us in His Word. May the Lord God open our eyes and ears to see and hear the instructions and the goodness that He has for each of us.

Many days we find ourselves struggling with one thing or another. It may be our faith, health, relationships, or just a lack of direction. We must open and use the most powerful tool and weapon, His Word, living and active. It has always been God's desire to get a message to His people about His plans for us and about who He is.

> "In the past God spoke to our ancestors at many different times and in many different ways through the prophets. In these last days he has spoken to us through his Son. God made his Son responsible for everything. His Son is the one through whom God made the universe." (Hebrews 1:1-2)

In the scriptures—Revelations chapters 2 and 3—God told the Apostle John to write letters to the seven churches. These churches were dealing with some of the same situations and challenges that our current churches today face.

> "'Write down what you have seen—both the things that are now happening and the things that will happen.'"
>   (Revelation 1:19, NLT)

LESSON † We can say today that God has his own private heavenly postal service, and He is still sending messages/mail from heaven every day. We have no excuses for not knowing God's plan. Have you checked lately? We've got mail!

Do you see the words of the Bible as being letters from God? How often do you read them?

I'm with You Always

Let us thank God for the gift and the start of a new week. Let us trust that with God's strength and wisdom, we will be able to endure and overcome.

We are here at the beginning of a new week, and as much as we want to plan and control it, there is no doubt that there will be some surprising and unexpected things by the end of this week. No matter what we face, it is true that God is with us always. He will go before us, walk with us, and stand behind us. It will be just as Jesus said:

> "'I am with you always, to the end of the age.'"
> (Matthew 28:20b, HCSB)

Often, God will use our times of struggle and difficulties to build character in us and to display His sovereign power. We may never get through or be removed from our troubles and struggles.

> **LESSON** † **Our God may not remove us from our struggles, but He is faithful to His promise never to let us be tempted beyond our strength.**

Knowing that God is always with us, has there ever been a time when you were struggling and you needed or wanted Him to help you get out so you wouldn't have to go through it?

For God, It's All or Nothing

We can face this Tuesday with faith and assurance. Let us surrender everything to the Lord and say, "Bless the Lord, O, my soul. With all that is within me, bless His holy name."

At some point and time in each of our lives, we may find ourselves struggling with our faith. If we profess that we're a Christian who is following Christ but struggle with our faith, we may feel uncomfortable or guilty and won't share how we're feeling with others of like faith for fear of being judged. On the flip side, we may not have chosen to follow Christ and are secretly seeking Him and don't want to share for fear of being ashamed or judged by others who do not believe. Either way, we are all expected to decide whether we're going to serve God. We have two options, with no in-between. We can either be cold or hot.

When it's a matter of our faith and trust in Him, it's all or nothing.

> "'I know your works, that you are neither cold nor hot. I wish that you were cold or hot. So, because you are lukewarm, and neither hot nor cold, I am going to vomit you out of My mouth.'" (Revelation 3:15-16, HCSB)

LESSON † There will be times we may lapse in our faith. However, if we are expecting the blessings of God, we must be aware daily of our spiritual temperature, and we must live our lives entirely devoted to God.

Would you say that your spiritual condition is hot or cold today? Are you living your life devoted to God?

Help When Climbing an Uphill Battle

Let us thank God for seeing another "hump day" Wednesday. We can finish this week strong if we don't get weary in well-doing. Let us look to the hills from where our strength comes.

We will all need help from time to time, so if you feel like you're climbing an uphill battle this week, you're probably not alone. Even when facing uphill struggles, we should remain joyful and never stop praying. Our heavy and mountain-size problems are nothing in our all-powerful God's hands.

> "The mountains melt like wax in the presence of the LORD, in the presence of the Lord of the whole earth." (Psalm 97:5)

As God's children, we have the opportunity to finish strong with the help of people who love us and with the strength of the Lord. We must also continue to pray for strength, keep the faith, and be determined to make it to the mountain top.

LESSON † What we're going through now will probably not be the most challenging mountain that we will climb in our lifetime. There will always be another one. The Lord will empower us to be in control of the uphill battles that we face.

Where do you seek your help and motivation when your life feels like you're climbing an uphill battle? Do you return help and motivation to others?

Hanging on by a Thread

On this "grateful Thursday," let's thank God for waking us up and giving us another chance to bless His holy name. May He continue to make us whole, and touch all who need a touch.

Happiness is the key to life and is a gift from God. However, there will be times when we don't think we can make it. We live daily hanging on by a thread, with issues in our lives that embarrass and isolate us and fill us with hopelessness.

If we want to be healed from our issues, we must first acknowledge that we indeed have an issue.

> "A woman in the crowd had suffered for twelve years with constant bleeding, and she could find no cure. Coming up behind Jesus, she touched the fringe of his robe. Immediately, the bleeding stopped. 'Who touched me?' Jesus asked. Everyone denied it, and Peter said, 'Master, this whole crowd is pressing up against you.' But Jesus said, 'Someone deliberately touched me, for I felt healing power go out from me.' When the woman realized that she could not stay hidden, she began to tremble and fell to her knees before him. The whole crowd heard her explain why she had touched him and that she had been immediately healed. 'Daughter,' he said to her, 'your faith has made you well. Go in peace.'" (Luke 8:43-48, NLT)

LESSON † **We must defy every obstacle, and with courage and faith, find Jesus Christ, the Great Physician, daring to touch Him through a relationship, having an encounter that will transform our lives and set us free.**

Are you faced with an issue today that needs healing that only Jesus the Great Physician can heal?

Lord, Prepare Me

Let us not forget to pray to God and thank Him for keeping us through the week. We have survived another week because He has saved us from the fiery darts of the enemy.

We are here, and each of us has survived this week, so we must move on to face what today holds. Let us accept where we are and know that we are where God wants us to be. We must keep moving, always preparing for what's before us.

> "Even when I go through the darkest valley, I fear no danger, for You are with me; Your rod and Your staff—they comfort me." (Psalm 23:4, HCSB)

We must trust and believe that every promise God has made, He will keep. Whether we find ourselves at the end of the week, on the mountain top, or down in the valley, every experience is a part of God's divine plan for our lives. Often, we pray to God for what we think we need or want, and that's okay. He tells us to ask, and it shall be given. We often fail to pray that He prepares us to handle what we have prayed for. Not all of God's answers to our prayers are enjoyable! However, we should always thank Him for answered prayers. They will end up being a blessing for us.

> "'She who has believed is blessed because what was spoken to her by the Lord will be fulfilled!'" (Luke 1:45, HCSB)

LESSON † The thing about God is that we never know what He is up to in our lives. Many times, we won't understand what He is doing. God uses each experience, good or bad, to prepare us. Even when it seems like we are in a season of waiting, God is actively preparing us for what He has already ordained for us to do.

Looking back over your life, can you see the preparation God used to get you ready to do what He has called you to do?

We are All God's Masterpiece

Thank God for loving us and seeing us to another blessed weekend. May He renew and strengthen each of us with purpose and a desire to walk even closer with Him.

Let us be grateful and appreciate the generation we belong to. I'm grateful to belong to a generation of women who have set the example of simple, hard-working women, who, although they struggled, continued to trust God, making a way out of no way.

They showed me that I don't have to measure myself against anyone because each of us has been created and given work to do.

> "God has made us what we are. He has created us in Christ Jesus to live lives filled with good works that he has prepared for us to do." (Ephesians 2:10)

LESSON † Many of us grown-ups are carrying the heavy weight and pain of childhood from parents and grown-ups and loved ones who hurt us and we can't move on to be the masterpiece that we are and fulfill the jobs we are created for. In almost all cases, those people just didn't have what we needed, wanted, or expected them to give.

Do you find it easy or difficult for you to see yourself as God's marvelous handiwork? If it's difficult, why?

Wages of Sin is Death

Praise God for waking us up on this blessed Sunday. I pray the meditations of our hearts and the words of our mouths be acceptable in His sight.

Life can often feel or even be complicated, especially when we're trying to live right. It seems like there are only rules of do's or don'ts, and they only seem to get more complex and stricter when trying to live a godly life. We have an enemy who wants to steal, kill, and destroy us, but fear not, we serve the God who moved heaven and earth to save us.

We all have a choice that we must make. When life feels complicated and bombarded with do's and don'ts, we must consider ourselves dead to sin and alive to God in Christ Jesus (Romans 6:11) and know who we are in Christ Jesus.

> "So you also should consider yourselves to be dead to the power of sin and alive to God through Christ Jesus. Do not let sin control the way you live; do not give in to sinful desires. Do not let any part of your body become an instrument of evil to serve sin. Instead, give yourselves completely to God, for you were dead, but now you have new life. So use your whole body as an instrument to do what is right for the glory of God. Sin is no longer your master, for you no longer live under the requirements of the law. Instead, you live under the freedom of God's grace." (Romans 6:11-14, NLT)

LESSON † Set before each of us is a broad and fun road that seems right but ends in death. All who are willing to be corrected are put on the pathway to life.

Has there been a time when your attitude kept you from hearing God's voice? Are you receptive and willing to be corrected?

Be the Change

May we give ourselves entirely to the work of the Lord this week so that we may see others and our situations clearly as He sees them and not as they are.

As we begin to navigate and see our way through this new week, let us start with a fresh and abundant dose of grace and mercy, knowing that our help comes from the Lord. Our God has the power to change this week from an ordinary week to an extraordinary week.

We must stop praying and waiting for God to change others or our situations. Sometimes, if we want to see change, we must be the change that we want to see or, more importantly, the needed change.

> "Don't say anything that would hurt {another person}. Instead, speak only what is good so that you can give help wherever it is needed. That way, what you say will help those who hear you. Don't give God's Holy Spirit any reason to be upset with you. He has put his seal on you for the day you will be set free {from the world of sin}. Get rid of your bitterness, hot tempers, anger, loud quarreling, cursing, and hatred. Be kind to each other, sympathetic, forgiving each other as God has forgiven you through Christ." (Ephesians 4:29-32)

LESSON † Change can be difficult for us, but we must follow what is known as the Golden Rule and show others the kind of love God shows to each of us every day!

Have there been times when you've expected situations and others to change? Or do you change your perspective on how you see them?

Living Fearlessly

On this Tuesday, let us acknowledge God in all our ways so that He can direct our path, and let us turn our fears over to Him.

We have to keep our trust in the Lord on this journey we call life because when we least expect it, fear will snatch the rug from right under our feet. To make things worse, fear will bring doubt along with it. If we haven't already, each of us and our loved ones will face some fears and worries at some point in time. But we must not fear. We must keep the faith and trust that God is directing and leading our loved ones and us.

> "God is our refuge and strength, a tested help in times of trouble. And so we need not fear even if the world blows up and the mountains crumble into the sea." (Psalm 46:1-2, TLB)

We are told repeatedly in the Bible to "fear not"! We must not forget that God keeps His promises to always be with us. We tend to worry and imagine the worst when: *F*alse – *E*vidence – *A*ppearing – *R*eal presents itself.

> **LESSON** † We must learn to trust God during all of the diffi-cult circumstances in our lives. We must learn to have faith be-yond our fears, realizing that things are not always how they look.

Have there been times when you allowed your fear to be bigger than your trust in God's protection?

On Bended Knees

On this "hump day" Wednesday, let us kneel in prayer and bless the Lord for who He is and for all that He has done and will be doing as we move through this week.

Prayer is essential in the kingdom of God, but, for many of us, the practice of prayer has become a quick and hasty rehearsed script that we call prayer. We seem to have abandoned the posture of kneeling. There is power in kneeling. Our posture and position of prayer not only represent our surrender, but they show our acceptance of being in the presence of the Most High God.

To be strong warriors, we must believe, stand firm in God's Word, and stay on our knees where spiritual battles are won. Let us not be weak or lazy when it comes to prayer because not only do we rely on our prayers to change our circumstances in our lives, but others also depend on our prayers. Kneeling may not be an option, but at some point when we pray, we should take on the posture of kneeling with open hearts and stretched-out hands.

> "Come, let's worship and bow down. Let's kneel in front of the LORD, our maker, because he is our God and we are the people in his care, the flock that he leads. If only you would listen to him today!" (Psalm 95:6-7)

LESSON † As prayer warriors on bended knees, in and for the kingdom of God, we must take on prayer as a way of living and not just a quick means of trying to change God's mind or to get what we want from Him.

What posture do you most use when praying to God? Do you think it matters to God the posture you take when communicating with Him?

A Seat at the Table

Let us thank God for this "grateful Thursday." May this indeed be a day of thanksgiving for all the answered prayers, for all we have, and for who we have.

Each of us is privileged and has a daily, open, and standing invitation to have a seat at the Lord's table.

Many of us are looking for peace, happiness, fellowship, health, or healing. Whatever we are desiring can be found in Christ. And what we don't need for ourselves, we can take for others.

> "Hearing this, a man sitting at the table with Jesus exclaimed, 'What a blessing it will be to attend a banquet in the Kingdom of God!' Jesus replied with this story: 'A man prepared a great feast and sent out many invitations. When the banquet was ready, he sent his servant to tell the guests, "Come, the banquet is ready." But they all began making excuses.'"
>
> (Luke 14:15-18a, NLT)

LESSON † Because God's plan is not yet complete, the invitation still stands. There is room at the Lord's table for many more. May God bless you!

At the Lord's table, He will serve us all that we need. What are you looking to be filled with today?

I Thanked God Yesterday for...

Thank God it's Friday. Let us thank God for protecting and watching over us through another week. May He continue to fill our lives with every good and perfect gift that comes from above.

I saw a picture that asks something like this: "What if you woke up the day after with only the things you thanked God for the day before?"

We can be grateful for our yesterdays. Let us continue to give the Lord our prayers of thanksgiving for a new day, and let us treasure our expectations of new hope for tomorrow and for the opportunity for God's blessings to flow through us.

> "I ask only one thing from the LORD. This is what I want: Let me live in the LORD's house all my life. Let me see the LORD's beauty and look with my own eyes at his Temple."
>
> (Psalm 27:4, NCV)

LESSON † As God's children, we should be like the psalmist who searched for and who enjoyed the Lord's presence, which provided him with confidence and security in his life. He lived in the promise of God's protection and looked forward every day to offering sacrifices of thanksgiving and praise.

If you were only going to receive what you thanked God for yesterday, what would you receive?

Never Give Up!

We have made it to the weekend, which means we didn't give up. Let's look to God to give us the determination to keep going no matter what challenges we may face.

As we have made it through this past week, I trust that each of us did whatever we had before us to do, and that we did it to the best of our ability, not giving up. Some things may have happened this week to us or others around us that we don't understand. We must know that God allows some things to occur in our lives that we may not understand. When these things happen, we must never give up. We must be patient, and we must trust God's will because He is our strength.

> "I will keep on expecting you to help me. I praise you more and more. I cannot count the times when you have faithfully rescued me from danger. I will tell everyone how good you are, and of your constant, daily care. I walk in the strength of the Lord God. I tell everyone that you alone are just and good." (Psalm 71:14-16, TLB)

LESSON † For those who are patient and not willing to give up and continue to believe that good things are on the way, the best is yet to come.

Often times things look like they are never going to change. What are you trusting God to do for you?

The Beginning of the Good News

On this Sunday, let us remain alert as we pray to our Heavenly Father and let us stay hopeful about the issues and concerns that we have. May each of us feel His presence as we worship and praise Him.

Throughout time God has used messengers, and He wants us to be His messengers of the gospel today, which is the Good News.

We often reject or miss our blessings because we judge or underestimate the messenger or, as they say, "shoot the messenger." On the flip side of it, if we are supposed to be the messenger, those same reasons of fear or shame can keep us from delivering the message. Two great messengers that we can learn a lesson from about delivering the message of God's Word are John the Baptist and the Apostle Paul. In the Word, Paul lets us know that:

> "This is the beginning of the Good News about Jesus Christ, the Son of God." (Mark 1:1 NCV)

LESSON † **Extra, extra, read all about it! As we think about the second coming of Jesus, may it stir up in us the memories of God's goodness and give us the expectancy of hope that comes with knowing that Christ is with us.**

Who was the first messenger to share with you the Good News of Jesus? Did you trust them?

Hope That Anchors Our Soul

As we face the start of this new day, let us prepare our hearts through prayer for what this new week will bring with it. May our lives be filled with great hope and strength as we recognize the many possibilities that present themselves for our spiritual growth.

Many struggle to find hope during dark and depressing times. Despite all the world's darkness, our hope in Christ is unshakably anchored to God's Word. God's Word is full of His will, His plans, and purposes for His people. We have a blessed hope that is steady and firm as an anchor to see us through our stormy trials of life so that we won't be tossed about with every changing wind of doubt and uncertainty.

> "Then we will no longer be immature like children. We won't be tossed and blown about by every wind of new teaching. We will not be influenced when people try to trick us with lies so clever they sound like the truth."
>
> (Ephesians 4:14, NLT)

LESSON † In His Word, God has given us His unchangeable and unshakeable promises that give us the strength to hold on to the hope that we have been given. As we find ourselves struggling to find hope, let us latch onto the blessed promised hope with both hands and never let go.

What one promise of God in His Word do you hold on to because it keeps you grounded?

Teach Us to Number Our Days

Let us open our mouths this day to give God all the honor and praise. He provides us with time, strength, and wisdom to enjoy and to overcome days of sorrow and trouble.

With the passing of each day, living through difficult times can remind us that life is short and we should make our days count rather than count our days.

We often find ourselves consumed with watching the calendar and counting down the days and months. Our focus has to change from counting days to being present and accounted for in the presence of God to gain a better insight into His Word.

When we learn to make the days of our lives count and not count our days, we will realize the beauty of life. Making our days count and seeing their beauty can only come when we go to God seeking to gain a heart of wisdom.

> "Teach us to number our days and recognize how few they are; help us to spend them as we should."
>
> (Psalm 90:12, TLB)

LESSON † No matter who we are, our days are numbered. We must all realize that only what we do for the Lord lasts. With each passing day, let us move forward, leaving a legacy of love, faith, and commitment for our loved ones and those who look up to us to follow.

Each day how are you making every effort to live for God in all you do and say?

Another Promise of Hope

Today is "hump day" Wednesday, and we have made it halfway through this week. Let us continue to remain hopeful that God will work everything out in our lives even though it looks impossible.

There will be times in each of our lives when we will face things that will appear to be impossible, and they may be impossible for us. The Gospels of *Matthew 19:26, Mark 10:27*, and *Luke 1:37*, also known as the synoptic Gospels, all share in similarity that things will be impossible with men but not with God.

We can continue to walk this week in the promise of hope in our Lord and Savior Jesus Christ.

When things seem impossible, we must know that we serve a God who is able. No matter what we may be facing, He is the God of possibilities and the God of impossibilities.

> "Then Moses stretched out his hand over the sea. All that night the LORD pushed back the sea with a strong east wind and turned the sea into dry ground. The water divided, and the Israelites went through the middle of the sea on dry ground. The water stood like a wall on their right and on their left." (Exodus 14:21-22)

LESSON † Despite our circumstances or situations that we may face today, this week, or in our life that seem impossible or feel like they're not going to work in our favor, we must remember who our God is. We must trust God for yet another one of His promises of hope because there is nothing too hard for Him.

Do you believe that when you worry, you are saying that your problems are bigger than God?

Hope of Being Blessed Abundantly

Let us thank God on this "grateful Thursday" for the abundance of hope that He continuously provides that allows us to live a life of abundance.

Thank God for the promised hope that He intends for us to have an abundant life—not always easy because of the evil one, but because of the Good Shepherd, abundant.

> "'A thief comes only to steal and to kill and to destroy. I have come so that they may have life and have it in abundance.'" (John 10:10, HCSB)

We often forget that God is more than able to meet our needs, so we tend to hold back when it comes to giving freely and generously to the cause of God. We worry about not having enough left to meet our needs. Each of us must figure out what an abundant life looks like for us. For us to say that we live in abundance means that we have more than enough of the things in life. For each of us to declare that we are blessed abundantly in life suggests that we are pleased and satisfied in every area of our lives.

> "And God is able to make every grace overflow to you, so that in every way, always having everything you need, you may excel in every good work." (2 Corinthians 9:8, HCSB)

LESSON † Although life is not always about what we can get, we have a promised hope that God can and will meet our every need. When it comes to being blessed abundantly, we must be mindful to accept even the most minor things in our life with gratitude and not with an ungrateful attitude.

How do you share the abundant blessings that God gives to you to meet the needs of others?

Looking Forward with Hope

Yay, it's Friday! Because God has brought us through this week, let us let go of everything not from God that tried to hold us back, and let us cling to the hope and power to move forward boldly.

Even though hope is the thing that keeps us going during tough times, when everything around us is going wrong, many tend to lose hope quickly. We find it hard to look or move forward because we allow things like our past, missed opportunities, fear of failing, and others' opinions to cause us to lose hope. And the list goes on.

> "Let's keep a firm grip on the promises that keep us going. He always keeps his word." (Hebrews 10:23, MSG)

As children of God, He is our source of hope. When we live an obedient life, we can look forward to hoping for all the promises that He has for our lives, especially the coming of our Lord and Savior.

> "Therefore, with your minds ready for action, be serious, and set your hope completely on the grace to be brought to you at the revelation of Jesus Christ. As obedient children, do not be conformed to the desires of your former ignorance."
> (1 Peter 1:13-14, HCSB)

LESSON † If we're going to be successful looking forward with hope, we must put and keep our trust in God. We must also stop looking back with regret and let go of what's gone and, with hope, focus on what's before us.

Do you find it harder or easier to focus on God's promises rather than your circumstances to give you hope?

Selah: Pause and Reflect

Let us thank God for His fresh and new grace this Saturday. We have come through a week full of hope. Let us rejoice in our confident hope today and, as we pray, let us pause, reflect, and meditate on the goodness of our protective and awesome God.

Coming through a week of having hope, we are encouraged to look to God and to press pause on the noise of life. Even if we are not where we want to be, we still need to take a breath, stop, and reflect on the goodness of God. Sometimes when God has a blessing for us, we are not in the proper position.

Selah is a Hebrew word that means to pause and take a breath, reflect, rest, and stop. *Selah* is used only seventy-four times in the Bible—seventy-one times in Psalms and three times in Habakkuk. When we're reading the Word of God, we do not need to say *selah* at the end of a passage. It's used to let us know to stop, pause, and reflect on what God has just told us. We can quickly get distracted and caught up in turmoil, forgetting that God is with us.

> "God says, 'Be still and know that I am God. I will be praised in all the nations; I will be praised throughout the earth.' The LORD All-Powerful is with us; the God of Jacob is our defender." (Psalm 46:10-11, NCV)

LESSON † We need to know that we don't always have to say anything or do anything in times of trouble because God is our refuge.

Can you pause, take a breath, and stop looking at your situation or what's going on in your life or the world today and reflect on God's goodness?

Love in Action

Let us pause today in worship to remember the love that God has for us that He would send his Son to earth for us!

Until we learn and understand the love of God, we live our lives in darkness. It brings joy and hope into our lives when we are aware of God's act of sending Jesus into the world to demonstrate His love.

God has set the perfect example of what love is. Our actions and our ways will tell everything about us, and we are called to show love to our families and our neighbors.

> "Dear children, we must show love through actions that are sincere, not through empty words. This is how we will know that we belong to the truth and how we will be reassured in his presence." (1 John 3:18-19)

LESSON † God is love, and anything being done that doesn't have God in it is empty. Let us seek to love like we have been loved.

How do you demonstrate God's love to others throughout the year? Do you expect anything in return?

Straight "Outta" Bethlehem

May we feel the love of God and the presence of His guardian angels that He has given charge over our lives. May His goodness and mercy follow each of us no matter where this week takes us.

God's plan for the world was presented and introduced from humble beginnings—straight "outta" the town of Bethlehem, the expected Messiah's birthplace. We are told in Zechariah 4:10 not to despise small beginnings because God is more pleased with what is right than what is big.

> "But you, O Bethlehem of Ephrathah, who are one of the little clans of Judah, from you shall come forth for me one who is to rule in Israel, whose origin is from of old, from ancient days. Therefore, he shall give them up until the time when she who is in labor has brought forth; then the rest of his kindred shall return to the people of Israel. And he shall stand and feed his flock in the strength of the LORD, in the majesty of the name of the LORD his God. And they shall live secure, for now he shall be great to the ends of the earth." (Micah 5:2-4, NRSV)

LESSON † Wherever we are from, we must not be discouraged by our own small and humble beginnings. Our first opportunity to show love is to show love for ourselves and accept who we truly are.

Do you allow the circumstances, the place of your birth, or your hometown to determine your worth or do you see yourself as God sees you?

God's Love is All We Need

Let us thank God for allowing us to see this new day. As we continue to navigate this week, may we continue to feel and know that God loves and cares for us.

In the chaotic world that we live in, it is of the utmost importance that we unite our lives with God each passing day. He loves us, He knows us, and He understands everything that we are going through and what we will face. It doesn't matter if we're lost, found, or searching. We can trust Jesus to take us to the Father. Once with the Father, we will experience all the benefits of being His children.

> "No one has ever seen God. God's only Son, the one who is closest to the Father's heart, has made him known."
>
> (John 1:18)

> "'Lord,' Thomas said, 'we don't know where You're going. How can we know the way?' Jesus told him, 'I am the way, the truth, and the life. No one comes to the Father except through Me. If you know Me, you will also know My Father. From now on you do know Him and have seen Him.' 'Lord,' said Philip, 'show us the Father, and that's enough for us.'"
>
> (John 14:5-8, HCSB)

LESSON † **Our Lord and Savior came down from heaven to pay the price for all our sins and to show us how much God loves us. As we look forward to finishing this week, if God is all we have, we have all we need!**

Are there times in your life you feel you need more? Do you have the faith to believe that God can fill that need?

The Lord Loves and Cares for Us

It is "hump day" Wednesday, and we have made it halfway through the week. Let us continue to place all our anxieties, cares, and troubles in the hands of the Lord because He cares for us.

One thing real about life is that we will encounter stormy weather. Not all storms are physical, but the turbulence can be just as bad. Our storms may be in the form of a broken relationship, bad diagnosis, prodigal children, financial crisis, and many more. It may feel like the Lord is asleep and not aware that we are weathering these storms. When it seems like our anxieties, cares, and troubles multiply, and our joy, peace, and faith are fading, we need to ask Jesus to help us. We need to ask Him in faith for the strength promised in the Word.

> "Turn all your anxiety over to God because he cares for you."
> (1 Peter 5:7)

While we understand that there will be storms, we must know that no storm or circumstances can stop God's love and care for us.

LESSON † Yes, Jesus loves and cares for us! We do not have to go through our storms alone. Sometimes our faith may turn to fear, and we sometimes may feel like we don't have anyone else.

When have you experienced God's care for you while you were in a storm in your life?

Our God's Love has No Limits

On this "grateful Thursday," let us give God all the honor, glory, and praise for loving us without limit.

There's a classic song that says: "What the world needs now is love, sweet love. It's the only thing that there's just too little of." [33] At times the world seems to experience a bit of compassion fatigue. Yes, what the world needs is love and not just any love. We need to demonstrate God's love, which has no limits.

> "'And so I am giving a new commandment to you now—love each other just as much as I love you. Your strong love for each other will prove to the world that you are my disciples." (John 13:34-35, TLB)

Let us stay focused and be reminded that even though it seems that evil is prevailing, God is still in control. We must remain focused on God and trust His limitless power and His unlimited plan for us.

> "Our Lord is great, and his power is great. There is no limit to his understanding." (Psalm 147:5)

LESSON † God shows His great limitless love for us in this way: He sent His Son, Jesus Christ, who "died for us while we were still sinners" (Romans 5:8).

Are you aware of the depth of God's love for you? No matter what happens or what you do, God will always love you.

God's Love Will Sustain Us

Thank God it's Friday! We have made it through this week sustained by the power and strength of God's love.

Many of us have come through this week and are wondering how we made it through. I'll tell you. We have made it through by the love of God. He's good like that; He's a keeper! No matter what we face, our times of trouble have a way of putting us in the presence of God when we cry out to Him. As God's people, we know the truth of God's Word that lets us know that God's perfect love has the power to sustain us and, more importantly, change us.

> "The righteous cry out, and the LORD hears, and delivers them from all their troubles. The LORD is near the broken-hearted; He saves those crushed in spirit."
>
> (Psalm 34:17-18, HCSB)

With the Holy Spirit's direction and help, we must stay focused and on the path of righteousness. We must not put our hope in things, those in our homes, jobs, or those in the world we encounter who don't know the Lord or His ways.

LESSON † We serve a compassionate and gracious God, slow to anger and rich in faithful love and truth. Because our Father in heaven loves us dearly, He provides everything that we need daily. God's love will sustain us!

What has been your experience of God's sustaining love while going through fearful and challenging times?

I Want to Believe God Loves Me

We have reached another weekend, and no matter what we have come through or where we are now, I pray that each of our hearts is filled with God's love.

The world offers us many things to believe in or not to believe in. During difficult times is when we have our doubts about the love that God has for us. We feel that, surely, He can't love us. We say, "You don't know what I've done," or we ask why this is happening to us. That is just where the enemy (the devil) wants us to place our focus. He wants us to hide in shame and guilt, making us live our lives feeling defeated. When we're living a defeated life, we are not drawing others to Christ.

> "The one who loves us gives us an overwhelming victory in all these difficulties. I am convinced that nothing can ever separate us from God's love which Christ Jesus our Lord shows us. We can't be separated by death or life, by angels or rulers, by anything in the present or anything in the future, by forces or powers in the world above or in the world below, or by anything else in creation." (Romans 8:37-39)

LESSON † After a long week, get some rest and be sure that no matter what we are going through or how many things we might have gotten wrong, we can believe God loves us!

Has there been a time when you've doubted God's love for you or your loved ones? What helped you to overcome that doubt?

The Peace Jesus Brings

As we worship and acknowledge the peace of God, I pray that our minds, bodies, and souls feel peaceful.

We are all living and longing for peace—peace in our homes, at our jobs, and in the world.

We often misunderstand what peace is. The peace that came with the birth of Jesus is not about our feelings. The peace that Jesus brings is based on *shalom*, the ancient Hebrew word that means unity and wholeness. This unity and wholeness are with God and all of humanity.

> "For Christ himself has brought peace to us. He united Jews and Gentiles into one people when, in his own body on the cross, he broke down the wall of hostility that separated us. He did this by ending the system of law with its commandments and regulations. He made peace between Jews and Gentiles by creating in himself one new people from the two groups. Together as one body, Christ reconciled both groups to God by means of his death on the cross, and our hostility toward each other was put to death. He brought this Good News of peace to you Gentiles who were far away from him, and peace to the Jews who were near. Now all of us can come to the Father through the same Holy Spirit because of what Christ has done for us." (Ephesians 2:14-18, NLT)

LESSON † We can have perfect peace in our lives when we depend on God and stop trying to do everything ourselves.

When you think of having the peace that God brings, do you have the assumption that you won't have any trouble in your life?

A Promise of Peace

On this Monday, let us ask God for the vision to see and an open heart of faith to believe and receive His promise of peace—a promise of peace that surpasses our human understanding.

As we press our way, let us shift our focus to peace that we often pray for with eager expectation, and let us make room for Christ in our hearts. No matter what chaos we may face, there is a promise from God that we can still experience peace here on earth. The chaos we face tests our faith and our will to trust in the Lord. We often expect peace to be immediate and for our lives to be free of trouble, pain, and disappointments. Our life experiences let us know that following Christ is not easy, and neither was it promised to be easy. Jesus said:

> "'I have told you all this so that you may have peace in me. Here on earth, you will have many trials and sorrows. But take heart, because I have overcome the world.'"
>
> (John 16:33, NLT)

> **LESSON** † God gives us peace in small and insignificant ways. He chose the humblest beginning to send Jesus, the King of Peace, into the world. He came as a baby, and the world couldn't comprehend His destiny.

God gives us peace in the midst of our trials and challenging times. What lessons have you learned while experiencing God's promised peace?

Peace of Heart and Mind

Chaos has a way of showing up in the world. I pray each of us on this Tuesday will be reminded of and feel the promised peace and comfort of God as we move through this week.

Despite the times in life when we are uncomfortable and faced with troubles, let us continue our daily walk, knowing that peace is not the absence of problems in our lives but the presence of the Lord, knowing that He is in control. We often consider being at peace as a state of being comfortable, feeling good, and successful. We often make the mistake of not understanding the peace that Jesus brings. God's peace often calls for a change in each of us and the world's nature and character.

> "'Don't think I've come to make life cozy. I've come to cut.'"
> (Matthew 10:34, MSG)

> "I came to set fire to the world, and I wish it were already burning!" (Luke 12:49, NCV)

> "'I am leaving you with a gift—peace of mind and heart! And the peace I give isn't fragile like the peace the world gives. So don't be troubled or afraid.'" (John 14:27, TLB)

LESSON † Having peace of heart and mind doesn't come naturally, Therefore, it can feel uncomfortable. Only we can stop God's promise of us having peace of mind and heart in our lives. We have the option to receive the gift or to reject it.

Knowing that having peace often brings with it some type of trials and troubles in our lives, are you open to receiving God's gift for peace of mind and heart?

Finding Peace in Our Struggles

We have made it to the middle of the week, "hump day" Wednesday. May we, and all those we are praying for and with, have the peace of God in any distress we may have today.

Our lives can be full of struggles, difficulties, battles, and setbacks. It doesn't matter what our lot in life—rich or poor, our race, and yes, our political affiliation—they often blindside us, and we find ourselves in situations where we question God, asking, "Why?"

We must know and understand that although our struggles are real, so is God's peace.

Struggles and difficulties will come to us. Whether we want them or not, they will come.

But just because they come to us doesn't mean we have to let them rob and steal our peace.

> "He will keep in perfect peace all those who trust in him, whose thoughts turn often to the Lord! Trust in the Lord God always, for in the Lord Jehovah is your everlasting strength." (Isaiah 26:3-4, TLB)

LESSON † We will never have all the answers to our life's struggles. Therefore, if we want to find peace in our struggles, we must always trust in the Lord God and not let our struggles discourage us.

What struggles are you not trusting God with today that are blocking you from finding God's peace He desires you to have?

The Ruling Peace of God

On this "grateful Thursday," let us give thanks to God. If for any reason we find that our inner spiritual peace is weak, we need to pray to God, for He has the ruling power to bless each of us with His peace.

Each day as we live and have our being, we should always be thankful and always pray about everything in our lives. It will be our prayers of gratefulness and gratitude that will shield and protect us from negativity.

> "Pray all the time; thank God no matter what happens. This is the way God wants you who belong to Christ Jesus to live." (1 Thessalonians 5:17-18, MSG)

Our prayers and thankfulness should not change with our circumstances nor with our feelings.

LESSON † There is power in being grateful and giving thanks! It emphasizes and magnifies our blessings and expands our ability to be a blessing to others. Let us have peace by remaining grateful, thankful, and wise as we follow God's ruling peace by being led daily by the Holy Spirit.

What does allowing God to rule and reign His peace in your life look like?

Called to Peace

May each of our days continue to be blessed with peace. Let us thank God for His presence and the peace that He gives as we come to the end of this week.

Whether it's in our homes or our jobs, life can be complicated. Many of us have asked, "What peace?" It seems like getting along with some folks is just hard to do. Despite everyone's failure to live in harmony, the Word lets us know that God strengthens us, and He blesses us with peace. However, we are called to get along with each other as best as possible in this world.

> "If possible, on your part, live at peace with everyone."
> (Romans 12:18, HCSB)

Living in total peace with everyone is impossible because there are so many hurt people who hurt people. Often, we find ourselves agreeing to disagree respectfully with each other to keep the peace.

> "And those who are peacemakers will plant seeds of peace and reap a harvest of goodness." (James 3:18, TLB)

LESSON ✝ As God's people living in harmony, we are called to do our part to keep the peace. We must strive to have a bond of peace with each other. Let us allow God to use us to sow seeds of peace. We do this by first focusing on God and not ourselves.

In what ways do you attempt to share God's peace with the difficult people you encounter?

Protect Your Peace

I pray that we can experience peace and take some time to rest our minds and our souls from the responsibilities, griefs, and thoughts you may have had this past week.

We are often told and advised that if we want to have peace in our lives, we need to limit or even let go of some people. That can very well be true, but if we don't keep our minds from being flooded with negative thoughts and unnecessary information, there goes our peace. While it may be important for us to be informed of what's going on in the world or with our loved ones, nothing is more important than our inner peace. Our peace is priceless!

Today, let's be protective of our peace and be mindful not to lose sight of ourselves and our values by others' negative energy. Don't allow anything or anyone, including family members, friends, those in traffic, other shoppers, and co-workers, to steal your peace.

> "Guard your heart above all else, for it determines the course of your life." (Proverbs 4:23, NLT)

LESSON † **We can't control others, but once we see that those we surround ourselves with are bent toward being negative, we are responsible for conducting ourselves and making a conscious and informed decision to protect our peace.**

God's Spirit produces in us the fruit of the spirit of peace. Are you aware of the things that try to steal God's peace from you?

Joy to the World

May our hearts overflow with the joy, hope, love, and peace that comes from Jesus.

Christ came to earth with a message of hope for the hurting. He brought joy to the world!

The world has a way of surviving. God keeps His promises. We must be patient and wait on the Lord because He will help us solve our problems or give us the strength to endure them.

More importantly, God will not leave us alone during our problems. He will stay close and help us have joy as we grow in our waiting.

> "Consider it pure joy, my brothers and sisters, whenever you face trials of many kinds, because you know that the testing of your faith develops perseverance. Let perseverance finish its work so that you may be mature and complete, not lacking anything. If any of you lacks wisdom, you should ask God, who gives generously to all without finding fault, and it will be given to you. But when you ask, you must believe and not doubt, because the one who doubts is like a wave of the sea, blown and tossed by the wind."
>
> (James 1:2-6, NIV)

LESSON † We belong to the God of hope. So no matter what we find ourselves faced with individually or collectively, as God's people, may we be filled with overflowing joy and peace as we trust in Him.

In spite of life's trials, how do you express the joy of Christ to the world?

Today, Choose Joy

As we start this new week, let us choose joy by first speaking it into existence by faith, and then let us accept and receive what God has for us this week.

Whenever things are going well for us, we feel happy and excited. It's not hard for us to feel down and out as we see and hear about the world's conditions. We don't have to look far to see many families are being affected by so much pain and grief every day. No matter how challenging this week is, let's not allow any circumstances to take away our joy and cause us to sink into depression and despair. Let us be reminded that the joy of the Lord is our strength.

> "I will lift up my eyes to the hills—From whence comes my help? My help *comes* from the LORD, Who made heaven and earth." (Psalm 121:1-2, NKJV)

> "The LORD is my strength and shield. I trust him with all my heart. He helps me, and my heart is filled with joy. I burst out in songs of thanksgiving." (Psalm 28:7, NLT)

> "Don't be dejected and sad, for the joy of the LORD is your strength!" (Nehemiah 8:10b, NLT)

LESSON † Life is hard, but having a constant and unwavering relationship and living every day with Jesus will strengthen us and keep us healthy, balanced, and joy-filled, no matter how challenging or easy our life's circumstances are.

Have you found that by choosing to have a relationship with Jesus, you are stronger and more joyful each day?

Joy is on the Way

Let us thank God for this new day and trust Him for our tomorrows. Let us remain joyful by allowing our first thoughts in the morning and our last thoughts at night to be about Jesus so that His joy never leaves us.

Yes, there will be weeping, and there will be dark nights. They will come to pass and will not last forever, but we must first learn how to endure and not be blinded by our nights if we want to see His glory in them. We must continue to remain strong when our pain and suffering seem like the darkest nights that last forever with no end or without a ray of light, love, hope, peace, or joy.

To get through our nights and dark times, we must praise God in them. We must surrender them to the Lord daily, and He will turn them into joy. He promises us that His mercy is sufficient, and it is new every morning. The key is for us to give everything to Him.

> "Oh, sing to him you saints of his; give thanks to his holy name. His anger lasts a moment; his favor lasts for life! Weeping may go on all night, but in the morning there is joy."
> (Psalm 30:4-5, TLB)

LESSON † **We must hold on and not give up in the night. Our joy and help will come from the Lord in the morning.**

Paul and Silas sang praises in the midnight to help get through their difficult times. What do you do to bring joy to your soul and to get you through your difficult and darkest times?

Hope Brings Joy

We have made it halfway through this week. On this "hump day" Wednesday, let us ask God to open our understanding so that we can be confident and faithful in our daily walk.

Only in God can the fullness of joy be found. Each day as we wait with anticipation for the joy and the happiness God has for us, let us be confident that what He has for us is for us. The joy that God has for us can't be taken, stolen, and no one can stop it. What we put our hope in or what we think will happen in the future will often determine and dictate how we live.

Each of us can either have our fears or our hopes come true. We make that choice by rejecting God and living our way or by accepting God and following His ways. As God's children living a righteous life before the Lord, we don't have to put our hope in this world or expect our joy to come from others.

> "The hope of righteous people {leads to} joy, but the eager waiting of wicked people comes to nothing."
>
> (Proverbs 10:28)

LESSON ✝ Joy is a fruit of the Spirit that comes to us when we put our hope and trust in Jesus Christ. Our righteousness is a gift from God, so we can have confidence that what God has promised will come to pass.

What does placing your hope in God's hands look like in your life? Does it bring joy?

The Gift of Joy

Welcome to this new day! Wherever we are and whatever we find ourselves facing on this "grateful Thursday," may we have and share God's gift of joy.

Being happy and having joy is essential to life. Much of our joy comes from having stuff and relationships with others. Many of us would find it hard to give the meaning of what joy is. We know that we like it, we want it, and we spend a large part of our lives looking for it.

As God's children, we receive good gifts that don't leave us feeling empty and unfulfilled, and it pleases Him to provide us with those good things!

> "Every good present and every perfect gift comes from above, from the Father who made the sun, moon, and stars. The Father doesn't change like the shifting shadows produced by the sun and the moon." (James 1:17)

LESSON † As we face each day living in the gift of joy, we can thank God, praise God, and tell others about God.

Do you find your joy from being in the presence of God or from the presents from God?

Good News that Brings Joy to All

Let us thank God for the Good News of Him sending His Son to earth as a baby to save us from our sins.

We live in some difficult times and can use some joy. The Word tells us that as God's children, our joy and happiness don't rest on our circumstances but on the Lord. We can have joy in the midst of chaos. Great joy comes to us once we welcome and embrace the message of Jesus Christ and have a consistent relationship with Him. His name is Jesus, and His birth is the Good News of great joy for all people.

> "The angel said to them, 'Don't be afraid! I have good news for you, a message that will fill everyone with joy. Today your Savior, Christ the Lord, was born in David's city. This is how you will recognize him: You will find an infant wrapped in strips of cloth and lying in a manger.'"
>
> (Luke 2:10-12)

> "You will teach me how to live a holy life. Being with you will fill me with joy; at your right hand I will find pleasure forever." (Psalm 16:11, NCV)

LESSON † While the news of the birth of Jesus is one of the most significant events in history, it is about a joyous occasion that has more to do with the promise of us having joy in our hearts daily. Who doesn't want to be the first to get the news hot off the press? While we are not the first to get the big headline news about Jesus's birth, let us remember that it is still and will always be the Good News that brings great joy to the world for everyone.

Does the news of Jesus's birth still bring you great joy?

Encouraging Words at the Well

Now What?

Let us thank God for this new beautiful and blessed and weekend. Let's not take anything for granted, especially our life and our health. Let us praise God for the gift of eternal life that He has given to us through His Son Jesus.

Celebrating special occasions, means different things to different people. And when they have come and has gone, the question is usually, "Now what"? But, do we make room for God to be in each of our hearts and our plans for the future? Life seems to go by so quickly. It's incredible to think of and to be reminded of what God has done for us! He has rescued us from the darkness, bringing us into the light and His kingdom.

> "God has rescued us from the power of darkness and has brought us into the kingdom of his Son, whom he loves. His Son paid the price to free us, which means that our sins are forgiven. He is the image of the invisible God, the firstborn of all creation. He created all things in heaven and on earth, visible and invisible. Whether they are kings or lords, rulers or powers—everything has been created through him and for him. He existed before everything and holds everything together." (Colossians 1:13-17)

LESSON † With the uncertainty of the days to come, we must make up our minds whether God will be supreme and rule in our lives. Let us serve God and trust Him to care for us according to His perfect plan and hold everything together. And let us not slip back into the darkness that the world has to offer.

Is your soul encouraged and stimulated spiritually with a renewed passion and commitment for God when you think about how He has rescued us?

Every Day's Forecast

Let us thank God for the blessing of seeing another day and for the benefit of being our Healer, Protector, and Provider.

Throughout God's Word, we read that He sent many messages to the people through His prophets. Still today, His Word continues to let us know what says the Lord. We see promises—promises of blessings and of judgments.

> "Jesus Christ (the Messiah) is [always] the same, yesterday, today, [yes] and forever (to the ages)." (Hebrews 13:8, AMPC)

When God's people obeyed, there would be peace in the land. If and when they disobeyed, there would be disaster and tragedy.

> "'It's because of you that the heavens withhold the dew and the earth produces no crops. I have called for a drought on your fields and hills—a drought to wither the grain and grapes and olive trees and all your other crops, a drought to starve you and your livestock and to ruin everything you have worked so hard to get.'"(Haggai 1:10-11, NLT)

> "'I will bless my people and their homes around my holy hill. And in the proper season, I will send the showers they need. There will be showers of blessing.'" (Ezekiel 34:26, NLT)

> **LESSON** † When tragedy or chaos impacts us, it's not always the result of sin and wrongdoing. What is clear and obvious is the truth and the forecast that our God is in total control. He reigns, and the "Son" shines.

Do you live each day trusting God and anticipating that He will fulfill His promises and blessings in your life?

It's a Setup – Better Days are Ahead

As we begin this new week, may we walk in faith with expectations to receive what God has for us.

When we face seemingly impossible situations, our first instinct is often to give up. We can all expect better days because not every situation or thing in our lives is permanent. There will be bad days and some good days, and we will have to press our way through some bad days to get to some good days.

We all need encouragement to make it through days that seem to be setbacks when things are not going well.

> "That is why we are not discouraged. Though outwardly we are wearing out, inwardly we are renewed day by day. Our suffering is light and temporary and is producing for us an eternal glory that is greater than anything we can imagine. We don't look for things that can be seen but for things that can't be seen. Things that can be seen are only temporary. But things that can't be seen last forever."
>
> (2 Corinthians 4:16-18)

LESSON † No matter what happens to us during this lifetime, we have the promise of eternal life, when suffering will end and all sorrows are no more. But until then, we need to walk with the Lord, focusing on our great reward for our faith and the joy that will last forever. God will turn our setbacks into a greater comeback.

Have there been discouraging times in your life when you felt like you couldn't go on? How did you recover to go on living with hope?

Only God Knows What Lies Ahead

Let us thank God for another day to make the most of our lives, for we know not what tomorrow holds.

There is nothing wrong with us looking ahead or planning for our future. However, we must put God in those plans. Only our God knows what lies ahead for any of us.

> "We can make our plans, but the LORD determines our steps."
> (Proverbs 16:9, NLT)

If you're one of the many people always saying that they are ready to abandon and leave the season you're currently going through, I urge you to slow down and make the best of the gift of time that God is giving to us.

> "Look here, you people who say, 'Today or tomorrow we are going to such and such a town, stay there a year, and open up a profitable business.' How do you know what is going to happen tomorrow? For the length of your lives is as uncertain as the morning fog—now you see it; soon it is gone. What you ought to say is, 'If the Lord wants us to, we shall live and do this or that.' Otherwise you will be bragging about your own plans, and such self-confidence never pleases God."
> (James 4:13-16, TLB)

LESSON † We all fall short of God's glory, and our lives are like a vapor or a mist. We can be here today and gone tomorrow. We must live each day for the glory of God! Why? Because life is short, but heaven is forever.

What's your reaction after coming through a good or bad season that went nothing like you planned? Do you take credit or give God the glory?

Encouraging Words at the Well

Our New Paths Come with Challenges

We have made it to "hump day" Wednesday. Hopefully we didn't have too many humps to go over. Moving forward, let us ask God to show each of us where He wants us to go and what He wants us to be.

Life is a journey that we must all make no matter the condition of the roads and the paths we must take. Often, we settle for the paths of least resistance, meaning we don't want to venture toward anything that may challenge us or cause us any hardship.

> "The Lord is good and glad to teach the proper path to all who go astray; he will teach the ways that are right and best to those who humbly turn to him. And when we obey him, every path he guides us on is fragrant with his loving-kindness and his truth." (Psalm 25:8-10, TLB)

As we move through life, we should not be in such a hurry to choose the easy paths or roads. Did you know that those difficult, problematic paths or roads can lead us to our most beautiful destinations?

> "So be careful how you act; these are difficult days. Don't be fools; be wise: make the most of every opportunity you have for doing good. Don't act thoughtlessly, but try to find out and do whatever the Lord wants you to."
> (Ephesians 5:15-17, TLB)

LESSON † Being the great teacher that He is, God will often use those challenging paths as teachable moments. Just because the teacher is quiet doesn't mean that He is not present. It only means that the test has begun!

How do you respond to new challenges in your life?

Change is Just Ahead

On this "grateful Thursday," let us thank God for being with us through all the days of our lives and let us release anything that is not from God.

When we leave one season of life for the next, we can't seem to praise God enough. If the truth is told, many do not like change, mainly because we want to be in control. Each new season brings with it things that change us. Nevertheless, despite what we go through or see others go through, we don't have to be afraid of what's to come as we move from year to year and season to season.

There is time when the changes of the seasons in our lives come in like a peaceful dove or like a roaring lion. We have reason to be grateful because God promises to be with us. It is the Lord who will go before us, be with us and never leave us nor forsake us.

> "And the one sitting on the throne said, 'Look, I am making everything new!' And then he said to me, 'Write this down, for what I tell you is trustworthy and true.'"
>
> (Revelation 21:5, NLT)

LESSON † Yes, we should look forward to each new change of seasons, but we should know that being in God's presence and having the mind of Christ is all that matters. We don't know what changes lie ahead nor what our future will be. However, we know who holds the future in His hands.

Knowing that Jesus holds the future in His hands, does that help you to trust whatever changes are ahead for your life?

Behold, I Will Do a New Thing

Let us thank God for the promise of doing new things in our lives. Let us not get in the habit of looking back on our past with regret and denial. Let us thank God in advance for what's ahead for us. May we experience His presence and all the good it brings, and may we love Him even more.

Despite the setbacks and the lows of life, the Lord has and can do great things for us!

> "'But forget all that— it is nothing compared to what I am going to do. For I am about to do something new. See, I have already begun! Do you not see it? I will make a pathway through the wilderness. I will create rivers in the dry wasteland. The wild animals in the fields will thank me, the jackals and owls, too, for giving them water in the desert. Yes, I will make rivers in the dry wasteland so my chosen people can be refreshed.'" (Isaiah 43:18-20, NLT)

When we reflect on all that we've seen and heard, let us not forget we serve a faithful God who is the master of making things new and unique. His mercies are new each day.

> "That is what the Scriptures mean when they say, 'No eye has seen, no ear has heard, and no mind has imagined what God has prepared for those who love him.'"
>
> (1 Corinthians 2:9, NLT)

LESSON † Throughout our years, God gives each of us enough of what we need and want according to His will to make all our plans succeed.

Are you sometimes reluctant to accept the new things that God wants to do in your life because you want to hold on to the old?

The New Me

Thank God for seeing us through this week and bringing us to the weekend. There is nothing impossible with the help of the Lord. His goodness is never-ending and never not enough.

We have made it this far with God's help, and we should only be thinking of and looking back at our yesterdays to see how far He has brought us. Please don't spend too much time thinking about yesterday. We are getting a do-over each new day and each new year we live.

> "Now we look inside, and what we see is that anyone united with the Messiah gets a fresh start, is created new. The old life is gone; a new life emerges! Look at it! All this comes from the God who settled the relationship between us and him, and then called us to settle our relationships with each other." (2 Corinthians 5:17-18, MSG)

If we're going to enjoy all the years God allows us to see, we must follow the instructions of Jesus to seek first the kingdom of God.

> "'Seek the Kingdom of God above all else, and live righteously, and he will give you everything you need.'"
> (Matthew 6:33, NLT)

LESSON † Each of us has the opportunity for a fresh start with Jesus by living right and thanking God for all that He brings us through, both the blessings and the hard times.

Throughout the years, how have you seen God change your life?

Have Not Because We Ask Not

On this glorious Sunday, let us not be nervous or anxious about anything. Let us boldly expect and look to God for an exciting, healthy, and prosperous future.

Each of us must believe that God is faithful and merciful to take care of our every need. We may have to do as the five daughters of Zelophehad in the scripture today and flip the script or step entirely out of the box to have something we want. We may have to boldly do something that has never been done before.

> "One day, the daughters of Zelophehad came to the entrance of the Tabernacle to give a petition to Moses, Eleazar the priest, the tribal leaders, and others who were there." (Numbers 27:1, TLB)

LESSON † What courage and determination they must have had in a patriarchal (male-dominated) society to take on such a challenge, asking for what they wanted!

Has there ever been a time when you needed to use courage and determination like those sisters to ask for what you wanted? What was the outcome?

Don't be Shaken

Let us trust God as we begin this first full week and let us not doubt His unfailing love for us. This week, as we reflect back or look ahead to the future, let us first pray and ask the Lord to help us with our faith in Him.

As we move and progress through life, at some point we must realize that with the Lord on our side, we don't have to be afraid when we are going through challenging circumstances because they only come to teach us lessons.

> "The LORD is my light and my salvation—so why should I be afraid? The LORD is my fortress, protecting me from danger, so why should I tremble?" (Psalm 27:1, NLT)

As God's children, each of us is given a measure of faith that provides us with a unique sense of security. However, we must grow our faith into a healthy, strong, and unshakeable faith if we want to be able to shake off doubt and unbelief in our lives.

> "I will bless the LORD who guides me; even at night my heart instructs me. I know the LORD is always with me. I will not be shaken, for he is right beside me."
>
> (Psalm 16:7-8, NLT)

LESSON † We don't have to be afraid, shaken, or have a sense of hopelessness. We must understand that we all experience challenging and painful times that will shake our faith. Let us continue to seek God as we move ahead confidently, doing what is right in the eyes of God.

What fears or thoughts of hopelessness are you facing today?

Keep Asking, Searching, and Knocking

It's a blessing to have the chance to experience another day. As we begin this Tuesday, it's comforting to know that we serve a God who knows and understands everything we are going through.

No matter what we go through, we must know that God knows all about it, and He doesn't want us to give up now. He also didn't bring us this far to leave us. Because God knows and understands everything we are going through doesn't mean we should sit around with our arms folded, waiting for Him to fix it or give us everything. We are instructed in the Word to keep praying. We must keep on asking, knocking, and searching.

> "'Ask, and you will receive. Search, and you will find. Knock, and the door will be opened for you. Everyone who asks will receive. The one who searches will find, and for the one who knocks, the door will be opened.'" (Matthew 7:7-8)

Although Jesus instructs us to persist in pursuing God, we tend to give up after a few times of uncertainty, and we assume that God cannot be found. If we're going to have a rewarding personal relationship with God, we must have faith, focus, and follow-through on our desire to seek Him.

LESSON † It's not wrong to come to God many times with the same requests. Jesus encourages persistent prayer, and He condemns the shallow repetition of words that don't come from pure intent. We can never pray too much, and our prayers should be honest and sincere. Before we pray, we need to make sure we mean what we say.

Do you easily give up on God about the things you have prayed about?

Hold On Until God Blesses You

As we begin this "hump day" Wednesday, a new day that is fresh and untouched, let us put aside yesterday and ask the Lord to make us new and forgive us for all the things we have done in our past.

When struggling, we often feel that we are all alone, and we find it hard to see God. We often want to get out, move on, or be set free. But God wants us to know more than anything who we are and that we need Him.

It's during those times of struggling, when we have done all that we know to do, that we can begin to feel alone. That's when God can come and do something in us and for us. Just ask Jacob.

> "So Jacob was left alone. Then a man wrestled with him until dawn. When the man saw that he could not win against Jacob, he touched the socket of Jacob's hip so that it was dislocated as they wrestled. Then the man said, 'Let me go; it's almost dawn.' But Jacob answered, 'I won't let you go until you bless me.'" (Genesis 32:24-26)

LESSON † **We may not wrestle physically, like Jacob, to be blessed, but we must always search for God, hold on, and never give up until God blesses us.**

Do you ever feel like you are struggling or fighting in this world all alone? Hold on to God to receive your blessings and don't give up. Don't fight against God. Instead, fight with Him. It can change you!

God is Making Room for Our New

Thank God for this day. On this "grateful Thursday," let us embrace this day with gratitude, thankfulness, and with God's grace so that we can move forward.

What's normal and what's new? "Normal" can change quickly in our lives. Each of us may have to face many unexpected changes at any given time. The way we have known things may never be the same for us again, so during those times we must make up our minds to embrace and accept that God is making room for our new. There will come a time when we will be able to settle our past and embrace our future with hope and expectancy.

> "I will create a new heaven and a new earth. Past things will not be remembered. They will not come to mind."
>
> (Isaiah 65:17)

God has a desire to guide us, so He will allow us to go through things to make room for our new. We shouldn't get so caught up or try to hold on to the things in this old world.

> **LESSON** † With joy, we can look forward to God restoring this world because we have been given a vivid and precise description of the new heavens and the new earth, which will be eternal. In them, none of the things of this world will exist. Only genuine love, safety, and peace will be available to all.

Are you willing to let go of certain things that don't belong in your life in order for God to replace them with your new?

Waiting on God

On this Friday, let us count our many blessings and not our troubles as we end this week. Let us thank God for the strength and patience that has helped us make it through.

If asked to make a list of the most challenging things in life we've had to do, waiting would probably rank high on that list. Many times, we feel like we are waiting for something that's never going to happen. Waiting doesn't have to be the most challenging thing we do in life. When we choose to trust in God's plan for our lives and wait on Him, we can expect to have some unexpected blessings.

> "I wait for the LORD, my soul waits, and with hope, I wait for his word. My soul waits for the LORD more than those who watch for the morning, more than those who watch for the morning." (Psalm 130:5-6)

> "Wait for the LORD; be strong and courageous. Wait for the LORD." (Psalm 27:14, HCSB)

LESSON † Waiting on God is not to torment us but to prepare us. We see many examples in God's Word of those who waited on God and the benefits that came. I'm sure there are some things each of us is waiting to see come to pass in our lives. However, we must wait patiently for God and not trade our time limits for His timing. He is in total control, and He brings everything together in each of our lives according to His sovereign plan.

We know that waiting is a hard thing to do. Do you think it is important for us to wait on God? Why?

Living Our Unlimited Potential

We have made it to a new weekend. May we experience the peace of God and strive for the limitless potential that we have in Christ.

When our world is confusing and looks bleak, it shouldn't surprise us. We are told in God's Word that we can expect to have trouble. And who wants trouble? No one!

Trouble will always be happening in our lives and this world. We need to focus not on the difficulties but on the fact that Jesus has overcome the world. No matter what happens around us, our potential's power and the ability to live our lives without limits come from being connected to Christ.

> "'Yes, I am the vine; you are the branches. Those who remain in me, and I in them, will produce much fruit. For apart from me you can do nothing.'" (John 15:5, NLT)

LESSON † As God's people, we shouldn't let fear and excuses stop us from living up to our potential. Despite us striving to be good and trustworthy people who do what is right, Jesus says that staying close to Him is the only way for us to live up to our unlimited potential.

By the unlimited power of the Holy Spirit, do you live your life in a way that empowers you to have a divine connection with Christ and bear the fruit of the Spirit daily?

Your Mess Turned into a Message

On this blessed Sunday, wherever we are at this moment and time in our lives, let us not give up but give God everything. He wants to turn our life's pain, suffering, and mess into a message.

To say that we won't have any difficult or painful times in life will be not true. Many of us have already faced many unexpected, painful, and challenging struggles that we have come to know all too well. We can pray that God takes away or stops any chances of us being affected by the tragedies of life, or we can trust Him to be with us through them.

> "At first I didn't think of it as a gift and begged God to remove it. Three times I did that, and then he told me, My grace is enough; it's all you need. My strength comes into its own in your weakness." (2 Corinthians 12:8-9, MSG)

LESSON † As believers, we must understand that God's grace is sufficient and that our spiritual condition is, without exception, more important than our physical condition. We don't know why God chooses to heal some and not others. What we know is that it's according to His divine purpose. We are required to pray, to believe, and to trust God to turn our life's pain, suffering, and mess into a message.

How have you seen God turn a "mess" in your life into a message?

Encouraging Words at the Well

Follow Your Moral Compass

As we began this new week's journey, let us look to God for His direction because He will never steer us wrong.

As we journey and travel through our daily lives, the Bible is our road map, and the Holy Spirit will be our compass. Keeping in tune with our moral compass can be challenging, and without it, we can and will justify anything. There are times when there is so much noise in our society that it's hard to know which way is right, wrong, up, or down. We shouldn't allow the ungodly and those in the world to chart our path. God asks that we listen to His voice!

> "Your words are a flashlight to light the path ahead of me and keep me from stumbling. I've said it once, and I'll say it again and again: I will obey these wonderful laws of yours."
>
> (Psalm 119:105-106, TLB)

LESSON † We must recognize ourselves as pilgrims, travelers here on earth who need to study God's map, the *B.I.B.L.E* (*B*asic *I*nstructions *B*efore *L*eaving *E*arth), to learn and know the way. If we don't study and pay attention to the map, we will lose our way in and through life and risk missing our proper destination.

Do you trust in the power of the Holy Spirit to help you understand scripture? Do you find that you are able to apply the scriptures that you learn to help you to navigate life and to grow more like Jesus?

When Facing Giants

On this Tuesday, let us start our day with prayer and faith that God will give us enough of what we need in order to accomplish what we need to do. May we feel the love of our all-powerful God and seek His protection from the enemies we live with and those who try to come up against us.

With each passing day, pressures and troubles in our lives are mounting one after another, seemingly growing to giant proportions. Because the evil and the ungodliness that we see around us appear to be giants and so much stronger than we are, it makes it easy for us to be afraid and terrified of them, but we must fear not and keep the faith.

God's Word promises us that we already have the victory in Christ because we are His.

> "But you belong to God, my dear children. You have already won a victory over those people, because the Spirit who lives in you is greater than the spirit who lives in the world. Those people belong to this world, so they speak from the world's viewpoint, and the world listens to them. But we belong to God, and those who know God listen to us. If they do not belong to God, they do not listen to us. That is how we know if someone has the Spirit of truth or the spirit of deception."
> (1 John 4:4-6, NLT)

LESSON ✝ No matter how strong we think that we are, more often than not, when facing our giants, we must depend on the Lord and His strength.

To help defeat the giants you may face in life, are you trusting that God will come through for you?

My Feet are Slipping; Lord, Help Me

We have made it to "hump day" Wednesday. Let us thank God that we have made it this far even in our weakness and that we can look forward to finishing this week strong with His help.

We serve an amazing God who understands that we sometimes fall short and will need to call on Him from time to time. The beauty of it is that when we are weak and it seems that the Lord has forgotten us, we can trust that He will never reject or abandon His people. When we find ourselves slipping and cry out to God, He steps right in. He doesn't force us to try to save ourselves. There will be times when we will be anxious, depressed, and overwhelmed by the cares of the world. God will comfort us and hold us when we are tempted to go off course.

> "GOD will never walk away from his people, never desert his precious people. Rest assured that justice is on its way and every good heart put right. Who stood up for me against the wicked? Who took my side against evil workers? If GOD hadn't been there for me, I never would have made it. The minute I said, 'I'm slipping, I'm falling,' your love, GOD, took hold and held me fast. When I was upset, and beside myself, you calmed me down and cheered me up."
>
> (Psalm 94:14-19, MSG)

LESSON ✝ Many times in our lives, if God hadn't been there for us when our feet began to slip and we were losing control, where would we be? When we cry out to God in our time of need, His love will always be there, strengthening and guiding us so that we can go on.

When you feel that your feet are slipping, do you feel comfortable enough to cry out to God for help?

Giving Thanks for What?

On this "grateful Thursday," let us have hearts of gratitude, thanking our loving and generous God for everything. He will make everything work together for the good of those who love Him according to His plan. Amen.

There will always be an opportunity for us to experience chaos, tragedy, pain, and suffering in our lives. So much so that we might be asking, "Give thanks for what"?

Despite going through certain hardships in our lives, we must choose to be grateful. There will always be opportunities for chaos, tragedy, pain, and suffering, but each of us will always have something to be thankful for.

> "Always thank God the Father for everything in the name of our Lord Jesus Christ." (Ephesians 5:20)

> "Whatever happens, give thanks, because it is God's will in Christ Jesus that you do this." (1 Thessalonians 5:18)

LESSON † Giving thanks for what? Everything! Because God is worthy of our praises! He is good, and His mercy endures forever. He is in total control of everything, even in the midst of our crises. What a privilege we have to carry everything to Him in prayer. We only need to respond with a heart of gratitude.

Are there times when you feel you don't have anything to thank God for? Thank Him for Jesus and what He did on the cross on your behalf.

The Way You Lean is the Way You Fall

Thank God that we have made it to the end of this week. Let us thank Him for our family, friends, and those who have helped us press our way through.

If, by chance, you have reached the end of this week and you are feeling weary and tired, there is still a chance that you can and will finish strong.

> "Trust GOD from the bottom of your heart; don't try to figure out everything on your own. Listen for GOD's voice in everything you do, everywhere you go; he's the one who will keep you on track. Don't assume that you know it all. Run to GOD! Run from evil! Your body will glow with health, your very bones will vibrate with life!" (Proverbs 3:5-8, MSG)

Despite all humanity being made in the image and likeness of the Triune God—Father, Son, and Holy Spirit—we tend to bend toward our sinful nature. We often seek popularity, power, and perfection instead of leaning into the One who can and will help us finish strong.

LESSON † God has designed, created, and equipped us to be strong enough to withstand the strong winds that blow in our lives.

Are there any areas of your life that have you leaning or struggling today? Ask God to help you to find the strength to lean on Him.

You Have Permission to Rest

Thank God for allowing us to reach the weekend! Let us take this Saturday to rest from the chaos and labor of the week.

There is no such thing as a life without a bit of trouble and some chaos. It's during these difficult times that we need to reevaluate and reset our purpose, plans, and values. Please take a moment to breathe and slow down the pace of life to enjoy it. You have permission to rest today!

Too many times, we feel that we must fix everything that is broken or going wrong. However, if for some reason you are the only one who handles everything, God bless you, and may you find rest in Him.

> "'Come with me by yourselves to a quiet place and get some rest.'" (Mark 6:31b, NIV)

LESSON † Although we are faced with chaos every day, life goes on, and doing the work of God must go on. We are encouraged not to get weary in well-doing. In scripture, we see that Jesus took His disciples away to get some rest. He wants us to recognize that while doing God's work is very important, we need constant rest and renewal to do it effectively and live a satisfying life.

In spite of what you may be going through, will you take some time to relax and rest in God's goodness and faithfulness today?

God Wants Full Custody

Thank God for this beautiful Sunday. No matter our place of worship, let us worship in a position of reverence by bowing before Him on our knees because He has made us, and we are His!

God has created us to worship Him!

The problem is that many of us count the cost of following Christ and belonging to God as being too high.

> "One day when large groups of people were walking along with him, Jesus turned and told them, 'Anyone who comes to me but refuses to let go of father, mother, spouse, children, brothers, sisters—yes, even one's own self! —can't be my disciple. Anyone who won't shoulder his own cross and follow behind me can't be my disciple.'"
>
> Luke 14:25-27, (MSG)

LESSON † **God wants full custody and not only weekend and three-times-a-year visits from those of us who say that we are committed to being Christians and disciples.**

Can you say that you have a life-sustaining relationship with Christ?

Bruised but Not Broken

As we begin this new week, no matter what we may face this week, we can be assured that God's powerful presence will be with us, and His ears are open to our prayers.

Throughout history and even today, with certainty, we can face whatever evil because of what God has done through Christ and because we know that God's face is toward the righteous and that He is close to the brokenhearted.

> "A Message from the high and towering God, who lives in Eternity, whose name is Holy: 'I live in the high and holy places, but also with the low-spirited, the spirit-crushed, And what I do is put new spirit in them, get them up and on their feet again.'" (Isaiah 57:15, MSG)

LESSON † As God's people, we are fortunate He promises to be "close to the brokenhearted" (Psalm 34:18, NIV) and be our source of power, courage, and wisdom. Because God is helping us through our lives and problems, we may get bruised, but we will not be broken!

Have you ever faced what you believed to be overwhelming or unbeatable odds that didn't break you? How did you experience God's care and protection for you?

God's Word is Precious

On this Tuesday, let us thank our precious and almighty God for another day! May we find the strength, wisdom, and whatever we need not in the physical consumption of our daily bread but by every word that comes from the mouth of God.

There is nothing in this world more important or valuable to us than God's Word. Yet, there was a time in history when God's messages were few and far between, and visions were uncommon. God was not communicating His will through prophets or priests. He was silent, and these times were spiritually dark.

> "The boy Samuel was serving GOD under Eli's direction. This was at a time when the revelation of GOD was rarely heard or seen." (1 Samuel 3:1, MSG)

God means what He says in His Word, so we should not take it for granted. Scripture also warns us to seek God while He can be found, and we are to pray to Him while He is reachable.

LESSON † The words of God are perfect, and they protect us, make us wise, and give us joy and light. God's words are pure, eternal, and just. They are more desirable and precious than gold. They are sweeter than honey from a honeycomb. They lead us away from harm and give success to us when we obey them.

How precious are God's words to you? Do you keep God's words front and center of your mind daily?

How Long, Lord?

Thank God that we have made it to another "hump day" Wednesday. We must trust the Lord with so much happening, trusting that His will be done on earth as it is in heaven.

The Word lets us know that there is nothing new under the sun. So no matter what difficulties we face, all of heaven is encouraging us to hold on by faith. Not one of us is immune from the difficulties and sorrows that each day can bring. From day to day, when we think that things can't get any worse, we find ourselves falling on hard times and having moments when we are wondering and asking God, "Are you there? Do you see what's happening to us?"

If you've been there, praying and asking God, "How long?" you are not alone!

> "How long, O LORD? Will you forget me forever? How long will you hide your face from me? How long must I make decisions alone with sorrow in my heart day after day? How long will my enemy triumph over me?" (Psalm 13:1-2)

LESSON † While many of us want to know how God intends to deal with evil and our problems, not many of us would ask Him openly. But when we are alone with Him? "Why, God? How long, God? Please, God?"

Do you believe that God is your ever-present help in good times and bad times? Or do you find yourself crying out, "Where are You"? and, "Why?"

Bitter People or Better People

On this "grateful Thursday," let us humbly release any bitterness from our past. Let's thank God for all the blessings this week, and let us boldly move forward into the number of gifts that He has for each of us.

Challenging times can cause pent-up emotions that sooner or later come bursting out. We should expect that every trial or test in our lives will have the ability to make us bitter or better. However, they only come to make us strong. We all have the responsibility to choose one or the other and to know that our characters will be revealed not by our efforts during happy and good times but by our actions when things are not going our way.

> "Don't let evil get the best of you; get the best of evil by doing good." (Romans 12:21, MSG)

LESSON † Bitterness is a miserable place to be. If we are going to live as God's people, we should strive not to be bitter people but better people. When we are bitter, we can block or delay the power and ability to do better and be better.

Has there been an experience in your life that once you came through it, you had to make the choice of becoming a better person or a bitter person? Which did you choose?

Change Takes Time

On this Friday, let us thank God for the time of experiencing His presence this week and the days to come. Let us keep the faith that God can restore everything that goes wrong and change it into something extraordinary and unbelievable.

During our lifetime it may look like we are in some tough times, and we probably will be. They will also probably get tougher before they get better. During tough times we tend to become desperate for change. We must understand that God knows all about it and has something in store for us. He is patiently and actively involved in the matters not only of each of our lives but of the world.

The Bible has repeated themes of restoration and refreshing that offer us hope when everything seems wrong. We should never give up, and we must keep our eyes on the prize because change takes time!

> "Then times of refreshment will come from the presence of the Lord, and he will again send you Jesus, your appointed Messiah. For he must remain in heaven until the time for the final restoration of all things, as God promised long ago through his holy prophets." (Acts 3:20-21, NLT)

LESSON ✝ **For every generation, God may seem slow in coming to deliver us as we face challenging times. We must be ready to meet Christ at any time, even today. Still, we must plan and live our lives as though He may not return for many years.**

We know that Jesus promises to return. Do you trust in His timing?

Yes and Amen

Let us thank God for allowing us to live in His amazing power every day. Making it to another weekend and being here says that we have pressed through every struggle, endured every trial, and overcome every hurdle we've faced with the help of the Holy Spirit.

No matter what obstacles or circumstances we may face in our lives, we can always count on the Lord to keep and fulfill God's promises to us.

> "Certainly, Christ made God's many promises come true. For that reason, because of our message, people also honor God by saying, 'Amen!'" (2 Corinthians 1:20)

We may never understand why God allows things to happen, but we must trust His will.

> "Commit everything you do to the Lord. Trust him, and he will help you." (Psalm 37:5, NLT)

Our response to what God allows in our lives should always be yes and amen. We must agree with God, move with God, end with God, and never doubt God. *Amen* is a Hebrew word which means, "It is true," "So be it," or "So let it be." God's people accepted His will in exile and His promise to be their God, and, today, we must do the same.

> "Thanks be to the Lord God of Israel from everlasting to everlasting. Let all the people say amen. Hallelujah!"
> (Psalm 106:48)

LESSON † We use "amen" to end prayers or to agree with something being said or that has been said.

Were you aware that amen *is the last word in the Bible? What are your thoughts about it?*

God Will Redirect Us

Let us thank God for His presence in each of our lives on this blessed Sunday. May He make every unfair and crooked way straight and show us the way.

We often ask God to direct our path, and then we wonder and doubt that He is redirecting us when He says no to the way we are going or what we are doing. Often we are moving and doing life happy and content, feeling confident in and on the path we feel God has called us to. Then suddenly, out of nowhere, when we least expect it, it appears that God is saying no to a lot of things.

> "If people can't see what God is doing, they stumble all over themselves; But when they attend to what he reveals, they are most blessed." (Proverbs 29:18, MSG)

Only when we listen to the voice and the call of God will we be most assured and confident in the path that He has chosen for us.

LESSON † God will redirect us in our callings which will sometimes call for us to step out of our comfort zones. But that is just where God wants us to be so that we can be comfortable in Him.

Can you think of any changes that God can make or redirect in your life that will move you out of your comfort zone?

Faith in God Changes Everything

Let us thank God for a new day and a new week that is before us and is full of His faithful love and promises. May He comfort those mourning, revive broken hearts, and heal all those in need of healing.

The only two things that can limit God are sin and unbelief. They both have the power to prevent God from moving and working in our lives. Because the resurrection from the dead is a necessary belief of the Christian faith, God used Lazarus's raising as an essential display of His power to change things.

> "After Jesus said this, he told his disciples, 'Our friend Lazarus is sleeping, and I'm going to Bethany to wake him.' His disciples said to him, 'Lord, if he's sleeping, he'll get well.' Jesus meant that Lazarus was dead, but the disciples thought Jesus meant that Lazarus was only sleeping. Then Jesus told them plainly, 'Lazarus has died, but I'm glad that I wasn't there so that you can grow in faith. Let's go to Lazarus.'"
>
> (John 11:11-15)

LESSON † As we navigate this week, even if our circumstances appear to be dead, let us not lose hope, but let us trust God and believe in the many good things to come. Let's not allow sin and unbelief to cause us to live our lives as if there is no God in heaven.

Do you believe that God has the power to change situations in your life? Has He ever changed a situation that you had given up on?

None Righteous, No Not One

Let's choose to do all that we can on this Tuesday to do the things God loves. May the words each of us speak and the meditations of our hearts be acceptable in God's sight.

Although we profess Christianity, we recognize that we live in an imperfect world and that not one of us are perfect beings, and we all have struggles. We need to stop expecting those around us to be perfect.

> "As the Scriptures say: 'There is no one who always does what is right, not even one.'" (Romans 3:10, NCV)

> "For everyone has sinned; we all fall short of God's glorious standard. Yet God, in his grace, freely makes us right in his sight. He did this through Christ Jesus when he freed us from the penalty for our sins." (Romans 3:23-24, NLT)

We have a sworn enemy, Satan, who wants to remind us that we are flawed and imperfect, so what does he do? He whispers daily to us, trying to tempt us to look back at our past mistakes. Thank God that our heavenly Father does not expect us to be perfect. However, we must not allow Satan and others' foolishness, hate, or negativity to hinder us from being the best person we can be.

LESSON ✝ Even as believers, we are not perfect, no not one, but we serve a perfect God we cannot fool. Like David, we must ask God to search our hearts daily, and then we must strive to live out and speak from the good that lies within us.

When your actions and choices are uncomfortably close to the actions of the world around you, do you ask God to help you to see and choose the fruit of righteousness in your life?

Encouraging Words at the Well

Separated by Healthy Boundaries

We have made it to another "hump day" Wednesday! Let's thank God for blessing us with the wisdom and strength He has given us to make it through each day and the hope to finish strong.

Too often, we fail to see the beauty of life, which is precious, because we tend to carry the burdens that others lay on us. God never intended for us to bear the burdens of others that weigh us down.

> "For each person will have to carry his own load."
> (Galatians 6:5, HCSB)

We must set healthy boundaries with love and stop spending so much of our time trying to cover and please those who are not living a life obedient to God's Word.

> "My prayer for you is that you will overflow more and more with love for others, and at the same time keep on growing in spiritual knowledge and insight, for I want you always to see clearly the difference between right and wrong, and to be inwardly clean, no one being able to criticize you from now until our Lord returns. May you always be doing those good, kind things that show you are a child of God, for this will bring much praise and glory to the Lord."
> (Philippians 1:9-11, TLB)

LESSON † We shouldn't be seeking the pleasures and comforts of this world, putting up with negative and offensive people, and allowing them to make us abandon our happiness for fear of hurting their feelings.

Who around you might need your understanding and compassion for the burdens they carry?

Grateful Prayer – I Won't Complain.

Every day is the perfect day to be grateful. On this "grateful Thursday," let us forget about our lack and our troubles. Let's thank God for His mercies and His grace that sustain and give us enough of what we need each day.

> "Do all things without grumbling *and* faultfinding *and* complaining [against God] and questioning *and* doubting [among yourselves]," (Philippians 2:14, AMPC)

The Lord cares for all those who love and fear Him. Not only can He provide, but it is His desire to so.

> "The LORD is my shepherd; there is nothing I lack."
> (Psalm 23:1, HCSB)

Often, it's because of a lack of faith and the fact that we don't believe that the best is yet to come that we sometimes grumble, complain, and fail to be thankful and remember that God is with us and that He is at work in our lives, even during our problems and when things look hopeless.

> **LESSON** † Grumbling, complaining, focusing on our current circumstances, and our desire to want our daily supply in advance all make us independent of God and blind us to the reality of God's glory and His willingness to provide for us.

Have you ever been found guilty of grumbling and complaining about your problems and what you perceived as lacking?

Keep Going

Yay! It's Friday, and we can thank God for His protection. Everything we have faced this week, whether small or large, we have endured, overcome, and prevailed over because of His help. No matter how large or small the mountains that we've faced this week, we can keep going, be comforted, and be assured that not a day had gone by that our God has not gone before us and carried us when we needed Him. His love for us is more than we can ever know.

> "Christ's love is greater than anyone can ever know, but I pray that you will be able to know that love. Then you can be filled with the fullness of God." (Ephesians 3:19, NCV)

> "'Family of Jacob, listen to me! All you people from Israel who are still alive, listen! I have carried you since you were born; I have taken care of you from your birth. Even when you are old, I will be the same. Even when your hair has turned gray, I will take care of you. I made you and will take care of you. I will carry you and save you."
>
> (Isaiah 46:3-4, NCV)

LESSON ✝ **By seeking God's presence and continuously seeking His strength, we can keep going with confidence because He is faithful.**

Is there a time when God has helped you to share your faith with someone who needed to be encouraged to keep going?

Dealing with Criticism

Thank God that we have reached another weekend. On this Saturday, let us not focus on any oppositions or criticisms, and let us remember that God promises to keep us in perfect peace when our minds and hearts stay on Him.

Everyone has an opinion and is a critic at some point in time. While criticism can be hurtful, not all criticism is harmful or destructive. Often, we're our own worst critics. Criticism can also bring about good results. However, we don't always know how to receive criticism and often allow it to make us lose our joy. We go wrong as critics when judging others and seeing ourselves only in a good light while seeing others' imperfections.

> "'It's easy to see a smudge on your neighbor's face and be oblivious to the ugly sneer on your own. Do you have the nerve to say, "Let me wash your face for you," when your own face is distorted by contempt? It's this whole traveling road-show mentality all over again, playing a holier-than-thou part instead of just living your part. Wipe that ugly sneer off your own face, and you might be fit to offer a washcloth to your neighbor.'" (Matthew 7:3-5, MSG)

LESSON ✝ Developing greater compassion and love for ourselves will help us not be such critics of ourselves and allow us not to criticize others but to build positive relationships with them. Jesus urged his disciples, and He urges us, to minister to others rather than condemn them.

Do you resist seeing yourself as better than others? Do you ask God to help you to let go of the impulse to criticize others?

On What Foundation are You Building Your Life?

On this Sunday, let us thank God that with His help and what He did through Christ Jesus, we will be able to endure whatever we may face today and always.

We must choose on what foundation we build our life. Having a stable and firm foundation is the most important and needed part of our faith for it to endure.

Jesus is the only sure foundation. However, many will attempt to build a life on their own strengths and abilities.

> "'These words I speak to you are not incidental additions to your life, homeowner improvements to your standard of living. They are foundational words, words to build a life on. If you work these words into your life, you are like a smart carpenter who built his house on solid rock.'"
>
> (Matthew 7:24, MSG)

The time will come to test what materials we've built our spiritual house on.

LESSON † So let us practice obedience, digging deep into God's Word, not only hearing but responding to and following it, which becomes the solid foundation that allows us to weather and survive the storms of life.

What are ways that we can ensure our foundation is built on Christ?

Our Main Priority

As we begin this new day, let us be reminded of the importance of prioritizing God daily in our lives. May He give each of us the grace and wisdom to serve Him and be a blessing to those we encounter.

Many of us have probably caused some trouble or chaos in our lives by having the wrong priorities. However, we can be thankful that we serve a loving God who loves us and will never give up on us.

If we're going to live our lives as God's people, we are told to set our affections on things above and not the things below. Meaning we should prioritize our affections by focusing on eternal things and not these temporal things such as materialism and fleshly desires.

> "Since you were brought back to life with Christ, focus on the things that are above—where Christ holds the highest position—the one next to God he Father on the heavenly throne. Keep your mind on things above, not on worldly things." (Colossians 3:1-2)

There's no denying that it can be a struggle to seek the things that we cannot see, but our priorities will fall in place with our efforts to seek first God's kingdom.

LESSON † First things first, each day we must ask ourselves what is most important to us because people, material possessions, success, and other desires all compete for priority in our lives every day.

What are ways that you are prioritizing God during your busy schedule?

Perfect Sympathy of Christ

Let us rejoice today in knowing that we can endure because we have Jesus, our Lord and Savior, and because He is our strength.

No one ever wants to feel alone, especially when going through difficult times. Many of us would agree that we would like someone who understands what we're going through to be with us. There is good news: we not alone! No matter what we're going through, we have a well-aware God who is no stranger to what we go through, and He understands all our pain and sufferings, and He wants to empower us with the strength to withstand whatever comes our way.

> "For we do not have a high priest who is unable to sympathize with our weaknesses, but One who has been tested in every way as we are, yet without sin."
>
> (Hebrews 4:15, HCSB)

> "Because Jesus experienced temptation when he suffered, he is able to help others when they are tempted."
>
> (Hebrews 2:18)

LESSON † **Jesus paid the price for our sins even though He knew no sins. He continues to be with us today, living inside us and strengthening us as we go through our trials.**

Is there someone you could encourage with the love of Christ as they go through a difficulty?

Living as Conquerors

On this "hump day" Wednesday, let us thank God for protecting us from everything that the evil one tries to bring into our lives to destroy our loved ones or us.

Because we're living in a fallen world, we can expect to see evil and even experience it in our lives. However, we don't have to be afraid and surrender to it. Despite weapons being formed, they will not prosper over us if we stay with Jesus. The Bible assures us that we are more than conquerors.

> "No, despite all these things, overwhelming victory is ours through Christ, who loved us." (Romans 8:37, NLT)

> "No weapon that has been made to be used against you will succeed. You will have an answer for anyone who accuses you. This is the inheritance of the LORD's servants. Their victory comes from me," declares the LORD." (Isaiah 54:17)

As God's children, we have a heritage of righteousness in the fact that God is fighting for us, and He has the power to block and remove fear, doubt, hate, worry, stress, and pain.

> "So be subject to God. Resist the devil [stand firm against him], and he will flee from you." (James 4:7, AMPC)

LESSON † **There is no need to be alarmed by the spiritual warfare battles and difficulties in our lives. In case you haven't heard, the "breaking news" is that there will be a final battle, and God has promised that He will be victorious, and so will His children.**

In what ways do you use the armor of God to help you through battles?

Promises, Promises!

On this "grateful Thursday," let us thank God for all the promises and blessings that He bestows upon us and for allowing us to make it this far. So many have not made it, but we are still here, still standing.

It's so crucial that we continue to pray prayers of thanksgiving, grow spiritually, and remain faithful. This will remind us that God is good all of the time and will allow us to thank Him when things are not so good.

> "The yes to all of God's promises is in Christ, and through Christ we say yes to the glory of God. Remember, God, is the One who makes you and us strong in Christ. God made us his chosen people. He put his mark on us to show that we are his, and he put his Spirit in our hearts to be a guarantee for all he has promised." (2 Corinthians 1:20-22, NCV)

> "Do not let this happy trust in the Lord die away, no matter what happens. Remember your reward! You need to keep on patiently doing God's will if you want him to do for you all that he has promised." (Hebrews 10:35-36, TLB)

LESSON † There is so much power in promises, especially in God's promises. His promises in scripture are like His assurance and guarantee to provide for all of our needs. Our prayer is how we can take possession of them, and there is no expiration on God's guarantee and His promises. They last forever!

Which promise of God do you hold onto during a time of need?

Life Can Sometimes Be Tough but So Can We

Let us thank God this Friday for the completion of another week.

As this week comes to an end, let us look forward to and enjoy the upcoming weekend, forgetting all those things that may have made life tough for us. Nothing in this life is guaranteed to be easy, and life can be challenging and unfair sometimes to good people. We must accept that we may never be good enough for everybody, but we are precious to God, and nothing happens that doesn't go through His hands.

> "You know that I have been insulted, put to shame, and humiliated. All my opponents are in front of you. Insults have broken my heart, and I am sick. I looked for sympathy, but there was none. I looked for people to comfort me, but I found no one." (Psalm 69:19-20)

When life gets tough, many times, we ask the question, "Why me?" Tough times in life are sure to happen, but we don't have to go through them without hope or help. No matter what tough times get thrown our way in life, God knows all about them.

> "I am able to do all things through Him who strengthens me."
> (Philippians 4:13, HCSB)

LESSON † Although life can be tough and challenging, we must keep going because the difficult roads we travel can lead us to places that reveal that we are much stronger and tougher than we think we are.

In what ways do life's challenges strengthen and shape us for the better?

Making the Right Move to Rest in Christ

On this Saturday, let us who are entering into rest from this past week's work continue to seek God and trust in His holy Word eagerly and with sincerity.

Many tend to be all about the business of living the good life, and while good things may be happening in our lives each day, God wants us, even in our rest, to focus on the best thing in life, which is Him.

> "The only thing good is if we come and rest in the life of Christ, who is the real Lamb of God. Then He can change our hearts, He can change our desires, and He can change our thoughts." – Russell M. Stendal [34]

> "It is useless for you to work so hard from early morning until late at night, anxiously working for food to eat; for God gives rest to his loved ones." (Psalm 127:2, NLT)

LESSON † **God is not against our hard work efforts. However, He did set the example for us at creation to rest. He does not want us to work so much that we do not rest or that we neglect our families. In life, we all need a reasonable amount of rest and times of spiritual refreshment. Our most earnest desire should be to have and maintain a relationship with God whereby we are lead, encouraged, guided, and have our hearts enlightened by the truth of His Word.**

Have you allowed yourself to enjoy God's many blessings and the fruit of your labor?

The Blessing of Being His Sheep

On this Sunday, let us serve the Lord with gladness because we know that we are His. May He continue to bless us, watch over us, and give each of us peace as we follow Him.

Everyone wants to feel that they have a connection to someone or something. However, sometimes we must relinquish our selfish desires if we genuinely want to have a healthy connection or relationship with others. Preparing today's devotional made me think of the toddler's creed, a poem I once read, that is used to prepare teachers and parents for the stage when toddlers start selfishly grabbing everything and claiming, "It's mine, mine, mine." It goes like this:

> "If I want it, it's mine. If I give it to you and I change my mind later, it's mine. If I can take it away from you, it's mine. If it's mine, it will never belong to anybody else, no matter what. If we are building something together, all the pieces are mine. If it looks like mine, it is mine." [35]

What a blessing it is that we belong to God. He calls us His sheep!

Unlike the toddler's selfish motives, when God declares that something is His, He has genuine motives, and He intends to shower us with His love. When we are hurting, lost, or when we end up going astray, our Shepherd is the first to see our needs, and He is forever listening. Most importantly, He loves us without judgment.

LESSON † The blessing of being God's sheep is that we can stop struggling when we are sincerely in God's hands because we are eternally protected never to perish, and no one can snatch us from His hands.

In what ways has God shown you His faithfulness?

Standing Firm

As we start this new week, let us look forward to a new week of promises. Let us stand firm and strong, not allowing any circumstances to take away our joy this week. May the joy of the Lord be our strength.

We all want to be better or to get better at doing what we do in each of our personal lives and what we do for the Lord. However, even as Christians, we will have our doubts and struggle in our faith about God's plan for us at some point and time in our lives.

The comfort and assurance that we have are that God never sends us into a situation or has us do life alone. God faithfully keeps His promise to always be with us. Better than that, He always goes before us and walks with us. God is now working everything out, so let's keep moving forward. Even though we don't know what this week holds, we know who controls this week.

> "Be alert. Continue strong in the faith. Have courage, and be strong." (1 Corinthians 16:13, NCV)

LESSON † Because Jesus has paved the way for us, nothing that we do is useless. Whatever task or situation we feel is draining or burdensome to us this week, let us not become discouraged but let us be strong and stand firm, looking at them as acts of worship or service to God.

How have you shown God's love through service to others?

Checking Your Mindset

On this Tuesday, let us have a blessed and beautiful day by putting things in perspective. Let us first give God the praise that He deserves and let us check our mindset. May we see God and His grace in every step we take.

When we allow our emotions to get the best of us, we often tend to be led solely by our feelings, which causes us to give up or not look on the bright side of things. There's a saying that says when we change the way we look at things, the things we look at change.

Our lives are only as good as our mindset, so each day, we must think positively and be confident of the things we can achieve. We must remember to see God on the throne, know that He is in control of our lives, and trust that He makes all things work together for the good of those who love Him.

> "Don't become like the people of this world. Instead, change the way you think. Then you will always be able to determine what God really wants—what is good, pleasing, and perfect." (Romans 12:2)

LESSON † **We are told that the things we put into our minds determine what comes out in our words and actions. Let us ask God to help us check our mindset, making every effort to program our minds to keep them focused and filled with positive and affirmative thoughts.**

Have you checked your thought process lately? Does it align with God's Word?

Strength From the Journey

On this "hump day" Wednesday, may we be filled with the strength of the Lord that gives us the hope and courage to make it. Let us thank Him in advance for the strength that we will receive from the experiences of the journey this week.

Often, I'm guilty of asking God to strengthen me before I even begin a journey or a season of life. More and more, I'm realizing and learning that my greatest strength comes not from a prepared strength that I ask for upfront but from the strength I've gained from the experience of going through the journey or the season of life.

> "I love you, LORD; you are my strength." (Psalm 18:1, NLT)

As God's children, we must learn that when we give God our weakness, He'll provide us with His strength and that our experiences in life are the gifts that keep on giving.

> **LESSON** † Sometimes it may seem like God has abandoned us, when in fact, He is still with us in our times of weakness. This way, we recognize our limitations and that we must depend on Him rather than our limited abilities and efforts.

What areas of life do you need to let God take care of?

But God

On this "grateful Thursday," let us be forever grateful for who God is and for all He has done, is doing, and will be doing—especially His love and sacrifice for us.

Many of us go through so much in life. It takes everything to hold on to our sanity. But God! God has done so much more for us than anything we will experience in this life. With God, we have a future glory that awaits us.

> "But God is so rich in mercy; he loved us so much that even though we were spiritually dead and doomed by our sins, he gave us back our lives again when he raised Christ from the dead—only by his undeserved favor have we ever been saved— and lifted us up from the grave into glory along with Christ, where we sit with him in the heavenly realms—all because of what Christ Jesus did. And now God can always point to us as examples of how very, very rich his kindness is, as shown in all he has done for us through Jesus Christ."
> (Ephesians 2:4-7, TLB)

LESSON † Although we live in a time when our world is so full of sin, death, and decay, because of who God is we have hope and so much to be grateful for. God's grace has saved us and will never abandon us!

Was there a time when God saved you or surprised you?

Every Chain Can Be Broken

On this Friday, let us call on the name of Jesus because of the power it has to free us from every sin and stronghold that is trying to hold us down and keep us captive.

God has brought us through another week. No matter what we have faced, there is no need for us to remain in bondage by chains that have bound us in our personal lives, on our jobs, or in our spiritual lives. Through prayer, God has the power to break every chain.

> "What then are we to say about these things? If God is for us, who is against us?" (Romans 8:31, HCSB)

> "The Spirit of the Almighty LORD is with me because the LORD has anointed me to deliver good news to humble people. He has sent me to heal those who are brokenhearted, to announce that captives will be set free and prisoners will be released." (Isaiah 61:1)

LESSON † Jesus has the power to bring hope into our lives when it seems like there is no hope. Every chain that holds us shall be broken today in the precious name of Jesus.

Has God freed you from any chains of bondage—fear, anxiety, depression, addiction, etc.?

Be Patient – God is not Finished Yet

Let us thank God for bringing us to the weekend. He helped us get started with the week, and He will allow us to finish.

We are told not to get tired or weary in well-doing because we can sometimes feel that we are not making progress in our personal and spiritual life. We often tend not to finish what we start, but not God. He always finishes what He starts.

> "And I am certain that God, who began the good work within you, will continue his work until it is finally finished on the day when Christ Jesus returns." (Philippians 1:6, NLT)

When God begins a project, he finishes it! As with the Philippians, God will help us grow in grace until He has completed His work in our life, which began when Christ died on the cross in our place.

LESSON † After completing this week, if you feel weary, discouraged, incomplete, unfinished, or overwhelmed, remember God's promise and provision to continue the excellent work throughout our lifetime and finish it when we meet Him face to face. God won't give up on us. So let's not let our current conditions or sins steal from us the joy of growing closer to Christ and knowing Him.

Is there something that you are still believing God for?

A Heart of Gold

On this blessed Sunday, may each of our hearts be bright, shiny, and so pure that they are inflamed with so much love today that all who we encounter feel and see the love of Christ radiating through us.

As God's people, we should do our best to love the Lord with all our heart, mind, and strength because we are commanded to do so, along with loving our neighbors as ourselves.

> ""So love the Lord your God with all your heart, with all your soul, with all your mind, and with all your strength." The second most important commandment is this: "Love your neighbor as you love yourself." No other commandment is greater than these."" (Mark 12:30-31)

One would think that it would be easy to love the God who Himself is love. However, we know that's not the case. It takes strength to love God and other people.

The current conditions we live in have managed to turn people's hearts of gold into cold hearts.

> **LESSON** † May we continue to pray for strength and thank God for those we encounter with hearts of gold, which encourage and inspire the spirits of each of us when we find ourselves with a most delicate and wounded spirit.

Is there someone in your life who you need God's help to offer love and compassion to? Are you willing to love them as yourself?

Love Your Enemies

On this Monday, let us continue to seek to draw closer to God so that we can grow spiritually stronger. This week, let us ask God for the strength not to let others bring out the worst in us, only our best.

We often find ways to pause and celebrate our loved ones and the people we love, making them feel special. If you ask anybody, they would say that it is easy to love those who love us.

Suppose we want this week to lead us on a path of love, possibilities, prosperity, and peace. In that case, we must not entertain the thought of hate and retaliation because they will ultimately lead us to destruction.

> "'You have heard that it was said, "Love your neighbor, and hate your enemy." But I tell you this: Love your enemies, and pray for those who persecute you. In this way you show that you are children of your Father in heaven. He makes his sun rise on people whether they are good or evil. He lets rain fall on them whether they are just or unjust.'"
>
> (Matthew 5:43-45)

> "{Nehemiah prayed,} 'Our God, hear us. We are despised. Turn their insults back on them, and let them be robbed in the land where they are prisoners.'" (Nehemiah 4:4)

LESSON † If we do not want to be the container or the vessel that corrodes by carrying hate and retaliation, we must put everything in God's hand. Granted, it will not be an easy task, but if we are going to love the world as Jesus did, we must start by loving, doing good, blessing, and praying for our enemies.

Are you doing a regular heart check and sharing your heart with others? Can you love those who simply and outright seek to hurt you?

Looking for Directions?

On this Tuesday, let us continue to choose God and trust Him as He orders our steps and guides us in our directions this week.

While difficult roads may lead to beautiful destinations, when we find ourselves looking for direction in our lives, our choices should always be to please God.

> "Show me Your ways, O Lord; teach me Your paths. Guide me in Your truth *and* faithfulness and teach me, for You are the God of my salvation; for You [You only and altogether] do I wait [expectantly] all the day long."
>
> (Psalm 25:4-5, AMPC)

LESSON † Walking God's path of righteousness calls for each of us to make a choice. We must make a decision that sticks when it comes to serving God. Serving God gives us a choice but ultimately offers us eternal life.

Are you seeking God's direction daily? What path have you chosen? Are you on the path of righteousness, or are you on the path that the wicked take?

Season of Repentance

On this "hump day" Wednesday, let us thank God for bringing us safely to the middle of this week, and let us ask Him to prepare our hearts for spiritual growth and repentance!

Death is a natural process of the life cycle. Ecclesiastes 3:1 tells us that there is a time for everything and a season for everything under the heavens. When thinking of death, one can't help but think of repentance, a time people of faith do a self-examination and and ask God to forgive us of our sins.. We also reflect on our mortality and the fact we are dust but God still loves us despite our uncleanliness.

> "Then the LORD God took dust from the ground and formed a man from it. He breathed the breath of life into the man's nose, and the man became a living person."
>
> (Genesis 2:7, NCV)

> "He said to the man, 'Go through Jerusalem and put a mark on the foreheads of the people who groan and cry about all the hateful things being done among them.'"
>
> (Ezekiel 9:4, NCV)

LESSON † It is our human nature to try to hide our sins and to overlook our mistakes. Let us reflect and realize our human frailty, admit our wrongdoings, and confess them, making it a season of redemption and a new life for each of us.

Have you shared your deepest mistakes with God and asked for His forgiveness? Are you accepting of the fact that when we repent, God doesn't always release us from the consequences of our sins?

Heirs of Everything

On this "grateful Thursday," let us humbly come before God with an appreciation for the many blessings that He has given us, and let us ask Him to help us in keeping our eyes and minds focused on the truth of His Word.

Even though we live in uncertain times when we don't know what to look forward to from one day to the next day, we still have much to be grateful for because we serve a faithful God. From Genesis to Revelation, God gives us as His children the assurance that He will keep all His promises to us.

> "So don't be anxious about tomorrow. God will take care of your tomorrow too. Live one day at a time."
>
> (Matthew 6:34, TLB)

LESSON † Thank God it's not what we do that makes us worthy, but because He chooses us. Today each of us is chosen out of God's goodness and grace to be a part of His cherished prized possession, receiving all of His promises.

As a child of God, have there been times when you have felt empty and your gifts have felt small and worthless? Were you still willing to offer them for the glory of God?

Our Hard Work Rewarded

As we come to the end of the week on this Friday, let us continue to persevere, knowing we have done our best according to the standards of God.

Early in our life, many of us are taught that hard work and being committed are the way to success. As we grow up, we learn that the path isn't always easy or necessarily smooth. However, the Bible has many encouraging words to guide and motivate us as we live and work even in the most challenging times in our lives.

> "Those who work hard make a profit, but those who only talk will be poor. Wise people are rewarded with wealth, but fools only get more foolishness." (Proverbs 14:23-24, NCV)

> "But you should be strong. Don't give up, because you will get a reward for your good work." (2 Chronicles 15:7, NCV)

LESSON † Being recognized and rewarded are the best encouragement and inspiration for us to persevere and keep up the good work. We must continue to live and work according to God's standards, and ultimately, we will receive our greatest reward, not in this life but in the life to come.

Has there been a time in your life when you had a job or ministry you worked hard at only for the applause and the approval of others?

No Looking Back

On this Saturday, let us put behind us all the regrets and failures from this past week and focus on the fact that we have conquered and survived another week.

We may have stumbled a little or a lot this past week, but because we cannot do anything about what happened this past week or in our day-to-day life, we don't have to worry or try to figure everything out. We must trust and believe that the Lord is leading and guiding us. There's going to come a time in life when we look back and realize that we have worried about things that we couldn't have done anything about.

> "'Can all your worries add a single moment to your life? And if worry can't accomplish a little thing like that, what's the use of worrying over bigger things?'" (Luke 12:25-26, NLT)

LESSON † We must stop worrying or allowing our negative past to affect us or prevent us from moving forward by looking back on what would have, could have, or have been.

Is there a past season in your life that's holding you back from reaching your destiny?

Stop, Wait, and Go

On this blessed Sunday, let us continue to stay focused and not be distracted by the many things that try to keep us from worshiping God and stop us from reaching the destination that He has prepared for us.

On this journey called life, we will encounter many traffic lights and road signs. Just like traffic lights and road signs are essential and vital in our daily lives, we need God's spiritual guidance through the Holy Spirit to help lead and guide us.

Knowing when it is the right time to stop, wait, or go is not always easy. God will always provide a timely answer, and it will be different in each of our situations.

> "The LORD showed them the way; during the day he went ahead of them in a pillar of cloud, and during the night he was in a pillar of fire to give them light. In this way they could travel during the day or night. The pillar of cloud was always with them during the day, and the pillar of fire was always with them at night." (Exodus 13:21-22, NCV)

God is the ultimate GPS, and He will not allow us to take a shortcut into our Promised Land. We, too, must be purged of sin that causes us to rebel and fear God before we can move on, no matter how long it may take. While God desires to guide and protect us, He is more interested in developing a loving relationship with us.

> **LESSON** † As God's people, we have the green light to keep going for Jesus. We must stay focused on God's promises and continue to travel to the place He is calling us to be.

Are you in the habit of running the spiritual traffic lights in your life? Or do you eagerly stop, patiently wait, and cautiously go when directed by God?

Thank God It's Monday!

On this Monday, let us set the tone for this new and blessed week, making it excellent as we give God nothing but our best by maintaining a Christian attitude.

Thank God for it's Monday! May each of us, as we begin this new week, declare, be reminded, and be inspired to make this week positive with changes to think and feel nothing but positive thoughts.

There are days when we don't feel like doing anything, and our moods are down. Mondays have such a bad reputation for being the most dreaded day of the week. God is so good to us that no matter what the day of the week it is, we should want to give Him our best in every aspect of our lives—our homes, jobs, school, and relationships, especially our relationship with Him.

> "Never be lazy in your work, but serve the Lord enthusiastically. Be glad for all God is planning for you. Be patient in trouble, and prayerful always. When God's children are in need, you be the one to help them out."
>
> (Romans 12:11-13a, TLB)

LESSON † Mondays are for a fresh start and new beginnings. What we put in our minds will determine our words and actions. If one small positive thought can change your whole day, make today count as an encouraging start of a new week.

Even when you are not having a good Monday, do you allow the faith of those around you to encourage you?

Invitation to Follow Jesus

As we awake to this Tuesday, may each of us find ourselves in the hands of the Lord. As we face today's challenges, let us not rely on our strength but receive His.

No matter what goes out of control in our lives or the world, we can survive this week and throughout life when we make the most uncompromised choice to follow Jesus.

> "And He said to them, Come after Me [as disciples—letting Me be your Guide], follow Me, and I will make you fishers of men!" (Matthew 4:19, AMPC)

Jesus is still saying today, "Follow me!" Never mind what we believe or what we are doing. Each of us has an open invitation to follow Jesus. Accepting His invitation means that we will do our best to walk the walk and follow in faith and obedience daily.

> "Calling the crowd to join his disciples, he said, 'Anyone who intends to come with me has to let me lead. You're not in the driver's seat; *I* am. Don't run from suffering; embrace it. Follow me and I'll show you how. Self-help is no help at all. Self-sacrifice is the way, my way, to saving yourself, your true self. What good would it do to get everything you want and lose you, the real you? What could you ever trade your soul for?'" (Mark 8:34-37, MSG)

LESSON † Only when we follow Jesus, no matter the cost, will we know what it means to live fully now and to have eternal life as well. Jesus made it clear that to be a faithful follower of His would not be easy. So let us get out of the driver's seat and let Jesus drive today!

Have you accepted the invitation to follow Jesus? If yes, has it been easy?

Feelings of Emptiness

On this "hump day" Wednesday, let us ask the Lord to allow His will to be done in our lives. May He fill us with His grace and mercy to be able to face whatever this day may bring.

Let us continue to reflect on our blessings and relationship with God. Let us not dwell too much on what we've gone through. While we also recall our many blessings, what we've gone through is still enough to make us feel tired and tapped out! But despite all that we go through, God is with us and is meeting us where we are, just like He did for the Israelites on their journey to the Promised Land.

> "Fill us with your love every morning. Then we will sing and rejoice all our lives. We have seen years of trouble. Now give us as much joy as you gave us sorrow. Show your servants the wonderful things you do; show your greatness to their children. Lord our God, treat us well. Give us success in what we do; yes, give us success in what we do."
>
> (Psalm 90:14-17, NCV)

Life can be a tough school of learning, and from day to day, we may sometimes feel empty or like we don't have all that we want. Truth be told, when we begin our day with the Lord and feed on His Word, each of us will have all that we need.

> **LESSON** † Let us use our feelings of emptiness to motivate us to draw closer to God and all the fullness and completeness of life that only He can give.

Has there been a time when you have felt an emptiness? Do you feel it came from a disconnection from the love of God?

Don't Forget God

Let us not forget to embrace this "grateful Thursday" with joy and gratefulness for all God has done for us and for all those He surrounds us with who are supportive and inspiring to us, making our lives more meaningful.

On those days when we find ourselves feeling down or feel it's too difficult to give God thanks, let us not forget that God deserves all of our praises.

> "After a meal, satisfied, bless GOD, your God, for the good land he has given you. Make sure you don't forget GOD, your God, by not keeping his commandments, his rules and regulations that I command you today. Make sure that when you eat and are satisfied, build pleasant houses and settle in, see your herds and flocks flourish and more and more money come in, watch your standard of living going up and up—make sure you don't become so full of yourself and your things that you forget GOD, your God, the God who delivered you from Egyptian slavery." (Deuteronomy 8:10-14, MSG)

Although Israel was given the deeds to the Promised Land and assured they would live a successful and satisfying life, there were three conditions. They had to listen to God's Word; they had to remember it; and they had to obey it.

> **LESSON** † These three necessary conditions are still applicable in our pursuit of having a successful and satisfying Christian life today. If we are going to succeed in our Christian walk, we must have God's guidance, protection, and provision, and it also helps to have the ability to recall what God has done for us.

Reflect on a time when you have depended on God for His guidance, protection, and provision.

Finishing the Week Strong

Let us give God the glory this Friday for allowing us to see another day. May He strengthen our faith to trust Him to provide us with the strength to finish and complete each task before us.

It may have been a rough week for some of us, and we may have had a few defeats and setbacks. However, by the grace of God we all have made it to the end of another week. Finishing strong can sometimes be a challenge when we don't make the necessary changes and adjust how we look at the obstacles and challenges we face.

> "But none of these things move me; nor do I count my life dear to myself, so that I may finish my race with joy, and the ministry which I received from the Lord Jesus, to testify to the gospel of the grace of God."
>
> (Acts 20:24, NKJV)

LESSON ✝ To finish our week strong, we must first do our best to start our week with faith, and then we must keep our focus on Jesus because, ultimately, He gives us the power to finish strong.

Do you believe that your ability to finish the week strong is dependent upon your attitude?

Nothing Can Stop God's Plan

On this Saturday, let us thank God for His sovereignty and that there is nothing too hard for Him. Even when things seem tough and we can't see our way, let us be assured and trust that He is the way maker.

Many are frustrated with the fact that we live during a time when it appears that evil is prevailing. The crazy thing about that is many are calling the wrong right and the right wrong. But there is nothing too hard for God.

> "'I have a plan for the whole earth, a hand of judgment upon all the nations. The LORD of Heaven's Armies has spoken— who can change his plans? When his hand is raised, who can stop him?'" (Isaiah 14:26-27, NLT)

No one and nothing can stop God!

> **LESSON** † We must not lose hope no matter the challenges and frustrations that try to hinder what God has for us. We must trust that God's plans and His timing for our lives are better than anything that we can dream or imagine for ourselves and that His will and plans, although the process and the wait can be challenging, will be what's best for us.

Have there been times when you felt like someone or something had stopped God's plan for your life, only to realize it wasn't stopped, it was only delayed?

The Power in Oneness

On this blessed Sunday, let us continue to pray that God fills each of us with the spirit of love and unity. Let us unite and pray for hope, healing, and love throughout this world.

In this world we're seeing so much more open judgment, prejudice, disruption, and division. Martin Luther King, Jr., said, "I look to a day when people will not be judged by the color of their skin, but by the content of their character." [36]

God has always been determined to break down the barriers that have stood between humanity, nations, and races. Not much has changed over the years since Martin Luther King, Jr., spoke those words and when Jesus prayed that prayer.

> "If anyone says, 'I love God,' yet hates his brother, he is a liar. For the person who does not love his brother he has seen cannot love the God he has not seen. And we have this command from Him: The one who loves God must also love his brother." (1 John 4:20-21, HCSB)

LESSON † Our power comes and is demonstrated only when we understand that we are on the same team and that we are all working for the same cause, to lift the name of Jesus. We are all in this together!

Oneness and unity are important in our homes, world, and the church. How have you been empowered by unity and the faith of others?

Stepping into Newness

On this new Monday, and new week, may our days ahead be filled with hope and happiness as we discern the many blessings that God has for each of us.

When the the time is right, flowering bulbs take the initiative to make their arrival.. It's like they are offering a forecast of hope that brighter days are ahead as they burst through the soil.

We must be like the flowering bulbs even when life seems complicated. We must wait on God's timing. Then we shall thrive by stepping into our sometimes newness and the purpose of being and doing what God has created us for.

Waiting does not always mean doing nothing. Often, we pray and ask God for His help and guidance, then we do nothing but wait, instead of taking some initiative to make something happen.

> "Show me the right path, O LORD; point out the road for me to follow. Lead me by your truth and teach me, for you are the God who saves me. All day long I put my hope in you."
> (Psalm 25:4-5, NLT)

There is an African proverb that says, "When you pray move your feet."

> **LESSON** † We should not ask God to order our steps or direct our way if we are not going to move our feet.

How does stepping into and walking in newness look for you as a Christian?

Let Us Encourage and Build Each Other Up

On this Tuesday, let us thank God for another day to get it right with Him and for another chance to be evidence of His kindness by encouraging and uplifting those we encounter.

Thank God for the good that we see from day to day, especially since there is so much distrust and negative thinking. We will not survive or live our best lives alone in this world. That is why we are encouraged in the Word to encourage and build each other up. This word is not only for the church, but this is applicable in our everyday life.

> "So speak encouraging words to one another. Build up hope so you'll all be together in this, no one left out, no one left behind. I know you're already doing this; just keep on doing it." (1 Thessalonians 5:11, MSG)

Not only does God equip us all, but He also blesses and comforts us so that we can do the same for others. He will use broken people to help broken people because it often requires an individual to have been encouraged before they can encourage others.

LESSON † Together we can do much more and better, so let us be the person that takes the time to encourage and make others feel like they exist and that they matter.

Who has God used to encourage you? Who can you encourage today?

A Promised Rest

On this "hump day" Wednesday, we may not understand all that is happening in our lives now, but let us continue to love and trust God because there is a promise of rest. Amen.

Many issues can present themselves in our lives, making us a somewhat tired and weary society.

> "Somewhere it's written, 'God rested the seventh day, having completed his work,' but in this other text he says, 'They'll never be able to sit down and rest.' So this promise has not yet been fulfilled. Those earlier ones never did get to the place of rest because they were disobedient. God keeps renewing the promise and setting the date as *today*, just as he did in David's psalm, centuries later than the original invitation: Today, please listen, don't turn a deaf ear... And so this is still a live promise. It wasn't canceled at the time of Joshua; otherwise, God wouldn't keep renewing the appointment for 'today.' The promise of 'arrival' and 'rest' is still there for God's people. God himself is at rest. And at the end of the journey, we'll surely rest with God. So, let's keep at it and eventually arrive at the place of rest, not drop out through some sort of disobedience." (Hebrews 4:4-11, MSG)

LESSON † Prayer is our way of approaching God, and we are told to come to Him boldly. No matter what we face, we must boldly know and boldly come to Jesus. Each day He invites us to obediently come to Him to rest and enter His finished work.

How does our faith in Christ secure the promise of rest?

Living an Abundant Life

On this "grateful Thursday," may each of us feel God's grace and mercy wherever we go today. May He abundantly bless us with everything we need and the desires of our hearts.

Whether we find ourselves feeling like we are lacking or feeling like we have everything we need or want, it's easy for us to have concerns about whether we're going to make it when things get tough. We don't have to lose hope. There is good news. God is the source of our blessings as our provider, "Jehovah Jireh." He values each of us, whether rich or poor, and can completely meet all of our needs. He desires to bless each of us, not only so that we can have what we need but also so that we can also bless others.

> "'For if you give, you will get! Your gift will return to you in full and overflowing measure, pressed down, shaken together to make room for more, and running over. Whatever measure you use to give—large or small—will be used to measure what is given back to you.'"
>
> (Luke 6:38, TLB)

LESSON † When we live our lives as God intends for us to live by treating others generously, kindly, and respectfully, we can live an abundant and full life.

Has there been a time in your life when you were lacking and didn't have enough? How did your blessing come?

Grace to Stand Strong

Let us thank God that we have made it to the end of another week. Let us choose to stay in faith, knowing that God's grace will give us the power and the strength to succeed.

Although we are Christians, we sometimes get weak and feel the pressure and the weight of a hard week. We can and we do make mistakes, stumble, and fall. However, it is God's grace that has gotten us this far, and it will be His grace that will get us through.

> "But because God was so gracious, so very generous, here I am. And I'm not about to let his grace go to waste. Haven't I worked hard trying to do more than any of the others? Even then, my work didn't amount to all that much. It was God giving me the work to do, God giving me the energy to do it." (1 Corinthians 15:10, MSG)

LESSON † **God may not remove our worries or the things that make us feel incomplete, but because we are His children, we do have the assurance that He is faithful and that we are never alone when feeling weak and feeling like life is too hard.**

To succeed in life, we all need God's grace!

Repeat this prayer: Lord God, when life gets challenging, help me learn to depend more and more on Your mighty power and grace to stand strong. Amen.

Under the Influence

On this Saturday, let us love the life that we have right now, and let us trust God to protect us from every influence not appointed by Him in our lives.

After a long week of physical and emotional work, many long for and seek some comfort. While we seek comfort from many things, we often fail to draw upon the power of the Holy Spirit, who is the ultimate Comforter that lives within us and helps us live the Christian life.

> "But the Comforter (Counselor, Helper, Intercessor, Advocate, Strengthener, Standby), the Holy Spirit, Whom the Father will send in My name [in My place, to represent Me and act on My behalf], He will teach you all things. And He will cause you to recall (will remind you of, bring to your remembrance) everything I have told you."
>
> (John 14:26, AMPC)

> "Those who are under the control of the corrupt nature can't please God. But if God's Spirit lives in you, you are under the control of your spiritual nature, not your corrupt nature. Whoever doesn't have the Spirit of Christ doesn't belong to him. However, if Christ lives in you, your bodies are dead because of sin, but your spirits are alive because you have God's approval." (Romans 8:8-10)

LESSON † As Christians, we have within us a portion of the very thoughts and mind of Christ. Being filled with or under the Holy Spirit's influence will help us please God daily and bring peace and comfort into our lives.

Do you trust the Holy Spirit to comfort you and to help you avoid seeking the comfort of the world that's not pleasing to God?

Jesus Flipping Tables

Thank God for allowing us to see another blessed Sunday. With all the distractions around us, let us not forget to ask the Lord to forgive us of everything we have done, said, or thought that is not pleasing in His sight.

Jesus is serious about faith and has never tolerated anything less than us being faithful. If we have a desire for Jesus to live in our lives, we must be willing to allow Him to do a clean sweep of our hearts and minds. Many say they are believers, but corruption is everywhere, and the church is no exception!

> "The Passover of the Jews was near, and Jesus went up to Jerusalem. In the temple he found people selling cattle, sheep, and doves, and the money changers seated at their tables. Making a whip of cords, he drove all of them out of the temple, both the sheep and the cattle. He also poured out the coins of the money changers and overturned their tables. He told those who were selling the doves, 'Take these things out of here! Stop making my Father's house a marketplace!' His disciples remembered that it was written, 'Zeal for your house will consume me.'" (John 2:13-17, NRSV)

LESSON † **He still wants to drive out all the things that can potentially hold us back from becoming the person or the people God wants us to be and from having sincere worship of God.**

How do you feel about the way Jesus cleansed the temple? Do you think that Jesus would be satisfied with what's going on in churches today?

Silenced

On this Monday and each day, let us start our day by talking to God. May our faith and belief remain strong enough to allow God to speak through our lips to declare His Word!

Women all over the world have had to struggle with the oppression of being second class or no class citizens when it comes to contributing to society. Yet we choose to challenge that oppression and are devoted to making contributions to our families, communities, jobs, and the world.

Since the beginning of time, dominant male societies have made being a woman challenging and complicated because of a lack of understanding in the church and community. Sadly, women also play a role in tearing each other down instead of building each other up.

> "Women should be silent during the church meetings. They are not to take part in the discussion, for they are subordinate to men as the Scriptures also declare."
>
> (1 Corinthians 14:34, TLB)

The purpose of Paul's words was to promote unity, not to teach about women's roles in the church.

LESSON † Women around the world today continue to fight to earn the right to speak up, challenge expectations, and be pioneers on the front line of change.

Do you think that women should be silent in church and only hold background roles? Explain. Is there a woman in your life or community who you think needs to be celebrated for her contributions?

Living Everyday Life
Walking in Faith

On this Tuesday, let us walk by faith through the doors of opportunities that God opens for each of us, knowing that He is already there wherever we go.

What happens when life doesn't always go the way we expect or plan? Yes, there will be those unexpected times when we will face life's challenges and problems that will cause us not to understand and to doubt.

> "Earn a reputation for living well in God's eyes and the eyes of the people. Trust GOD from the bottom of your heart; don't try to figure out everything on your own. Listen for GOD's voice in everything you do, everywhere you go; he's the one who will keep you on track. Don't assume that you know it all. Run to GOD! Run from evil!"
>
> (Proverbs 3:4-7, MSG)

> "Give your entire attention to what God is doing right now, and don't get worked up about what may or may not happen tomorrow. God will help you deal with whatever hard things come up when the time comes."
>
> (Matthew 6:34, MSG)

LESSON † As Christians, we are encouraged to live each day trusting God with our lives, which will not be as easy as it sounds. During challenging and uncertain times, we will need to see things through the eyes of Jesus, let go of what we think we know, and live every day walking and going in faith.

How does your faith help you in your daily life? Does it help you to get through dark and troubled times?

Jesus Says, I Am Willing

On this "hump day" Wednesday, let us thank God for the strength that has helped us make it here. May He continue to energize each of us with our purpose and direction and heal us of anything that will separate us from Him.

We're halfway through the week, and if you feel discouraged, hopeless, tired, or needing healing, Jesus is saying to each of us that whatever it is that we require to be made whole, He is willing!

> "When Jesus came down from the mountain, large crowds followed him. A man with a serious skin disease came and bowed down in front of him. The man said to Jesus, 'Sir, if you're willing, you can make me clean.' Jesus reached out, touched him, and said, 'I'm willing. So be clean!' Immediately, his skin disease went away, and he was clean."
>
> (Matthew 8:1-3)

> "That evening, after the sun went down, the people brought to Jesus all who were sick and had demons in them. The whole town gathered at the door. Jesus healed many who had different kinds of sicknesses, and he forced many demons to leave people." (Mark 1:32-34a, NCV)

LESSON † **Today, God is still healing and restoring sick bodies and tormented spirits. He desires, according to His will, to heal every place we're hurting. Whatever it is that each of us is looking for today, God is more than able, and there is no limit to God's healing power! The beauty of it is that His power is personal to each of us, and He says, "I am willing!"**

Have you come to the point in your life where you are asking Jesus to give to you what you don't have and what He is offering?

Our Prayers Have No Expiration Date

On this "grateful Thursday," let us thank God for the power of prayer as our daily armor. Let us thank God for blessing and protecting each of us, our loved ones, and our friends.

Sometimes it may look and feel like our situations will never change or get better, but prayer is powerful, and we should never underestimate its power. Prayer can change the unchangeable and can move the unmovable if it is within the will of God.

> "'Remember what happened long ago, for I am God, and there is no other; I am God, and no one is like Me. I declare the end from the beginning, and from long ago what is not yet done, saying: My plan will take place, and I will do all My will.'" (Isaiah 46:9-10, HCSB)

> "If any of you are having trouble, pray. If you are happy, sing psalms. If you are sick, call for the church leaders. Have them pray for you and anoint you with olive oil in the name of the Lord. (Prayers offered in faith will save those who are sick, and the Lord will cure them.) If you have sinned, you will be forgiven." (James 5:13-15)

LESSON † Although our prayers do not move God when they are not according to His will, we should keep faith in whatever we pray for because He never changes. He wants us to pray, and He lets us know that all things are possible with Him. God hears our prayers and the prayers that have been prayed on our behalf by others, and although they can be hindered, they have no expiration date.

Have you ever stopped to think about the journey of your prayers from this temporary earth into the hearing of God in the eternal heavens? Does that thought help you to keep praying?

What's Your Next Move?

Thank God it's Friday, and let us thank Him for the way He has made for us to move through this week.

Often, we think that the world has everything we need in life, only to regret the chances we didn't take because what we were looking for is not found in the world but within us. Yes, in our immaturity, we may have made mistakes or missed some opportunities, but we must keep moving. Those mistakes can serve as evidence that we are trying.

> "Dear friends, since you already know about this, be careful. Do not let those evil people lead you away by the wrong they do. Be careful so you will not fall from your strong faith. But grow in the grace and knowledge of our Lord and Savior Jesus Christ. Glory be to him now and forever! Amen."
>
> (2 Peter 3:17-18, NCV)

Some things that can hinder us from growing spiritually or evolving are not praying, not reading God's Word, missed opportunities, negative people, and painful situations.

I read a quote from Tupac Shakur that said, "You can spend minutes, hours, days, weeks, or even months over-analyzing a situation; trying to put the pieces together, justifying what could've, would've happened... or you can just leave the pieces on the floor and move on." [37]

Spiritual development and spiritual growth do not happen overnight and are beautiful things.

> **LESSON** † Our evolution and spiritual growth will come when we realize that we can choose not to focus on the bait of Satan to keep us stagnant in our Christian walk.

In what ways are you still easily moved or led by those who try to lead you astray? How can you continue to grow spiritually?

The Bridge to Life

Let us thank God for another Saturday and thank Him for giving His angels charge to watch over us even on the weekends, guiding us as we bridge the gap of what's before us with what's behind us.

There is no need for any of us to feel imperfect or sinful. We all have the same opportunity and the choice to walk a spiritual path. Once we choose, we must not quit or give up on ourselves or God. There is but one God, and He loves us. He is the God of Abraham, Isaac, and Jacob. We become separated from Him by sin. Despite there being only one pathway back to Him, we try many ways to bridge the gap between God and ourselves.

> "There is a way which seems right to a man *and* appears straight before him, but at the end of it is the way of death."
> (Proverbs 14:12, AMPC)

LESSON ✝ On our spiritual path, we must be one hundred percent straight with ourselves, walk the straight and narrow path with Jesus, and not get separated from God. We will all eventually have to decide whether to cross the only bridge that will connect us back to God.

Do you always acknowledge sin in your life that separates you from having connection with God? And do you seek God's direction back to Jesus, the bridge that connects you back to Him?

Something to See

Let us thank God for seeing another Sunday and give Him all the glory. Let us seek the vision to see this day and all that He has for us to hear, do, and see.

We live in a time like the Israelites coming out of the wilderness needing God's guidance, healing, and protection. Like them, we can become impatient and speak against those trying to help us by wanting to have and see more. God instructed Moses to use the bronze serpent on a pole as a cure for healing. It served as a metaphor and foreshadowing of Himself, God our healer, being lifted up.

> The LORD said to Moses, "Make a snake, and put it on a pole. Anyone who is bitten can look at it and live." So Moses made a bronze snake and put it on a pole. People looked at the bronze snake after they were bitten, and they lived."
>
> (Numbers 21:9-9)

> "Do everything without complaining or arguing."
>
> (Philippians 2:14)

LESSON † There is nothing new under the sun! The next time you see an ambulance, pay attention to the medical symbol. You will see the serpent on a pole. God is all-powerful and all-knowing. He wants us to learn from the experiences of those of time past. He wants us to see Him and not focus on our circumstances.

Even after grumbling and complaining, how have you seen God care for you and your loved ones in the past?

"God-fidence"

On this Monday, let us praise God and ask Him to give us the courage and God-fidence to make it through this week. Let us be confident in Him and ourselves.

It feels good and reassuring when others accept and appreciate us for who we are or what we do. When it doesn't go the way we expect it to, there goes our courage and confidence. We must stop looking outside for our courage and confidence and look inside and to the Lord.

> "For You are my hope, Lord GOD, my confidence from my youth. I have leaned on You from birth; You took me from my mother's womb. My praise is always about You. I have become an ominous sign to many, but You are my strong refuge. My mouth is full of praise and honor to You all day long." (Psalm 71:5-8, HCSB)

LESSON † Fear can be our worst enemy! Let us not go into this new week feeling devalued and underestimating who we are. After all, none of us can make anyone like us. All we can do is show others who we are, how we feel, and what we believe. It's up to them to figure out what our value is to them.

Do you recognize your value? At all times? And do you feel like you are living out your worth at all times?

While I'm Waiting, I Will Worship

On this Tuesday, let us pray and trust God to reveal to each of us how we can best serve and honor Him with our life despite what's going on or what we may be waiting on.

Regardless of who we are or what season of life we find ourselves in, we will experience the struggles of waiting on something or someone. When we find ourselves waiting on God, Satan knows that many of us tend to worship only when we are being blessed, and the first thing he tries to do is get us not to praise and worship God.

> "I will praise the Lord no matter what happens. I will constantly speak of his glories and grace."
>
> (Psalm 34:1, TLB)

LESSON † While it may be hard for us to know what it looks like to wait on God, there shall be no reason or season in our life that we should not give Him praise. When nothing makes sense and waiting seems more than we can bear, we must continue to trust God and pray that He gives us the strength to take our eyes off the waiting, whatever is going on, and look to Him.

Reflect on a time when you found it hard to praise God because you were waiting on Him, something, or someone. You didn't want to wait any longer but you waited. Was it worth the wait?

Not All Hope is Gone

On this "hump day" Wednesday, let us thank God for life, health, and strength. Let us keep the vision of His promise of new life both physically and spiritually.

When we find ourselves in the midst of despair and down in the valley, we long to be restored or revived to a place of abundant life and hope. We must realize that God is only a breath away. He has the power to restore our life and bring the situations back to life no matter how dry they are, or even if we have given them up for dead.

> "Then he said to me, 'Human, these bones are like all the people of Israel. They say, "Our bones are dried up, and our hope has gone. We are destroyed." So, prophesy and say to them, "This is what the Lord GOD says: My people, I will open your graves and cause you to come up out of your graves. Then I will bring you into the land of Israel."'"
>
> (Ezekiel 37:11-12, NCV)

No matter what seems dead in our lives, all hope is not gone. Knowing that we are never alone and that God is always with us, whether on the mountain top or down in the valley, should give us a sense of security.

> **LESSON** † Our hope is lost when we lose our connection with God. The dry bones represented the people's spiritually dead condition. Let us not lose our connection/relationship with God and become spiritually dead people.

How might you share God as the reason for your hope even when it seems like all hope is gone?

I Believe in Miracles

On this "grateful Thursday," let us thank God for His goodness and faithfulness and for being the miracle-working God who turns our impossible into the possible.

Even though we can't physically see God, we can see the evidence of His existence through everyday miracles. Although we are God's people, many of us are waiting for a miracle because we, too, face situations in our life that seem impossible. It is crucial that we believe and understand that God exists and that He is the source of miracles. Only then will we see our impossible situations as miracles waiting to happen.

> "I am the Lord, the God of all mankind; is there anything too hard for me?" (Jeremiah 32:27, TLB)

When God gets ready to bless us, no one can stop Him.

> "He is your praise and he is your God, the one who has done mighty miracles you yourselves have seen."
> (Deuteronomy 10:21, TLB)

LESSON † For those of us who have hope and believe God for a miracle today, He specializes in the impossible, and He will use His power to fulfill His purpose in each of our lives. If we want God to do what seems impossible in our lives, we must have the faith to believe that when God steps in, miracles do happen.

Have you ever had the need for a miracle? Did you have enough faith to believe for what you asked God?

Do Not Drift Away

On this Friday, let us not drift away from what we know, but let us continue to build our "God-fidence" and draw closer to God because He will always be the safest place to be.

Maybe you have come to the end of this week feeling alone, and you haven't felt God's presence. Be assured it's not because He is not with us. We can become so occupied with life's challenges that we drift away from Him. He desires to care for us, and He is saying to us, "I am your helper," and "I am here." Do not drift away.

> "We must, therefore, pay even more attention to what we have heard, so that we will not drift away. For if the message spoken through angels was legally binding and every transgression and disobedience received a just punishment, how will we escape if we neglect such a great salvation? It was first spoken by the Lord and was confirmed to us by those who heard Him."
> (Hebrews 2:1-3, HCSB)

> "For God has said, 'I will never, *never* fail you nor forsake you.'" (Hebrews 13:5b, TLB)

LESSON † Drifting away can be easy but dangerous. Paying attention to what God says to us in His Word can be challenging but so worth it. It involves us focusing our mind, body, and senses for the Word to sink in. By listening to God as we stay the course each week and not drifting away, we are reminded of who we are and whose we are.

When you feel that you are drifting in your relationship with God, do you ask Him to renew your vision so that you can focus on His continual presence and live with an eternal outlook in all circumstances?

You're Not Buried, You're Planted

We have the privilege of experiencing the changing of the seasons. Let us be reminded to give God the glory because it is He who changes the seasons.

> "Like the ground that brings forth its crops and like a garden that makes the seed in it grow, so the Almighty LORD will make righteousness and praise spring up in front of all nations." (Isaiah 61:11)

The expression is, "Bloom where you are planted." Unlike the trees and the flowers, we tend not to bloom wherever we are because we see ourselves as buried and not planted.

LESSON † Sometimes, depending on what season of life we are in, our lives can be challenging. But that doesn't mean we shouldn't make our lives the best. Blooming where we are doesn't mean we should not be transplanted, especially if we feel buried and trapped or have an opportunity to grow and improve ourselves.

As we witness the trees and flowers blooming in full color, they are doing what they are intended to do—being fruitful and multiplying. Are there seasons when you are being fruitful and multiplying the Kingdom of God through your work?

Jesus Leads the Way

Let us thank God for this new day. Let us reflect on Jesus's relentless desire to be our Savior and always go before us, showing us the way.

Many want to be great but don't want to do what it takes. During Jesus's life on earth, He showed us what it takes to be a great servant-leader by leading the way. God has chosen and appointed many of us, and there are times we will be like those during Jesus's days on earth. We are easily tempted to give up and want to quit.

> "As Jesus and the people with him were on the road to Jerusalem, he was leading the way. His followers were amazed, but others in the crowd who followed were afraid. Again Jesus took the twelve apostles aside and began to tell them what was about to happen in Jerusalem. He said, 'Look, we are going to Jerusalem. The Son of Man will be turned over to the leading priests and the teachers of the law. They will say that he must die, and they will turn him over to the non-Jewish people, who will laugh at him and spit on him. They will beat him with whips and crucify him. But on the third day, he will rise to life again.'"
>
> (Mark 10:32-34, NCV)

LESSON † We can learn a lesson from the example that Jesus shows as He does not give up as He leads the way to Jerusalem. Jesus knew what would happen to Him.

Do you find it easy to walk humbly with God, the way that Jesus did? Do you ask for training so that your steps are in tune with God and His will?

Enter Not into Temptation

As we begin this new week, let us acknowledge that we cannot make it on our own in this world and that we need the Lord every day in our lives to help us overcome temptations that come.

Life can sometimes feel like a war zone, and navigating and surviving through each day can be a struggle, especially when we fall into the traps set by those who mean us no good.

> "'Stay alert; be in prayer so you don't wander into temptation without even knowing you're in danger.'"
>
> (Matthew 26:41, MSG)

> "So use every piece of God's armor to resist the enemy whenever he attacks, and when it is all over, you will still be standing up." (Ephesians 6:13, TLB)

> "Take the helmet of salvation, and the sword of the Spirit, which is the word of God." (Ephesians 6:17, NRSV)

LESSON † **Temptation is a choice, so we don't need to stop at every one of them. However, no matter which ones we face, God can help us through and make a way out. So let us choose to follow God and avoid people and situations that tempt us.**

Do you ask God to help you choose to stand against temptation before or after you've faced it?

God's Word – Our Spiritual Anchor

As we move through life this week and things are not going as we expect them to, let's consider what foundation we are standing on and let it be God's Word because we can trust it to anchor us.

Merriam-Webster Dictionary defines *infallible* as "incapable of error,"[38] and we know and believe the Bible is the infallible Word of God. We should follow, stand, and hold on to it. There is nothing in life that God cannot see us through. During hard times, we can fully put our trust in the Word of God because it will last forever, and it speaks with God's authority.

> "Every word of God is pure; He is a shield to those who take refuge in Him." (Proverbs 30:5, HCSB)

> "The grass withers, the flowers fade, but the word of our God remains forever." (Isaiah 40:8, HCSB)

> "Every Scripture passage is inspired by God. All of them are useful for teaching, pointing out errors, correcting people, and training them for a life that has God's approval. They equip God's servants so that they are completely prepared to do good things." (2 Timothy 3:16-17)

LESSON † Having God in our lives and standing on His Word in our life doesn't mean that our lives will be smooth sailing, but it assures us of being anchored during rough times and will indeed sustain, guide, and keep us from sinking in despair.

Have there been times in your life during hardships and troubled times you found God's Word to be an anchor that held you up?

Blessed Are Those Who Listen and Obey

On this "hump day" Wednesday, let us continue to grow stronger and deeper by listening for the voice of God and by obeying His Word.

We often listen to many things. There are those who we are in relationships with, plus the many other voices and opinions of those we tend to listen to. And that's okay. However, we must know that God still speaks to us in many ways. We must position ourselves and be ready to listen!

> "Jesus replied, 'Rather, how blessed are those who hear and obey God's word.'" (Luke 11:28)

> "Do what God's teaching says; when you only listen and do nothing, you are fooling yourselves." (James 1:22, NCV)

> "Just as a person's body that does not have a spirit is dead, so faith that does nothing is dead!" (James 2:26, NCV)

If we are looking to be blessed, it's not enough for us only to hear the Word of God. We must also obey it. Obeying and applying God's Word is what helps us grow spiritually, mentally, and physically in our lives.

LESSON † Let us live a life of faith and not grow weaker but stronger by applying God's Word that we have learned.

Do you have the faith to stay spiritually strong? Or are you lacking faith and feeling weak?

Consider Yourself Hugged by God's Word

Let us thank God on this "grateful Thursday" for the strength, energy, and His protection to make it this far. May He continue wrapping His loving arms around everyone and bless each of us one by one.

How many times have you felt down and out wishing for a hug from someone you know cares about you? During our life's hardships, we can feel like we need a hug. Although we serve a God who sits high on His throne, He reaches low to comfort and make us feel safe. He desires to be our omnipresent, never-ending, and constant help in our most desperate times of need! He's with us and has His arms wide open.

> "You who sit down in the High God's presence, spend the night in Shaddai's shadow, Say this: 'GOD, you're my refuge. I trust in you and I'm safe!' That's right—he rescues you from hidden traps, shields you from deadly hazards. His huge outstretched arms protect you—under them you're perfectly safe; his arms fend off all harm." (Psalm 91:1-4, MSG)

LESSON ✝ Jesus says He will never leave us and will always be with us. However, it's up to each of us to step into His loving, open arms daily. Today, consider yourself hugged by God's Word!

Do you want or need God's loving hug today?

Dance and Be Happy

Let us thank God for another Friday and getting us through another week. May we remain strong, stay calm, and let our Friday dance be for the Lord.

No matter what we may have faced this week, we should be able to do the Friday happy dance and be glad. God specializes in saving us from whatever fears, anxieties, health concerns, or enemies may try to triumph over us. He says that He will turn our mourning into joy! He comforts us to the point of having our past sorrows be just that—a thing of the past.

> "I give you all the credit, GOD—you got me out of that mess, you didn't let my foes gloat. GOD, my God, I yelled for help and you put me together. GOD, you pulled me out of the grave, gave me another chance at life when I was down-and-out." (Psalm 30:1-3, MSG)

> "'LORD, hear me and have mercy on me. LORD, help me.' You changed my sorrow into dancing. You took away my clothes of sadness, and clothed me in happiness. I will sing to you and not be silent. LORD, my God, I will praise you forever." (Psalm 30:10-12, NCV)

LESSON † Not everyone can praise God with a physical dance. However, each of us can praise Him from our hearts.

What has God saved you from this week?

An Emptiness Only God Can Fill

On this Saturday, let us thank God for filling us with His Holy Spirit, who helps us when we go through the daily trials and struggles of life.

The way we feel is not who we are, and despite being filled with the Holy Spirit, there are days and times when we allow hurts, trials, and struggles that we face in life to cause the feeling of empty hearts to overcome us because we try to fill our hearts with things, not with God. As God's people, only He can fill our hearts so that they don't feel empty. When the Lord fills our hearts, He uses His love, joy, and peace, which allows us the ability to say that all is well!

We can feel safe, complete, healthy, and strong because the Lord provides us with everything we need, along with the Holy Spirit.

> "Philip said to him, 'Lord, show us the Father. That is all we need.' Jesus answered, 'I have been with you a long time now. Do you still not know me, Philip? Whoever has seen me has seen the Father. So why do you say, "Show us the Father?"'" (John 14:8-9, NCV)

LESSON † To have all of our spiritual needs met, we need to confess and acknowledge the Lord as our Shepherd. We also must know that the Lord will meet our every need.

How long have you been in relationship with the Father? Do you really know Him as Abba Father, fulfilling your needs?

Being a Donkey for Jesus

On this Sunday, let us be reminded that while life is not always easy, we don't have to carry the burden of sins because Jesus has taken them all to the cross.

We can find the events of Jesus's triumphal entry into Jerusalem on His way to the cross in all four Gospels. It is written about in Matthew 21:1-11, Mark 11:1-11, Luke 19:28-44, and John 12:12-19.

In many cases, when the story is told, the focus is on Jesus and the crowd, not the donkey. But we can learn lessons from the donkey. Like the donkey, we are chosen to lift Jesus up and carry Him through to the many people in our daily lives.

> "Rejoice greatly, people of Jerusalem! Shout for joy, people of Jerusalem! Your king is coming to you. He does what is right, and he saves. He is gentle and riding on a donkey, on the colt of a donkey." (Zechariah 9:9, NCV)

LESSON † Jesus needed the donkey, and He needs each of us. To be used like the donkey that Jesus sent for, we need to realize that He chose us, be humble, and, more importantly, be available.

Are you today willing to be a donkey for Jesus, carrying Him into the crowds?

Being Fruitful and Humble

Let us thank God for the opportunity to have our hearts renewed and strengthened and that we have a closer walk with Jesus as we reflect on His determination to journey to the cross.

With each new day, we have our expectations of what the day will bring. Many of us are hungry for a new beginning. Let us be the best that we can! We can only form a mental image of what it must have been like for Jesus as He moved closer to fulfilling the purpose and plan of His Father, giving His life up for ours.

> "The next day as Jesus was leaving Bethany, he became hungry. Seeing a fig tree in leaf from far away, he went to see if it had any figs on it. But he found no figs, only leaves, because it was not the right season for figs. So Jesus said to the tree, 'May no one ever eat fruit from you again.' And Jesus' followers heard him say this." (Mark 11:12-14, NCV)

> "Jesus stood before Pilate the governor, and Pilate asked him, 'Are you the king of the Jews?' Jesus answered, 'Those are your words.' When the leading priests and the elders accused Jesus, he said nothing." (Matthew 27:11-12, NCV)

LESSON † Despite the approaching end of Jesus's earthly life, He continued to teach His disciples and us important lessons about being fruitful and show us a great example of remaining humble in the face of our accusers. Don't let our lives be unfruitful. When Jesus comes our way, we don't want to be found having nothing but leaves and bearing no fruit. Let us not focus on being right but humble.

Take some time and reflect on the best promise and possibilities of having a fresh and new start in your spiritual life.

ACKNOWLEDGEMENTS

Recognizing God in my life at an early age, I would like to give God His glory, for without Him, where would I be? It was He who sustained me and planted a seed in my heart with the courage to write His words allowing them to grow and spread throughout His Kingdom.

With much love to my mother, the late Mrs. Dorothy Edwards, and my grandmother, the late Mrs. Century Braham, who introduced and taught me about Jesus and how to invite Him into my heart to live a life worthy of His calling.

With the highest love and respect for my husband, Rock, and our four children, thanks for believing in me, encouraging me to reach for my goals, and always telling me it is now my time. "They coming."

My sister, Jacqueline Williams, my number one cheerleader, has been cheering me on, assuring me that God is with me. God's timing is perfect and I love and cherish our "now" time together. "You know the way."

To my friend who is like a daughter, Latoisha G. Smith, I'm so grateful for all your encouragement and help. Cross your bridges with courage!

To my editor, Rebekah Benham, and my book designer, Nelly Murariu, thank you for taking on the task of getting my manuscript book ready!

Last but not least: To Renee Fisher, my coach, friend, and #DreamDefender, a God-sent. From our first encounter, you challenged and encouraged me to go after my dreams. Not only are you Spirit-led, but you are also patient and so passionate about seeing others complete their dreams. I will never forget you!

ABOUT THE AUTHOR

Norma Sims, was born and raised in Folkston, Georgia, and considers herself a small-town girl. Living life as a military wife gave her family the opportunity to travel and live in a number of interesting places both in the United States and overseas. She appreciates the blessed life the military has given her family, but is most grateful for the lasting friendships.

She now resides in Blythewood, South Carolina, and is a licensed minister of the gospel, serving alongside her husband. Norma truly believes that God has created and gifted each person, enabling them to give of themselves no matter what place or places they may find themselves.

Romans 8:28 is the scripture that most reveals to her who God truly is and has been in her life. "And we know that all things work together for good to them that love God, to them who are the called according to his purpose." (Romans 8:28, KJV)

Motto: **With God, live life looking forward.**
Understand life looking back!

NOTES

1 "The Story of the Glass of Water," Health Positive, accessed April 3, 2020, https://healthpositiveinfo.com/the-story-of-the-glass-of-water.html#

2 Lexico, https://www.lexico.com/en/definition/hypocrisy , accessed April 20, 2020

3 Ziad K. Abdelnour, "Life is like a camera," Quote Fancy, accessed May 11, 2020, https://quotefancy.com/quote/1633821/Ziad-K-Abdelnour-Life-is-like-a-camera-Focus-on-what-s-important-Capture-the-good-times

4 Author unknown, "God created the Rose in the likeness of the woman," Google Images, accessed May 12, 2020. https://i.pinimg.com/originals/1d/ce/c4/1dcec4cfbc709e2725d1e20aa0c71996.jpg

5 Anthony Liccione, "We can't rewind the past, nor fast-forward the...", Good Reads Quotes, accessed May 16, 2020, https://www.goodreads.com/quotes/689461-we-can-t-rewind-the-past-nor-fast-forward-the-future-so

6 Mental Health Foundation, "Why did we pick kindness as the theme?", accessed May 19, 2020, https://www.mentalhealth.org.uk/campaigns/kindness/why-kindness-theme

7 J. Vernon McGee, *Thru The Bible with J. Vernon McGee*, (Nashville, TN: Thomas Nelson, 1983), _Job, chapter 23___, WORD*search* CROSS e-book.

8 Eleanor Brownn, "God, grant me the serenity to stop beating myself up...", Good Reads Quotes, accessed May 25, 2020, https://www.goodreads.com/quotes/7415267-god-grant-me-the-serenity-to-stop-beating-myself-up

9 Iyanla Vanzant, "Until you heal the wounds of your past, you are going to bleed into the future...", Good Reads Quotes, accessed June 6, 2020, https://www.goodreads.com/quotes/1015925-until-you-heal-the-wounds-of-your-past-you-are

10 "The good old days," Merriam-Webster Dictionary, accessed 16 June, 2020, https://www.merriam-webster.com/dictionary/the%20good%20old%20days

11 David Guzik, "Isaiah 43: 18-19", *The Enduring Word Bible Commentary*, accessed July 13, 2020, https://enduringword.com/bible-commentary/isaiah-43/

12 *Holman Study Bible*, Blum, Edwin and Jeremy Howard, ed. *Holman Study Bible: NKJV Edition*. Nashville, TN: (Holman Bible Publishers, 2013), Psalms 1, WORD*search* CROSS e-book.

13 Elizabeth Barrett Browning, "Earth is Crammed," The Famous People Quotes, accessed July 14, 2020, https://quotes.thefamouspeople.com/elizabeth-barrett-browning-220.php

14 *Life Application Study Bible*, (Wheaton, IL: Tyndale, 1988), _page: 1919____, WORDsearch CROSS e-book

15 Kristen Butler, "Don't Judge," Quotespedia.org, accessed July 20, 2020, https://www.quotespedia.org/authors/k/kristen-butler/dont-judge-you-dont-know-what-kind-of-storms-someone-has-just-walked-through-kristen-butler/

16 Thomas Adams quote, Thomas Adams quote: accessed July 21, 2020, Satan like a fisher, baits his hook according to the appetite of the fish. (inspiringquotes.us)

17 Charles H. Spurgeon, "Quote...", QuoteFancy.com, accessed July 23, 2020, https://quotefancy.com/quote/785745/Charles-H-Spurgeon-Whenever-God-means-to-make-a-man-great-he-always-breaks-him-in-pieces

18 Joseph Medlicott Scriven, "What a Friend We Have in Jesus," public domain.

19 William MacDonald, *One Day at a Time: 366 Soul-Stirring Daily Meditations* (Ontario, Gospel Folio Press, 1998), p. 30, quoted on "4 Reasons Not to Worry", CreativeKids.com, accessed August 5, 2020, https://creativekkids.com/thoughtful-thursdays-4-reasons-not-to-worry/

20 John Donne, "No Man is an Island," Quotes.net, accessed August 10, 2020, https://web.cs.dal.ca/~johnston/poetry/island.html

21 "Hope," *Famous Paintings* (1913), quoted on Garden of Praise, accessed August 24, 2020, https://www.gardenofpraise.com/artprint12.htm

22 Lao Tzu, "Lao Tzu Quotes," Brainy Quote, accessed August 25, 2020, https://www.brainyquote.com/quotes/lao_tzu_137141

23 Martin Luther King, Jr., "Martin Luther King, Jr., Quotes," Brainy Quote, accessed August 25, 2020, https://www.brainyquote.com/quotes/martin_luther_king_jr_105087

24 "You Can Lead a Horse to Water, But...," Know Your Phrase, accessed September 4, 2020, https://knowyourphrase.com/you-can-lead-a-horse-to-water

25 Whatcha Lookin' 4 lyrics, https://www.invubu.com/music/show/song/Kirk-Franklin/Whatcha-Lookin%27-4.html accessed, September 16, 2020

26 Mirror mirror on the wall" quote, https://slideplayer.com/slide/9307325/ accessed, September 20, 2020

27 Alice Walker, *Living by the Word,* (Boston: Houghton Mifflin Publishing, 1988), quoted in "Some periods of our growth are so confusing tha...," Good Reads Quotes, accessed September 23, 2020, https://www.goodreads.com/quotes/856195-some-periods-of-our-growth-are-so-confusing-that-we

28 *Life Application Study Bible*, (Wheaton, IL: Tyndale, 1988), page: 2070_____, WORDsearch CROSS e-book

29 *Life Application Study Bible*, (Wheaton, IL: Tyndale, 1988), _page: 2108____, WORDsearch CROSS e-book

30 *Life Application Study Bible*, (Wheaton, IL: Tyndale, 1988), _page: 1514____, WORDsearch CROSS e-book

31 Doe Zantamata, "Understand," Eminently Quotable Quotes, accessed October 17, 2020, https://www.eminentlyquotable.com/its-easy-to-judge-its-more-difficult-to-understand/

32 Mother Teresa quote, https://quotefancy.com/quote/869090/Mother-Teresa-Never-let-anything-so-fill-you-with-sorrow-as-to-make-you-forget-the-joy-of#:~:text=Mother%20Teresa%20Quote%3A%20%E2%80%9CNever%20let,the%20joy%20of%20Christ%20risen.%E2%80%9D, accessed October 23, 2020

33 Burt F. Bacharach and Hal David, "What the World Needs Now is Love,"

34 Russell M. Stendall, "Change," Christian Quotes for Reflection and Inspiration, accessed November 28, 2020, https://www.quoteschristian.com/quotesaboutchange.html

35 Anonymous, "Toddler's Creed,"https://teisinc.com/blog/toddler-creed/ accessed February 7, 2021

36 Martin Luther King, Jr., "Martin Luther King, Jr., Quotes," Brainy Quote, accessed June 3, 2020, https://www.brainyquote.com/quotes/martin_luther_king_jr_297516

37 Tupac Shakur, "You can spend minutes, hours, days, wee...," Quotes.pub, accessed March 12, 2021, https://quotes.pub/q/you-can-spend-minutes-hours-days-weeks-or-even-months-over-a-596891

38 "Infallible," Merriam-Webster Dictionary, accessed _March 23, 2021_____, https://www.merriam-webster.com/dictionary/infallible